ON THE CAUSES OF WAR

On the Causes of War

HIDEMI SUGANAMI

CLARENDON PRESS · OXFORD

This book has been printed digitally and produced in a standard design
in order to ensure its continuing availability

OXFORD
UNIVERSITY PRESS

Great Clarendon Street, Oxford OX2 6DP

Oxford University Press is a department of the University of Oxford.
It furthers the University's objective of excellence in research, scholarship,
and education by publishing worldwide in

Oxford New York

Athens Auckland Bangkok Bogotá Buenos Aires Cape Town
Chennai Dar es Salaam Delhi Florence Hong Kong Istanbul Karachi
Kolkata Kuala Lumpur Madrid Melbourne Mexico City Mumbai Nairobi
Paris São Paulo Shanghai Singapore Taipei Tokyo Toronto Warsaw

with associated companies in Berlin Ibadan

Oxford is a registered trade mark of Oxford University Press
in the UK and in certain other countries

Published in the United States
by Oxford University Press Inc., New York

ISBN 0-19-827338-X

PREFACE AND
ACKNOWLEDGEMENTS

THIS book is an expanded version of a paper presented at the
1989 London Convention of the International Studies Association
and its British counterpart, BISA. Excerpts from the paper appeared
a year later in the eighth edition of W. C. Olson's *The Theory and
Practice of International Relations*. In the same year, a revised
version of the paper was published in *Millennium: Journal of
International Studies*. In the course of coming to write the initial
paper and transforming it into its present shape, I have been helped
by very many people.

The origins of the book go as far back as 1970, when I left
Tokyo for Aberystwyth. There, at the University College of Wales,
I was fortunate enough to meet Brian Porter, who introduced
me straight away to the works and ideas of C. A. W. Manning,
Martin Wight, and Hedley Bull. Together, these writers gave me
confidence in International Relations as an academic pursuit, and
strengthened my belief that History and Philosophy are its two
key components. At Aberystwyth, I was also extremely lucky to
have Moorhead Wright as my supervisor. He immediately saw
that my strength was in conceptual analysis, and encouraged me
to follow my inclination.

It was in Wales, in the spring of 1971, that I read Kenneth Waltz's
Man, the State and War for the first time. This was an exciting experience. I read the book again in the autumn of 1973, when Andrew
Linklater, then with me at the Graduate School of the LSE, alerted
me to Waltz's theoretical bias, which had escaped me entirely: I
wanted to see it for myself (see Linklater 1982: 28–9).

For some years after 1975, when I took up a lectureship at
Keele, I used *Man, the State and War* for undergraduate teaching,
and every year I glanced at it. On one occasion, I read the entire
work very carefully as though I were writing it myself. In the
process of my many encounters with the book, I began to realize
that there are some serious errors and inexactitudes of a conceptual or logical nature in Waltz's argument. By 1980 I began to toy
with the idea of writing a book on the causes of war which would
transcend Waltz's contributions.

It was about this time that the philosopher Jonathan Dancy agreed to teach a short course with me on the causes of war. This was designed to introduce philosophical thinking to Keele's foundation-year students interested in international affairs. On the basis of this experience, I developed for the final-year students in International Relations my own special subject entitled 'The Causes of War: History and Theory'. The present volume stems from this course.

In preparing a reading list for this option, I came across a very useful book by Keith Nelson and Spencer Olin, Jr., called *Why War?* This book demonstrated to me the importance of analysing historical controversies about the origins of particular wars, a dimension which was lacking in Waltz's work. In this connection, Nelson and Olin's book directed me to W. H. Dray's excellent article entitled 'Concepts of Causation in A. J. P. Taylor's Account of the Origins of the Second World War' (1978). This was a good illustration of what a philosopher can do to heighten the level of debate among historians. Although Dray's article was concerned with a historical controversy about a particular case, it seemed to me possible to extrapolate from his somewhat tentative discussion a more general analytical framework for the understanding of the causes of war. By 1987 my aim was clear: to rewrite *Man, the State and War* by paying attention to particular wars and different interpretations about their origins, and by incorporating and expanding some of Dray's philosophical insights and arguments.

In the following year, I was fortunate enough to receive a Keele University Research Award, and spent the autumn term as a Senior Associate Member of St Antony's College Oxford. Much of my work, however, was done in a cottage in Steeple Aston which Moorhead and Rosemary Wright generously offered me. Once a week, I would attend my friend John Vincent's graduate seminars on theories of international politics, and on a number of occasions had him listen to my ideas as they began to take shape. Through Vincent, I met Martin Ceadel, Iver Neumann, and Elizabeth Cousens, among others, and benefited much from attempting to explain to them the argument of the book which began to emerge.

The 1989 ISA/BISA Convention was my first opportunity to publicize the argument. In writing the paper for the occasion, and revising it for publication in *Millennium*, I received much help from many scholars. David Walker alerted me to Vladimir Propp's study of Russian fairy tales, which my study of the war-origins literature resembles. Richard Godden directed me to the writings of Hayden White and Louis Mink, which influenced my view of history. And, above all, W. H. Dray and Jack S. Levy responded most encouragingly to the argument I was developing. I am also grateful to Christopher Brewin for making me read R. G. Collingwood carefully.

It has taken me five years to expand the paper into the present volume. The first draft of its five chapters was completed in the summer of 1993, when Alex Danchev and Andrew Linklater, the latter having just joined us at Keele, offered to read the whole thing. A historian and a theorist, they acted as though they were my joint supervisors. The final draft was completed a year later, and out of sheer generosity Danchev and Linklater read and commented on the work again. Richard Devetak was also helpful in reading the final draft very carefully, and correcting some of my errors.

A long journey has now come to an end. I dedicate this book collectively to five persons: Mrs Shige Suganami, who made it possible for me to come to Britain to study in the first place; Mrs R. S. Britton, who has enabled me to continue to study and work in this country; the late John Vincent, who treated me as though I were one of his younger siblings; Miho Suganami, who brought me profoundest happiness; and Amane Suganami, who taught me love. They deserve a book each, but a chapter each is all they get for the moment.

H.S.

CONTENTS

INTRODUCTION

> Some knowledge of politics, of international relations, of economics, is obviously necessary in order to understand the causes which lead to war. Philosophy, theology even, might come in usefully.
>
> (Woolf 1938: 157)

> Thinking is also research.
>
> (Samuel Alexander, cited in Bull 1977: x)

INTELLECTUAL dispositions of different sorts rarely coexist in a single mind. Either one is philosophically inclined or one is not, in a great many cases.

Those who are philosophically inclined—let us call them 'philosophers', though they may not, by profession, be such—tend to stare at a question, and ask: 'What is it that this question is asking?'; 'What might an answer look like if indeed there could be an answer to this type of question at all?' Those who are not philosophically inclined (or 'non-philosophers') would rather have some plausible answer to their question than to have it analysed, and get none at all. 'Philosophers' are dismayed by how readily substantive answers are offered by 'non-philosophers' even before preliminary questions have been taken care of. 'Non-philosophers' are frustrated by the philosophically inclined, who, to them, never seem to get anywhere.

'Philosophers' and 'non-philosophers' have their respective contributions to make in rendering the world a more intelligible place to live in. It stands to reason, therefore, that they must not only divide the intellectual labour, but cooperate. Yet collaboration across the boundaries of academic disciplines is relatively rare. The meeting of different intellectual dispositions is rarer still. *Explaining and Understanding International Relations* by Martin Hollis and Steve Smith (1990) is one recent exception to this.

'Causes of War' Viewed from the Causal End

The study of international relations in general, and that of the causes of war in particular, is dominated by 'non-philosophers'. Empiricism rules among historians and social scientists concerned with matters international. Historians in particular appear on the whole to mistrust conceptual analysis. Even among International Relations specialists, who are by and large more tolerant of conceptual enquiry than are historians, it is relatively rare to find a philosophical mind at work. When investigating 'the causes of war', they will study wars, and, contrary to the approach taken in this book, they will not begin by looking at the causal end of the stick.

This state of affairs is not so disturbing but for the almost self-congratulatory tendencies of some for being 'non-philosophical'. This unfortunate tendency is complemented by the lack of sufficient care on the part of some 'philosophers' to make themselves intelligible to wider audiences, and to demonstrate, where appropriate, the relevance of their contributions to improving our understanding of the world.

The self-congratulatory tendencies of 'non-philosophers' are noticeable in the contemporary British intellectual environment, and perhaps elsewhere. They have made use of certain lamentable expressions in order to dismiss the more philosophically inclined. They would say: 'He is only a logic-chopper'; 'You are splitting hairs'; 'We are more down to earth'; and even 'What we are saying is common sense, not too philosophical.'

It should be stated here that this book is *not* 'down to earth' in the sense in which 'non-philosophers' use that term. It is hoped, however, that there is little in what follows that contradicts good sense. This book also contains a good deal of what might appear as 'logic-chopping' and 'hair-splitting'. However, it certainly is not 'too philosophical' for the purpose it sets out to achieve. This is to think straight about the causes of war.

After all, how can we hope to think straight about the subject without drawing distinctions whenever the failure to do precisely that has drowned many a writer on the topic in the mire of confusions? In any case, what point is there in being 'down to earth' if the 'grounding' is not secure? There is, of course, no wisdom in drawing distinctions for the sake of it, or being stratospheric for sheer exhibitionism. But philosophical habits of mind can usefully be applied to problems in the empirical disciplines. This book is an attempt to demonstrate this with respect to the subject of the causes of war. It endeavours to do so in a way that can readily be appreciated by the less philosophically inclined, without at the same time doing too much injustice to the complexity of the discourse in which philosophers professionally engage.

But surely, it will be said, to find 'the causes of war' we must identify 'the causes of wars', and study as many wars, one by one, as time allows. Eventually, we may find relatively common causes of a large number of wars, and this is what is meant by 'the causes of war'. The knowledge thus acquired may be useful in giving some ideas about how to reduce the future frequency of war. What is fundamental, therefore, is a search for the causes of particular wars.

This seems a sensible thing to say. But, of course, what caused a war cannot be understood unless we know what it means to say that something 'caused' something else. As soon as this is admitted, and the question asked, we are in the realm of conceptual analysis, faced with a philosophical issue, whether we like it or not. This issue will be addressed in Chapter 4.

There is a view, however, that since each war is unique, we are unlikely in fact to be able to identify such things as 'the causes of war': the most we could do is to establish 'the origins of particular wars'. This also appears a sensible remark to make. To say, however, that we should only talk of 'origins', but not 'causes', and to say no more about the supposed difference between the two, is thoughtless hair-splitting, quite common, as it happens, in the 'non-philosophizing' camp. As will be argued in Chapter 4, the distinction turns out to be misconceived.

Further, the contention that each war is unique, though correct, is not in fact incompatible with an attempt to identify, at a certain level of abstraction, some similarities among the origins of different wars. The extent and sources of such similarities, among other things, are investigated in Chapter 5.

There is also a view that since it is difficult to establish the causes or origins of any particular war, we should look for the 'correlates of war'. Whether or not they are also 'causes of war', 'correlates of war' may be useful to identify since they may work as 'early warning indicators of war'. This, too, appears a sensible view to hold. One exemplary outcome of this line of enquiry, among other things, will be studied in Chapter 3.

But what is 'an early warning indicator'? Presumably we are not in search of 'an omen' whose link with the outbreaks of war is beyond rational comprehension. Scientifically minded as they are, most investigators of the 'correlates of war' would deny this. But if 'an early warning indicator of war' is said to be 'an early symptom of deteriorating international conditions likely to end in war', we are back to the realm of causality, for, undoubtedly, 'a symptom' is 'an effect', and 'an effect' is 'that which is caused'. This much can be found in any dictionary. But we do not yet know, in any deeper sense, what it means to say that something was 'caused' by something else.

But surely, it may be said, we already know what causes war: man's selfishness, aggressiveness, stupidity, and so on. So why go any further? 'Philosophers' will not be impressed by such complacency. For one thing, the notion of 'cause' still remains to be explicated. Besides, we now have a handful of other concepts: 'selfishness', 'aggressiveness', 'stupidity', and so on. Those 'non-philosophers' who claim that these, and the word 'cause', are just 'common-sense' words, and that 'philosophers' are creating an unnecessary problem for themselves, and being a nuisance to others, by demanding an analysis are unaware of their own confusions in insisting, for example, that war is 'caused' by 'human selfishness'.

If we are to point to the supposed selfishness of human nature as the cause of war, we will have to square that assertion with an awkward fact: that in addition to war there is also peace in human relationships. This point is often noted. As Kenneth Waltz has remarked, 'Human nature may in some sense have been the cause of war in 1914, but by the same token it was the cause of peace in 1910' (1959: 28). Of course, there is no denying the fact that war would be impossible in an imaginary world in which all human beings are entirely unselfish. But, it is easy to fail to notice, war would be impossible also in an imaginary world in which all human beings are entirely selfish: war demands varying degrees of self-sacrifice. Clearly, the precise character of the relationship between 'human nature' and 'war' requires a closer scrutiny, and is one of the topics to be discussed in Chapter 2.

Some readers may feel alienated by this kind of talk. Perhaps contrary to their initial expectation, not a single war has even been mentioned so far. But facts, events, and examples are interesting, not intrinsically, but because of what, on reflection, they reveal. A number of actual wars will in fact be discussed in Chapter 5 because, as we shall see, they illustrate in part some interesting points about the causes of war.

In any case, conceptual problems would not go away even if we were to wipe them off a blackboard, and decide merely to concern ourselves with more concrete 'real-world' issues. After all, in this book, we are interested in facts and events only to the extent that they are 'causally relevant' to the outbreaks of war, but we do not yet know how to find out which factors are causally relevant, or even what the term 'causally relevant' means.

In attempting to tackle the subject of 'the causes of war' from the causal angle, this book does not assume any prior familiarity with philosophical ideas about 'causation'. Discussions of philosophical writings are kept to a minimum, and appear mainly in Chapter 4. All that is required of the reader is a certain amount of tolerance: what might initially appear as 'logic-chopping' and 'hair-splitting' in a not so 'down-to-earth' world is indispensable in getting us out of a conceptual muddle, which writers on the causes of war have very often slipped into.

Three Questions before Three Answers

So what do these writers say are the causes of war? Much needed efforts have been made to bring some order to the plethora of answers which are often contradictory. By far the best known in this respect is Kenneth Waltz's tripartite classification, contained in his classic work, *Man, the State and War: A Theoretical Analysis* (1959). Much less well known, but worthy of serious attention, is another tripartite scheme offered twenty years later by Keith Nelson and Spencer Olin, Jr., in their little book *Why War? Ideology, Theory, and History* (1979). The former makes use of three levels of analysis, and the latter three underlying ideologies, in their respective classifications.

However, one of the primary reasons why there is such a bewildering variety of answers concerning the issue of war causation is that a number of distinct *questions* are in fact asked under the rubric of 'the causes of war'. There are at least three such questions, the distinction among which constitutes the organizing principle of the present volume. These are:

(a) 'What are the conditions which must be present for wars to occur?';

(b) 'Under what sorts of circumstances have wars occurred more frequently?'; and

(c) 'How did this particular war come about?'

Briefly, (a) asks for necessary conditions of war; (b) is about correlates of war; and (c) is in search of the full sequence of events which led to a particular outbreak of war.

A detailed analysis of Waltz's *Man, the State and War* and Nelson and Olin's *Why War?*, conducted in Chapter 1, will reveal how the failure to separate these three questions consistently has misled Waltz, and Nelson and Olin, in reaching their respective substantive conclusions about the causes of war. The discussion also shows that separating these questions is more fundamental than classifying existing answers in terms of the three levels of analysis, as is done by Waltz, or in the light of their ideological underpinnings, as is done by Nelson and Olin.

Chapter 2 then discusses some standard answers given to question (a). It examines their status and assesses their quality. Chapter 3 evaluates a number of answers which some leading specialists have suggested to question (b). It also investigates what inferences may be drawn from these answers. Chapter 4 is intended as a philosophical interlude. On the basis of the analysis conducted there, and with reference to several historical cases, Chapter 5 discerns the ways in which answers to questions of the form (c) are formulated. It also investigates, among other things, whether there is any limitation to the range of answers which can be given to this type of question. This leads eventually to a theory of war origins which takes seriously the fact that wars come about in different ways, but which also identifies the nature and sources of similarities among the origins of wars.

Linkages with Waltz

This book may be said to engage in three kinds of activity concerning the issue of the causes of war: 'mapping', 'theorizing', and 'bridge-building'. It endeavours to map the intellectual terrain in which multifarious answers are found by various avenues of research on the causes of war; it does so with a view to formulating a theory of war origins; and for this purpose it tries to bridge a gap between the philosophical analysis of causation and empirical enquiry into the conditions resulting in war.

One of the most important contributors to a similar set of goals—particularly the first two of the three just noted—has undoubtedly been Kenneth Waltz. The present volume has in fact been inspired by his example, and attempts to add another step in the direction he took forty years ago.

Any claim to go beyond a classic work, however, is liable to incur all forms of sceptical rejection. A certain myth is likely to have come to surround a classic work in such a way that its details are no longer discussed, and its pivotal role in the development of thought is almost ritualistically acknowledged. The present volume recognizes the pivotal role that Waltz's *Man, the State and War* played in the development of thought concerning the causes of war. But it seeks to refine some of his contentions.

Chapter 1 below therefore contains a very detailed re-examination of Waltz's *Man, the State and War*. Following this, in Chapter 2, the central thesis of Waltz's book that international anarchy is the permissive and underlying cause of war, explaining its possibility and recurrence, is critically assessed. One of the main topics to be discussed in Chapter 3 is a recent consensus among many leading researchers that there has been hardly any instance of war between any two constitutionally secure liberal states—a finding which potentially undermines Waltz's long-held position that war is bound to happen even among 'good' states (Waltz 1959: 114 ff.; cf. Waltz 1991: 670). Chapter 4 takes the analysis of the concept of causation beyond what is usually done by writers on the causes of war, including Waltz himself. Chapter 5 complements Waltz's almost exclusive concern with the *recurrence of war*, as opposed to the *occurrence of any particular war*, by investigating the variety of ways in which actual wars came about. The upshot of all this is a theory of war origins markedly different from Waltz's own.

The theory offered here does not explain why war occurs by any simple formula because it acknowledges that war is a multicausal phenomenon. It rejects Waltz's central contention that international anarchy is the most fundamental cause of war, explaining its possibility and recurrence. Instead, it points to various ways in which background conditions of many kinds, unexpected chance coincidences, and war-conducive mechanisms of different sorts combine to curtail governments' freedom of action, in the process leading to the outbreaks of wars. Like Waltz's theory, it acknowledges the actions of governments to be the key factor in explaining the origins of *particular* wars (Waltz 1959: 232). But, unlike Waltz's theory, it also identifies what types of action there are which governments perform in the process of deterioration from peace to war, and it goes on to explicate the status of that particular typology of government actions.

The present volume could thus be viewed as aspiring in part to deconstruct and transcend Waltz. It should be noted here that, through his later work, *Theory of International Politics* (1979), Waltz came to be associated with an approach called 'neo-Realism'. He is indeed a leading figure of that theoretical orientation. For some time, it has been a preoccupation of several International Relations theorists, when discussing Waltz's contributions, to scrutinize his 'neo-Realist' claim that certain observable regularities of international relations can be explained in terms of what, he considers, are the structural characteristics of the international system (e.g. Keohane 1986; Wendt 1987; Dessler 1989; Hollis and Smith 1990; Wendt 1992; Buzan, Jones, and Little 1993; Linklater 1995). The present volume's treatment of Waltz is compatible with such interests, and can be viewed as a partial critique of Waltz's neo-Realist stance.

However, this is not a book about Waltz. Its aim is to demonstrate how to reason about the causes of war. Waltz enters the discussion because he has some important things to say about this, and has also made some errors in his reasoning, which are worth correcting if only because of the far-reaching influence of his ideas among the students of international relations worldwide.

The Scope of Analysis

A few things had to be excluded from the scope of this book's analysis. Of these, two items should be mentioned here.

First, the focus of this book is on war among states: although it does not definitionally equate 'war' with 'international war' (see Chapter 2), actual wars which this book deals with are all instances of 'international war'. Some civil wars resemble international wars to such an extent that many of the points made in this volume may apply to them equally well. But this is not to be assumed in all cases. A comparable treatment of the causes of civil wars must await a separate study. It may be said, however, that the analysis of the concept of causation, and of historical explanation, developed in Chapter 4 will be relevant to such a study.

Secondly, this book is concerned with the processes through which war comes to be chosen as a means to some ends, but its focus is on the processes, not on the ends. It does not deal with the question of war aims. Recently, a number of writers began, quite rightly, to notice the importance of studying what states fight about (e.g. Diehl 1992), and a few pioneering works exist on this subject (e.g. Luard 1986; Holsti 1991; Vasquez 1993). More work needs to be done on this topic particularly with respect to the problems of identifying and classifying issues over which wars are fought, but this is left to another study.

Such limitations notwithstanding, the range of discussion in the main body of this volume is in fact quite broad, embracing History, Political Science, Quantitative International Politics, Expected Utility Theory, International Relations Theory, Ethology, Philosophy, Philosophy of Science, Philosophy of Social Science, Philosophy of History, Literary Theory, and Legal Theory. This is necessitated by the multidisciplinary nature of the existing causes-of-war research, coupled with this book's desire to learn from philosophical writings on causation and explanation, which are in turn scattered in some of philosophy's sub-branches and neighbouring disciplines.

Nearly twenty years ago, in a short but insightful article, Berenice Carroll and Clinton Fink made the following remarks:

classifications of theories of war causation according to the causes emphasized or included tend to ignore, or at best give inadequate attention to, the serious philosophical difficulties involved in all causal explanation in social theory. It is not possible to enter into these complex difficulties here, but it will be evident that any philosophical challenge to causal explanation itself must call in question all theories of the causes of war. (1975: 59–60)

The present volume rises to the challenge implicit in the above paragraph. It not only maps the intellectual terrain of the causes-of-war research with a view to formulating a plausible theory of war causation, but, for this purpose, it also makes an effort to bridge a gap between philosophical and empirical investigations. Complex difficulties are entered into.

Kenneth Waltz has argued that attempts to explain war in terms of the nature of man and the nature of the state are unsatisfactory because they fail to take into account the nature of the international system. This book argues that earlier attempts, such as those of Waltz, and Nelson and Olin, to select or construct a plausible theory of war by classifying and scrutinizing existing theories are unsatisfactory because they failed to take seriously the philosophical problems of causation and explanation. 'Theorizing' via 'mapping' needs to incorporate 'bridge-building' between the empirical and the conceptual.

I

QUESTIONS

It is often the case that when questions have failed to be
answered for a long time, as is the case with many of the
questions on war, it is because the questions themselves have
been posed in an unelucidating way.

(Vasquez 1993: 153)

There are at least three ways in which two answers may
differ. They may be different answers to the same question,
or answers to different questions of the same kind, or they
may be answers to questions of different kinds.

(Manning 1975: 129)

THIS chapter examines two major contributions to the study of
how to reason about the causes of war. They are Kenneth Waltz's
Man, the State and War, published in 1959, and Keith Nelson and
Spencer Olin's *Why War?*, which appeared twenty years later.
Correspondingly, there are two main sections to this chapter.

In Section 1.1, Waltz's contentions are examined in detail. A
critical exposition of the structure of his argument is followed by
a statement of what is believed to be a better starting-point than
Waltz's own for the discussion of the causes of war. In Section
1.2, we turn briefly to Nelson and Olin's main argument. Their
work is included in this preliminary study partly because of its
intrinsic merits, and partly also because—importantly from the
viewpoint of this chapter—it shares one major shortcoming with
Waltz's *Man, the State and War*.

The two works classify a large variety of *answers* which have
emerged concerning the causes of war, and they do so in different,
though partially overlapping, ways. But neither of them pays sufficient attention to the important fact that, under the rubric of the
causes of war, a number of distinct *questions* arise. This common
defect is partly responsible for leading Waltz, as well as Nelson
and Olin, into advancing their own causal theories of war, which
are in turn defective.

The aim of this chapter is to indicate how we might improve on the two works. In what follows, therefore, the remarks about them are almost exclusively critical. Needless to say, these works, in their own ways, are important contributions to the study of how to reason about the causes of war, and in the case of Waltz's book, a pioneering one.

1.1 MAN, THE STATE, AND THE INTERNATIONAL SYSTEM

Many of those who have read, or know about, *Man, the State and War* appear to think of Waltz primarily as someone who has identified the three levels of analysis regarding the causes of war. These are the levels of man, the state, and the international system. Waltz's doctoral dissertation, upon which his book was based, was therefore called 'Man, the State, and the State System in Theories of the Causes of War' (see Waltz 1979: 238). Waltz is famous for this tripartite classification, and for what he calls the first, second, and third 'images' of war.

'The first image' finds the major cause of war in the first level of analysis, or the level of man; 'the second image' in the second, state or domestic, level; and 'the third image' in the third, international or system, level (Waltz 1959: 12). However, in adopting this tripartite scheme, Waltz is not concerned simply to classify. His main aim is to point to the unique significance of the third level of analysis.

Waltz's Central Argument

In Waltz's judgement, the anarchical structure of the international environment—or the fact that there is nothing in the international system to prevent war—is of particular importance.

In his view, this fact—we may call this 'international anarchy'— is 'the underlying', or what he also calls 'the permissive', cause of war (Waltz 1959: 232, 233). It reveals why war is a constant possibility (Waltz 1959: 188, 227), and why states find it rational to be prepared to fight all the time (Waltz 1959: 160, 201, 220); it shows why prescriptions for peace aimed at the first two levels of analysis are inadequate (Waltz 1959: ch. 3 *passim*, 119–20,

122–3, 222, 231, 233–4); and it also explains how in some cases a power competition between states spirals into war (Waltz 1959: 234). In short, Waltz is himself a third-image theorist. Waltz is of course not unusual in treating 'international anarchy' as the fundamental cause of war. This is in fact a very popular view (see e.g. Wight 1978: 101).

This characterization of Waltz's own position is commonly accepted by most contemporary specialists in the theory of international relations. Some commentators, however, appear to feel that this is not in fact an accurate interpretation of Waltz's views as expressed in *Man, the State and War*. The reason is not far to seek.

For one thing, Waltz is critical of what he regards as mono-causal theories of war. Thus he finds the first image inadequate to the extent that it suggests human nature to be the *single* determinant of war (Waltz 1959: 81). Further, he treats J. A. Hobson's theory of imperialism (and war) as an example of a second-image theory, and criticizes it for its supposedly mono-causal character (Waltz 1959: 146–7). Waltz even states explicitly that 'no single image is ever adequate' (1959: 225), and that the 'prescriptions directly derived from a single image are incomplete because they are based upon partial analyses' (1959: 230). Accordingly, in his own estimates of the causes of war, Waltz never in fact neglects the first- and second-level factors (Waltz 1959: 184–5, 218, 232, 238). How then can he be treated as a third-image theorist? Surely, it may be said, Waltz is, or was in 1959, really an eclectic, the definitive contribution made by *Man, the State and War* to the causes-of-war research being that it has alerted the investigators to the inadequacies of any mono-causal theory, including, of course, the third-image one.[1]

However, this picture of *Man, the State and War* as essentially a critique of mono-causal theories in turn ignores two important facts. First, though often unnoticed, or entirely forgotten, by many commentators—and Waltz himself appears to forget this point

[1] See e.g. K. J. Holsti (1989: 3; 1991: 3). Martin Hollis and Steve Smith (1991: 116, 117, 146, 198) are inaccurate in their suggestion that only in his more recent response to his critics (in particular, Waltz 1986) did Waltz revise his position, and grant 'that a systems approach cannot explain everything' (Hollis and Smith 1990: 116): Waltz conceded this even in 1959, and has done so consistently (Waltz 1979: 48–9, 174; 1989: 44).

from time to time—he defines his three images, initially, in terms
of where one locates the *major* cause of war. He writes (1959: 12):

Where are the major causes of war to be found? The answers are bewildering in their variety and in their contradictory qualities. To make this
variety manageable, the answers can be ordered under the following three
headings: within man, within the structure of the separate states, within
the state system . . . These three estimates of cause will subsequently be
referred to as images of international relations, numbered in the order
given, with each image defined according to where one locates the nexus
of important causes.

Clearly, the major cause of war need not be, and is unlikely in
fact to be held to be, the *sole* cause of war. On the contrary, it is
natural to assume that one's selection of a particular kind of cause
as the major one is concomitant with one's judgement that there
are also *some other* less important kinds of cause. Therefore, it is
reasonable to suggest that all the three images, as defined by Waltz
himself, are in fact at least implicitly multi-causal ones, with each
image containing its own major *and minor* causes of war. In short,
Waltz's three images are not about mono-causality, which he rightly
rejects, but about causal weighting. Since this is so, there would
be no contradiction involved in Waltz's explicit rejection of mono-
causal theories of war, on the one hand, and his subscription to
any of the three images as defined by himself, on the other.

Secondly, even though, quite coherently with his multi-causal
view, Waltz never fails to recognize the relevance of first- and
second-level causes, he nevertheless distinguishes qualitatively between them and the third-level cause. According to him, the first two
levels contain 'the efficient causes' of war, or those factors which
make particular wars occur. By contrast, the third-level cause, he
maintains, constitutes 'the permissive cause' of war, or the condition
which accounts for the very possibility of war (Waltz 1959: 231–
3). Waltz's distinction between the two kinds of cause, 'efficient'
and 'permissive', is another thing that is not often remembered by
many readers of his book. But, as will be exposed shortly, this
conceptual distinction plays a critical part in his overall argument.

Suffice it to note for the moment that Waltz characterizes 'efficient causes' also as 'immediate causes'; and that he equates the
'permissive cause' with the 'underlying cause' of war (Waltz 1959:
232). In his judgement, 'efficient causes' are 'accidental causes'

TABLE 1.1. *Waltz's two types of cause*

Efficient causes of war	The permissive cause of war
make *particular* wars occur	accounts for *the very possibility* of war
are *accidental*, and often *trivial*	gives a *final* explanation of the origins of war among states
are also *immediate* causes of particular wars	constitutes *the underlying* cause of war

(1959: 231), and 'the immediate causes of many wars are trivial' (1959: 235). By contrast, he suggests that 'the permissive cause, the international environment' (1959: 233) gives a 'final explanation' (1959: 231) of the origins of war among states.

Waltz's views here are summarized in Table 1.1. Waltz's contrasting remarks about the two kinds of cause, listed above, cannot fail to reveal that in his judgement the 'efficient causes' are less fundamental than the 'permissive cause'. Moreover, as will be demonstrated presently in some detail, he also holds, unconvincingly in fact, that *all* the 'efficient causes' of war are found in the first two levels of analysis, and that the *sole* 'permissive cause' is located in the third level (Waltz 1959: 230–8; see Table 1.2 below). It follows, therefore, that in Waltz's view the first two levels are less fundamental than the third. It is correct then, after all, to characterize Waltz as a third-image theorist as defined by himself.

This interpretation finds further support in Waltz's more recent work, *Theory of International Politics* (1979), in which the first two images are collapsed into one category, a unit-level 'reductionist' theory, and the third image remains commended as a system-level 'structural' theory of international politics. This work has brought much fame to Waltz as a leading theorist of the so-called neo-Realist school, which claims to explain certain regular features of international politics, such as the recurrence of the balance of power among the major powers, in terms of the structural characteristics of the international system.

With respect specifically to the phenomenon of war, however, Waltz's initial defence of the third-image thesis, and, more fundamentally, his tripartite classification itself turn out to contain a

number of interrelated conceptual and logical problems which he
has failed to resolve in his works. In the next two subsections,
these problems are identified through a close analysis of his classic
1959 text. Where appropriate, his 1979 work will also be brought
into the discussion, and where convenient, the term 'unit level'
will be used to denote the first two levels of analysis, and 'system
level' to refer to the third.

Problems with Waltz's Tripartite Classification

Perhaps we should begin by asking from where the idea of the
three levels of analysis arose. Why does it seem so natural that
there are these three levels, or even that, as some would say, they
are the only ones?

It is interesting to note in this connection the manner in which,
even before Waltz, C. A. W. Manning referred to the very same
three levels when commenting on the failure of the League of
Nations. He wrote simply: 'If the League was to succeed it must
do so in spite of the nature of men, the nature of states and the
nature of the society of states' (1942: 115). It apparently seemed
to Manning quite natural to structure and express his thought
about the causes of the League's poor record in terms of the three
analytical levels, which have subsequently become almost insepar-
ably associated with Kenneth Waltz's name. No evidence is found
in *Man, the State and War*, however, to suggest that Waltz borrowed the tripartite scheme from Manning.

There seems little doubt that this tripartite analysis is accepted
with great ease because it reflects a very common view of how
modern political life is organized: human beings, as citizens, belong to separate states, and these in turn form a system. What is
more natural than to extract the three levels from this political
experience? Modern political philosophers and Natural Law writers on the Law of Nations articulated and reinforced this popular
perception by their theory: men left the state of nature and formed
separate states, and these, while in turn formally in the state of
nature, constitute a system or society of a kind. In fact, many
theories of war which Waltz examines in his book are those of
political philosophers. This may have made it seem to him all the
more natural to adopt the tripartite analytical scheme.

But we must ask: even though this scheme accords well with our conventional view of world political order, does it necessarily supply a good classificatory device for the multifarious causes of war? Can all the relevant causes be placed neatly in the three categories? Are the three in fact exhaustive?

Waltz does not say that the three are exhaustive, but he writes as if he thinks they are. Since there are likely to be very many kinds of thing which contribute to actual outbreaks of war, however, we may suspect that Waltz perhaps neglects those items which fall outside the three categories; or perhaps he inflates the categories somewhat to ensure that all the items he has taken into consideration can be contained conjointly by the three.

In fact, Waltz has made both these moves. However, the latter move, and, in particular, his quite artificial inflation of the first two categories in the concluding part of his book, is especially noteworthy. This is because this move, turning the first two categories into a 'dumping ground' for what he regards as insignificant explanatory variables, constitutes one of the key steps in reaching his conclusion in favour of the third level of analysis. These critical allegations, opaque as they stand, are substantiated below.

Inflating the first image

Let us start with Waltz's treatment of the first image. A close reading reveals that he initially gives it a relatively narrow definition, but that, in the course of his discussion, he surreptitiously enlarges the category.

Initially, Waltz defines this image as theories of war according to which the major cause of war is to be found in 'the nature and behavior of man' (1959: 16). Most of the time he treats this first level of analysis as the level of human nature. This point is well known. Yet he also includes in his discussion of the first image an explanation of war in terms of personality traits (e.g. Waltz 1959: 218). That is why he examines under the rubric of the first image a suggestion advanced by some to the effect that in order to lessen the frequency of war we should institute some form of psychological screening system so that only those who are peacefully inclined would be elected to high office (Waltz 1959: 62 ff.). Such a suggestion is based on a relatively common hypothesis that, not infrequently, the bellicose character of some national leaders was a major cause of war.

Human nature and personality traits, however, are not of the same order: there is a qualitative difference between what human nature is, and what some people are like. Human nature is a set of characteristics which are part of the human make-up; it is common to *all* human beings, and to them exclusively. Personality traits, by contrast, are characteristics only of *some* of them.

In relation to investigation into the causes of war, human nature is typically a starting-point for political philosophers and biologists, whereas personality traits are the concern of historians and psychologists. As will be formulated more clearly later, the type of question regarding the causes of war to which an insight into human nature may be able to suggest an answer is of a different category from the kinds of question to which the knowledge of personality traits may be of some relevance. This point is not brought out clearly by Waltz, who places the two quite separate things together under the same rubric of 'the first image'.

This, however, is a negligible sin perhaps. What is considerably more problematic, and must not go unchallenged, is Waltz's further enlargement of the first category in the concluding part of his book. Certain concrete mental states of the leaders, such as their desire for a particular piece of territory, or fear of aggrandizement on the part of a rival state, are now included in this category. Furthermore, according to Waltz, concrete acts undertaken by the leaders are also to be counted as among the first-level factors (Waltz 1959: 218, 232, 234). According to this line of argument, Admiral Jorge Anaya's desire for the Falkland/Malvinas Islands, leading to the war of 1982, the Saudi king's fear of Iraqi expansionism in the Gulf War of 1990–1, and President Nasser's request that the United Nations Emergency Force be withdrawn from the Sinai, resulting in the Six Day War of 1967, are all examples of Waltz's 'first-image' factors.

Now, admittedly, the ability of human beings to have any desire or fear at all, a greedy or paranoiac personality, and a concrete desire or fear on the part of a particular leader in a given instance may all be said to be 'within man', the expression Waltz uses in referring to his first image (Waltz 1959: 12). But they are not so in the same sense: these quite disparate items belong to all human beings, certain kinds of people, and a specific individual in concrete circumstances, respectively. The 'within-man' category becomes inordinately large when all these things have to be accommodated in it.

As far as particular acts of individual leaders are concerned, they are obviously performed by human beings. To be fair to Waltz, moreover, he defines his 'first image' in terms not solely of 'human nature', but 'the nature and *behavior* of man' (1959: 16; emphasis added). It might therefore be suggested that subsuming particular acts of specific leaders would not in fact stretch the category beyond its initial definitional boundary. However, in the first two chapters of his book, which he devotes to a critical exposition of the first image, 'behaviour' means 'behavioural tendency', not particular acts of specific individuals in a given instance. The latter enters the discussion only towards the end of the book, where the first image becomes overstretched (Waltz 1959: 218, 230 ff.).

Waltz may complain that all this is pure hair-splitting. A category is what one defines it to be, and there is no natural size to it; and, after all, it might be said, various desires, fears, and acts of particular leaders, relating to war, are all to some extent manifestations of their personality traits, and human nature at rock bottom. But if this is hair-splitting, it is by no means pointless. On the contrary, it helps reveal that Waltz's enlargement of the first category, particularly in the concluding part of his book, has enabled him unduly to depreciate the category's overall significance. How is this so?

In the earlier part of his book, where he treats the first category essentially as an argument from human nature, he complains, rightly, that the category fails to explain war specifically, in contradistinction to any other forms of human activity. In his own words, 'the importance of human nature as a factor in causal analysis of social events is reduced by the fact that the same nature, however defined, has to explain an infinite variety of social events' (1959: 27). More strikingly, he remarks, 'human nature may in some sense have been the cause of war in 1914, but by the same token it was the cause of peace in 1910' (1959: 28).

Towards the end of his book, however, where he treats the first category as also containing such things as specific thoughts or acts on the part of a given leader, he now considers the category as inadequate because such things only (partly) explain particular instances of war, and entirely fail to explain war as such. The ultimate explanation of the latter, which interests him more, is found, he insists, in the structural framework of the international system, not in the particular acts of individuals (1959: 230 ff.).

But this shift is quite unfair. The first image is criticized twice over—initially for being hopelessly too general, and later for being trivially too specific. A determined defender of Waltz may respond that he is criticizing different versions of the first-level analysis in different ways at different places in his book. If so, Waltz should have identified and separated these versions from the start, and assessed their respective merits independently. Instead, he draws a consistently negative picture of the first image on inconsistent grounds as though he were waging a smear campaign against it. The first image becomes a dumping ground. And this ('dumping-groundification') could not have been achieved without Waltz's enlargement of the first category beyond its initial definitional boundary.

The term 'dumping ground' here has been borrowed from Robert Keohane and Joseph Nye (1987: 746), who criticize Waltz's later (neo-Realist) theory for assigning to the unit level any explanatory variable of international political behaviour other than the (system-level) distribution of power. But Waltz's tendency counter-productively to stretch his unit level goes back to his 1959 work. It also continues to this day. In one of his publications thirty years later, Waltz (1989: 48) categorizes the presence of nuclear weapons as a unit-level phenomenon rather than, more naturally it would seem, as a phenomenon of the technological dimension. As Barry Buzan (1995: 208–11) rightly complains, there is no such dimension in Waltz's tripartite (and more recently, bifurcated) scheme.

Another enlargement

To the above exposition, we must add another critical observation: in the course of his discussion, Waltz also stretches his second category. According to the basic definition he gives it, the second image sees the major cause of war as lying in the internal structure of a given kind of state (Waltz 1959: 12). This point is quite well known. What is hardly noticed, by contrast, is his later inclusion of quite incongruous items within the category. Not only does he, as we just saw, treat concrete thoughts and acts on the part of specific individuals as 'within man', and therefore as belonging to the first (human) level of analysis, but he now considers such items also as features of the second (state) level.

To help reveal this rather elusive point, here are some key statements by Waltz which occur in his discussion of the immediate causes of war. First, he writes: 'If they [State *A* and State *B*] fight against each other it will be for reasons especially defined for the occasion by each of them' (1959: 232). Later on, he includes among such reasons a desire for something a country lacks, and a concern for its future security (1959: 234). He also maintains that 'these special reasons become the immediate, or efficient causes of war' (1959: 232). Then he offers a key observation: 'the immed iate causes of every war must be either the acts of individuals *or the acts of states*' (1959: 232; emphasis added), and that the immediate causes of war 'are contained in the first *and second* images' (1959: 232; emphasis added).

Waltz's reasoning here appears to be as follows: the immediate causes of war are what the leaders think and do; since the leaders are human beings, what they think and do can be treated as features of the first (human) level of analysis; at the same time, what they think and do, *as key decision-makers*, can be imputed to their state inasmuch as it is in the name of their state that they perform their thinking and acting; and, therefore, the immediate causes of war can also be said to be located in the second (state) level of analysis.

It is in this way that Waltz comes to speak of the first two levels of analysis in conjunction, as in the passage from *Man, the State and War* quoted above. Now, admittedly, the leaders' thoughts and acts can be imputed to their state. The Argentinian leaders' desire for, and decision to invade, the Falkland/Malvinas Islands were also, it is conventional to say, Argentina's desire for, and decision to invade, the islands. But, clearly, there is a difference between the sense in which a desire for, and the decision to invade, the Falkland/Malvinas Islands can be *attributed* to the Argentinian state, and the sense in which, for example, military dictatorship was an *attribute* of that state. The former is a matter of imputation. The latter sort of condition (regime types) is what Waltz's second image is initially and supposedly about. Adding the former type of item (state acts) to the category is quite inconsistent with the definition he gives it at the outset.

In any case, such an expansion of the category hinders its clear-headed assessment. Certain internal structural attributes of a given state may constitute an underlying cause of a series of wars in which it engages. By contrast, particular acts of the state can only be part of the explanation of a given instance of war. It is bound

TABLE 1.2. *Waltz's (1959) location of the two types of cause*

	First level of analysis	Second level of analysis	Third level of analysis
Efficient causes	Present	Present	Absent
The permissive cause	Absent	Absent	Present

to be quite counter-productive then to try to assess the *overall* significance of the second category of war's causes in which not only internal structural characteristics but also particular state acts have been accommodated.

The theoretical rationale

Waltz's expansion of the first and second categories is therefore troubling to say the least, and even harmful: it gets in the way of clear thinking. We may therefore wonder about the underlying theoretical rationale of such a move. What function does expanding the two categories in such dubious ways serve in the overall structure of Waltz's argument?

The answer turns out to be this: this move forms part of Waltz's argument in favour of the third image. How is this so? To answer this, it is necessary to return to the observation that his argument in support of the third image is constructed along the following lines: (i) that there are two kinds of cause with respect to war, efficient and permissive; (ii) that all the efficient causes are located in the first two levels; (iii) that the permissive cause is found exclusively in the third level; (iv) that therefore the third level contains a different kind of cause from the rest; (v) that the permissive cause of war is the underlying cause of war; and (vi) that, therefore, the third level of analysis contains the most fundamental cause of war. This is presented schematically in Table 1.2 and, using Waltz's later terminology, in Table 1.3 (see also Table 1.1).

In order to argue in the way summarized by these tables, Waltz needs to be able to say that the permissive cause is located *exclusively* in the third, system, level. But this assertion, which we shall discuss in the next section, needs to be complemented by the other claim that *all* the efficient causes are found in the first two levels of analysis, or the unit level. Without this supporting assertion,

TABLE 1.3. *Waltz's (1979) location of the two types of cause*

	Unit level	System level
Efficient causes	Present	Absent
The permissive cause	Absent	Present

the whole argument collapses: it is only on the basis of the *combination* of these two assertions that Waltz manages to draw a neat qualitative distinction between the first two levels and the third; and, as we saw, this distinction is in turn at the base of his third-image thesis.

Here then is the underlying theoretical rationale of Waltz's insistence that all the efficient causes of war are found in the first two levels. Among the efficient causes of war, Waltz notes, are such things as particular motives and acts on the part of key decision-makers. Waltz is therefore compelled to say, within his scheme of analysis and argument, that such items as concrete motives and acts on the part of particular leaders at a given time belong to the levels of man and the state, even though he is thereby forced to expand the unit-level categories beyond their initial definitional boundaries to the point, as we saw, of undermining their utility as units for coherent appraisal.

This move, it must now be clear, constitutes one of the important steps in Waltz's overall argument in favour of the third image. The other important move, as we just noted, is his assertion that the permissive cause of war is found *exclusively* in the third level. This and other related aspects of Waltz's third-image contentions are examined in the next subsection.

Problems with Waltz's Emphasis on the System Level

One of Waltz's main concerns in his book is to warn that prescriptions for peace aimed at the unit levels of man and the state are useless, or worse than useless, since they are applied within the existing international framework (Waltz 1959: 54–5, 108, 113–14, 119–20, 122–3, 222, 233–4). Thus he complains, for example, that even if the aforementioned psychological screening system for government officials could be instituted in one country, peace would not result, and the chances of war might be enhanced, unless all the other countries in the world were made to adopt the same measures simultaneously, which, given the decentralized nature of the international system, could not be done effectively (Waltz 1959: 62–3, 66).

As an assessment of the suggested prescription, and any other prescription of this kind, aimed exclusively at the levels of man and the state, Waltz's criticism appears in the main correct. But this does not show that the characteristics of the units, that is, the personality traits of the key decision-makers or the internal structural characteristics of some of the states involved, are not an important *part* of the cause of war in *some* cases. They clearly are. Saddam Hussein's Iraq in relation to the Gulf War, or Wilhelmine Germany in relation to the First World War, comes to mind. Of the Gulf War of 1991, Alex Danchev remarks: 'Profound causes must embrace Saddam and his system, its pathology and its political economy' (1994: 105). And the influence of domestic factors upon Germany's foreign policy before 1914 is well known (see e.g. Mommsen 1973).

Waltz may appear to concede such points when he states that the 'efficient causes' of particular wars are located in the first two levels of analysis. As we showed earlier, however, this is not the point he is making by this remark: his point is rather that the efficient or immediate causes of particular wars, being *acts* of individuals and states, are located in the first two levels of analysis. In any case, Waltz is so determined to reveal the inadequacies and misguidedness of prescriptions emanating from unit-level analyses that he fails to give sufficient attention to the part which unit-level factors play in producing particular wars or particular kinds of war.

Positive discrimination in favour of the third level

Coupled with Waltz's relative lack of emphasis on the unit level is his partiality towards the system level. As we saw, Waltz contends that 'the permissive cause' of war is found *exclusively* in the international environment. Quite transparently, however, this cannot be so: if the fact that there is nothing in the international system to prevent war is a permissive cause of war, then, by the same token, the fact that there is nothing of the sort, for example, in the make-up of man, or anywhere else for that matter, must also count as war's permissive cause. Impartiality dictates this.

In Waltz's assessment, we may recall, the fact that the third level of analysis yields an explanation, not of any particular war, but of the possibility of war as such, is the very strength of that level of analysis (see Tables 1.1–1.3). He is therefore in no position to complain, for example, that human nature fails to explain any specific war: this issue does not interest him. His main complaint about the first level is rather that human nature does not even explain war *as such* since, given the same human nature, not only war, but also peace, can result (Waltz 1959: 28). This is a legitimate complaint.

But the same complaint can in fact be aimed at the third-level explanation. Given international anarchy, sometimes there is war; sometimes there is peace. As Arnold Wolfers has remarked, 'the anarchical condition inherent in any system of multiple sovereignty constitutes one of the prerequisites of international conflict; without it, there could be no international relations, peaceful or non-peaceful' (1962b: 67). The division of the world into sovereign states is a precondition for international cooperation as well as conflict.

Thus there is qualitative equivalence between the view that human nature is a cause of war and the assertion that war is possible because there is nothing in the international system to prevent war. This point will be discussed further in the next chapter. Interestingly, Waltz himself in effect acknowledges that human nature qualifies as 'a permissive cause' of war, although he does not use this term explicitly in this context. He writes: 'Human nature is a cause then only in the sense that if men were somehow entirely different, they would not need political control at all' (1959: 28–9). To this, however, he adds the following observation: 'This calls to mind the runner who, when asked why he lost the race, replied: "I ran too slowly." The answer, though correct, is not very helpful' (1959: 29).

Even more interestingly, Waltz also notices that exactly the same criticism can in fact be aimed at the parallel assertion that war is possible because there is nothing in the international system to prevent war. He writes:

The third image, like the first two, leads directly to a utopian prescription ... It is of course true that with world government there would no longer be international wars, though with an ineffective world government there would no doubt be civil wars. It is likewise true, reverting to the first two images, that without the imperfections of the separate states there would not be wars, just as it is true that a society of perfectly rational beings, or of perfect Christians, would never know violent conflict. These statements are, unfortunately, as trivial as they are true. They have the unchallengeable quality of airtight tautologies: perfectly good states or men will not do bad things; within an effective organization highly damaging deviant behavior is not permitted (1959: 228–9)

Despite all this, Waltz ends by crowning 'international anarchy' as '*the* permissive cause' of war, and attaches a very special significance to this particular cause: it is said to give a 'final explanation' (Waltz 1959: 231) of the origins of war among states.

Waltz's continued stress on the system level

In his later work, *Theory of International Politics* (1979), Waltz continues to hold essentially the same position on the explanation of war. A slight difference of emphasis is observable, however. Whereas, in his 1959 work, he stresses that international anarchy explains the very *possibility* of war, now, in his 1979 work, he emphasizes that it explains the *recurrence* of war. The latter position is based on the following line of reasoning.

War is a recurrent phenomenon, and occurs in spite of variations at the level of the units (i.e. in the characteristics of individuals and states); only a constant factor can explain the recurrence of a given type of phenomenon; the anarchical structure of the international system is such a factor; therefore this, rather than the nature of the units, explains the recurrence of war; since what explains the recurrence of war is more fundamental than what explains the occurrence of a particular war, international anarchy is more fundamental than other conditions of war (Waltz 1979: 66 ff.). This, as will be shown below, is a strangely skewed argument, even if we were to concede for the moment that only a constant factor could explain the recurrence of any given type of phenomenon.

In the above line of reasoning, Waltz points to variations in the characteristics of individuals and states. But the characteristics of the international environment, too, show historical variations, for example, in terms of the patterns of power distribution or types of normative constraints imposed. Waltz, of course, knows this. His point is rather that, despite such, not unimportant, variations, international anarchy as such has remained a constant feature.

Now, of course, we have to concede that there is nothing in the international system to make war impossible, and also that this has been a constant factor in the international environment. But, correspondingly, the make-up of man or of the state, despite many changes, has also remained a constant factor to the extent that there is, and continues to be, nothing in either which can rule out the very possibility of war. Therefore, consistency demands that whatever privilege one gives to international anarchy on the basis of its constancy be accorded also to corresponding, equally constant, unit-level conditions. Waltz fails to notice this.

More fundamentally, however, Waltz's initial supposition that what explains the *recurrence* of a given type of phenomenon must be a *constant* factor is quite mistaken. Clearly, a factor need only be recurrent, not constant, to qualify as a candidate. What explains the recurrence of rain in England is not any *constant* factor, but the *recurrence* of those conditions which bring about the rain. Furthermore, although international anarchy, as defined here, is a constant factor, its constancy does not in fact explain war's *recurrence* as such. It shows only part of the reason why the recurrence of war is *possible*. Clearly, 'possibility of recurrence' and 'actual recurrence' are not of the same order.

Waltz neglects this last point, and apparently believes that he has given a theoretical explanation of a regular feature of international relations, the recurrence of war, in much the same way as physicists explain regular features of the physical world (Waltz 1979). But all that he has done is simply to point to one of the permissive causes of war. As far as explaining war is concerned, therefore, Waltz's 1979 publication does not go beyond his work twenty years earlier.

International anarchy, the underlying cause?

If we return, therefore, to his earlier work, Waltz's positive discrimination in favour of the third level—complementing what was earlier depicted as a smear campaign against the first two—is further exacerbated by his ready equation of 'the permissive cause' with 'the underlying cause'. 'International anarchy', which Waltz himself concedes at one point (1959: 228-9) is no more than one of the trivial permissive causes of war, becomes inflated, in his scheme, into 'the underlying cause of war', which may be understood to mean 'the most profound cause of war as such'.

To be fair to Waltz, he does not in fact write that the frame-work of international relations is '*the* underlying cause of war'; he merely states that, 'if the framework is to be called cause at all, it had best be specified that it is *a* permissive or underlying cause of war' (1959: 232; emphasis added). Immediately afterwards, how-ever, he refers to 'the international environment' as '*the* permissive cause' (1959: 233; emphasis added). Therefore, it is legitimate to assume Waltz to be thinking that international anarchy is '*the* underlying cause of war', and this interpretation coheres with his overall argument.

Now, 'anarchy' can mean a number of things. A continuously tense and unstable situation where war is effectively part of every-day expectations might perhaps be called 'international anarchy'. And we might say, with respect to some specific cases, for example, Arab–Israeli wars, that such a tense and unstable condition was 'an underlying cause' of the war that ensued. Even in such cases, however, we would not necessarily suppose that 'international anarchy', in the sense just specified, is the *sole* underlying cause of war; there may be a number of others. Moreover, 'international anarchy' in this sense is most definitely not 'an underlying cause' of war in *every* case. Witness, for example, the Falklands/Malvinas War. War was not part of everyday expectations at that time in Anglo-Argentinian relations, and in a sense that was part of the problem (see Sect. 5.4). In short, 'international anarchy' in the sense of a continuously tense and unstable situation is at best *an* underlying cause of *some* wars.

But 'international anarchy' in this sense is not the same as 'in-ternational anarchy' in the sense of 'the fact that there is nothing in the international system to prevent war'. The former points to an extremely—and exceptionally—disorderly situation. The latter is an inescapable fact. And it is the latter which is one of the permissive causes of war, accounting for the very possibility of war. Clearly, we cannot conclude that 'international anarchy' in the sense of 'the fact that there is nothing in the international sys-tem to prevent war', which is *a permissive cause of war as such*, is also *the underlying cause of war as such*, by demonstrating that 'international anarchy' in another sense, signifying a tense and unstable condition, is *an underlying cause of some wars*. But this does not appear to have concerned Waltz (see 1959: 217 ff.).

Waltz might have noticed a category mistake involved here if he had been more careful in his use of the concept of 'possibility'. Part of the time he thinks of a permissive cause of war as a factor which makes war 'possible' in the strict sense that in the absence of this factor war would be 'impossible' (1959: 228–9). Yet, by adding a temporal dimension to the idea of 'possibility', and calling it 'constant possibility' (1959: 188, 227), Waltz activates it, so to speak, and almost imperceptibly turns it into something rather more menacing than a sheer possibility.

By the time the 'constant possibility of war' is made interchangeable with the idea that 'any state may at any time use force to implement its policies' (1959: 160), or that 'war may at any moment occur' (1959: 232), Waltz has transformed the idea of 'possibility' from its strict sense, contrasted with 'impossibility', into something close to the 'imminence' of war. Correspondingly, he has failed to distinguish between one sense of 'international anarchy' which makes it a permissive cause of war (such that in its presence war may occur somewhere sometime), and another sense of 'international anarchy' which is an underlying cause of war in some cases (such that in its presence war may break out at any moment at a particular place).

Two related issues may be raised in this connection. One is Waltz's apparent neglect of an important distinction between a 'pre-emptive war' and a 'preventive war'. The other concerns his use of two elementary scenarios of war origins.

A 'pre-emptive war' is where State *A*, sensing the imminence of State *B*'s attack upon *A*, resorts to anticipatory self-defence. Israel's attack on Egypt in 1967 is a standard example. By contrast, a 'preventive war' is where A thinks that, in order to achieve its aims, war with B will be necessary sometime in the near future, perhaps within the next few years, and resorts to it now when in its own calculation it has a better chance of winning. According to one interpretation now accepted by some notable historians of the First World War (e.g. Gordon 1974: 195), the German motive for war against Russia in 1914 was 'preventive'.[2]

The awareness of the fact that there is nothing in the international system to prevent war is a particularly decisive element in

---

[2] It is possible for a preventive war by State *A* against State *B* to be initiated by *B*'s pre-emptive strike: 'prevention' is a quality of the motive which underlies engagement in war, whereas 'pre-emption' relates to who strikes first. See Levy (1987) for a very thoughtful discussion of 'prevention' and 'pre-emption'.

A's calculation leading to a pre-emptive strike. By contrast, the same awareness plays a less significant part in preventive wars, and there may be many cases of preventive war where unit-level factors are decisive as the war's 'underlying causes'. For example, it may be partly owing to an unusually strong position of the military in its government that A comes to consider war with B as inevitable in the near future, and judges that it is better to go to war now rather than later. In such a case, though clearly not in all cases, A's internal structure is an important causal factor which may well qualify as the war's 'underlying cause'.[3]

Waltz does not discuss these points, apparently determined that 'the underlying cause of war', which he readily equates with 'the permissive cause of war', is always to be found in the third level of analysis. It is worth noting here that because of this ready equation there is no room in Waltz's scheme for the idea of 'an underlying cause of a particular war, which is specific to that, or that type of, war'. To him, 'the underlying cause of war' is always 'the underlying cause of war as such', located, as he insists, in the system level.

This reveals a highly questionable limitation which Waltz imposes upon the extent to which war comes about in different ways: wars may be different as regards their immediate causes, but they are all the same as regards their underlying cause, according to him. A theory of war which does not allow for a multiplicity of underlying causes is not, strictly speaking, mono-causal, but would still seem quite unnecessarily impoverished—'reductionist' in fact. This point will be explored further in Chapter 5.

The other issue, relating to the above point, concerns the two elementary scenarios of war origins which Waltz (1959: 234) very briefly makes use of in his discussion: one where war results from State A's desire for x (say, a piece of territory) which is in State B's hands; and the other where war arises out of a power competition between A and B.

Waltz refers to these scenarios solely to explain his view of the relationships between the unit level and the system level, and to argue that the efficient causes of war are located in the former, and the permissive cause in the latter. Accordingly, his reference

---

[3] See further Levy (1987: 104–5); and Sect. 5.3. Major democratic powers appear never to have launched preventive war (Schweller 1992).

to these elementary scenarios is extremely brief, and he does not consider whether there may be other kinds of scenario depicting the origins of wars. This question needs to be explored further since there are many ways in which war comes about, and Waltz's two models are insufficient both in detail and variety for the purpose of understanding this important point.

As a matter of fact, Waltz's selection of these two particular scenarios tends to exaggerate the significance of the system level. Here we must note Waltz's comment (1959: 234) that in the second scenario, where war results from a power competition, the efficient cause of war (namely 'fear') 'is derived from' the permissive cause (the fact that there is nothing in the international system to prevent war). Thus the system level is depicted by Waltz not only as containing the permissive cause of all wars, but also as playing a somewhat more active or direct role in one out of the two likely kinds of situation leading to the outbreak of war. As will be shown in Chapter 5, exploration of other scenarios leads to a different assessment.

An overview of Waltz's third-image contentions

The discussion so far shows that Waltz's apparent belief that it is exclusively in the system level that the permissive or underlying cause of war is located cannot be sustained; and further that his argument attaching special importance to the system level involves a number of highly questionable moves. However, in case it is thought that the picture of Waltz presented here distorts his central contentions, or that it is excessively critical of them, some qualifying observations should be added to the foregoing exposition and critique.

It is not suggested here that Waltz is mistaken in attaching *some* importance to the system-level factors. At one point, he writes: 'the international political environment has *much* to do with the ways in which states behave' (1959: 122–3; emphasis added). It has indeed. This is accepted wholeheartedly.

Further, the fact that there is nothing in the international system to prevent war is here conceded to be *a* permissive cause of war. An awareness of this fact is a particularly decisive element in calculations leading to a pre-emptive strike, we noted. We may wonder, however, where national leaders' *consciousness* of this fact should be located in Waltz's tripartite scheme. His own logic would appear to suggest that this belongs, not to the third, but to the first two levels of analysis.

More generally, the fact that there is nothing in the international system to prevent war is a key to understanding why states perceive it to be rational to be prepared to fight at any time. This perception may exacerbate competition for security especially where there is much mistrust between the contestants. This familiar argument will be employed in Chapter 3 to show why the presence of an acute arms race may not be a useful early warning indicator of war: in a predominantly self-help system, escalation once under way is very difficult to contain. There is nothing objectionable in drawing attention to this difficulty, which is part of what Waltz is doing in his work. We also noted that international anarchy in the sense of a highly tense and unstable situation may be an important underlying cause of war in *some* cases.

Further, Waltz appears in the main right, we agreed, to stress the inadequacies of prescriptions for peace aimed at the first two levels of analysis. In connection with this, it should also be noted that, as part of his third-image view, Waltz (1959: 230) believes that war-conducive elements located in the first two levels are to some extent the product of the anarchical international environment. This point is worth considering, and will be discussed in the next chapter.

Such important qualifications notwithstanding, Waltz's apparent belief that the fact that there is nothing in the international system to prevent war is *the single, permissive, underlying cause of war as such* must be rejected. Accordingly, his rationale for expanding the first two categories weakens. As we saw, this has led Waltz to place incongruous items in each of these categories even at the cost of reducing their utility as units of appraisal. Such a price might perhaps have been worth paying if, as Waltz apparently believes, the three levels of analysis were the only ones, and the third level of analysis were the only place where a permissive cause of war was located.

However, a permissive cause of war can be found in places other than the third level: for example, in defective human nature. Besides, there is no compelling reason to insist that all the causally relevant factors *must* be slotted into the three places. A rigid adherence to the tripartite scheme is neither necessary nor desirable, even though the scheme accords well with our conventional view of world political order, and is hence easily comprehensible, which no doubt accounts for its immense popularity.

But if we are to abandon the Waltzian tripartite scheme, how are we to proceed? And where should we begin?

A Fresh Start

An opening move we must make in order to launch a successful attack on the question of what causes war is to note that the question is answered in different ways depending on which of the following three types of question is in fact being asked. These, as we noted, are:

(a) 'What are the conditions which must be present for wars to occur?';
(b) 'Under what sorts of circumstances have wars occurred more frequently?'; and
(c) 'How did this particular war come about?'

In (a), the term 'the causes of war' is implicitly taken to mean 'the necessary conditions of all wars', and, accordingly, the question 'What causes war?' is approached from the viewpoint of identifying such conditions. War is here assumed to be such that for any war to occur there are certain common conditions or prerequisites which must be satisfied.

In (b), 'the causes of war' (or the more important of them) are presumed to have a statistical association with the occurrence of war, and, accordingly, it is assumed that, in order to find a worthwhile answer to the question 'What causes war?', we should first identify the 'correlates of war'. Here war is considered as a type of phenomenon with regard to which statistical generalizations can usefully be made.

By contrast, (c) treats 'the causes of war' to be, at least initially, events and actions in a given sequence which in the circumstances led to the outbreak of a particular war. Here each instance of war is seen as resulting from a potentially unique sequence of occurrences.

These three questions thus embody different ideas about what 'cause' is and how to look for one, and require different methods of enquiry. They also make different assumptions regarding what sort of thing 'war' is from the viewpoint of identifying its causes.

Therefore, separating these questions clearly and consistently is a more fundamental move to make in clarifying how to reason about the causes of war than is noticing the three levels of analysis or the three images as Waltz has done.

Moreover, it turns out that the unsatisfactory aspects of Waltz's defence of the third image have resulted partly from his failure to adhere consistently to the distinction which he himself draws between questions (a) and (c).[4] Had he separated the two questions consistently, he would have hesitated to place together in the first level of analysis such incongruous items as (1) human nature, (2) the personality traits of key decision-makers, and (3) their specific thoughts and acts under given circumstances.

Of these three items, (1) is relevant to (a), (2) is relevant to (c) and perhaps also to (b), and (3) is relevant to (c). As we saw, however, Waltz unhesitatingly places all the three items in the first category, and this, especially his inclusion of item (3) in this category, enables him to make the first important move in his overall thesis: that all 'the efficient causes' of particular wars are found in the first level of analysis and, by imputation, in the second level also.

His second important move, as we saw, is his assertion that the sole permissive cause of war is located in the system level. Furthermore, he equates the 'permissive' with the 'underlying' cause. Waltz might be right to consider that a tense and unstable situation among particular states at a given time was a system-level underlying cause of war among them. But, clearly, this sort of assertion relates to question (c). Had Waltz separated this question from (a) consistently, he would not have treated a historical interpretation that a tense and unstable international situation was the system-level underlying cause, for example, of the First World War as though it were the same kind of assertion as his central thesis that the fact that there is nothing in the international system to prevent war was the permissive cause of war as such. Indeed, he might have suggested that the underlying cause of war would vary according to which war (or type of war) we had in mind.

[4] Waltz points to the distinction between questions (a) and (c) when he separates 'permissive' from 'efficient' causes. Recall that his 'permissive cause' relates to the possibility of war, whereas his 'efficient cause' relates to the occurrence of particular wars.

As for (*b*), Waltz is of course aware of its existence as a question which arises in the causes-of-war research. He correctly notes, however, that a statistical correlation is not sufficient to establish a cause-and-effect relationship (1959: 13), and perhaps because of this, he does not give question (*b*) a full treatment: he is concerned with the causes of war, not mere correlates.

None the less, there is some evidence in Waltz's book to suggest that he at times considers 'a cause of war' to be such that its removal should lead to a reduction in the frequency of war (see Waltz 1959: 8, 47, 83, 231–2). This reveals that Waltz at times implicitly accepts the view that 'a cause of war' must also be 'a correlate of war' (although he knows the reverse not to be the case): otherwise, removing 'a cause of war' could not be presumed to reduce the frequency of war in the first place. Clearly, however, there can be 'a cause of a war' which is not at the same time 'a correlate of war'. Waltz might have noticed this point had he paid fuller attention to the distinction between questions (*b*) and (*c*).

Furthermore, Waltz not only asserts that war is possible because there is nothing in the international system to prevent war; he also writes (1959: 231–2) as though he believes that this assertion is of the same kind as the assumption that the relatively decentralized institutional structure of the international environment explains the relative frequency of war. If Waltz had clearly distinguished between questions (*a*) and (*b*), he would have avoided this error. In any case, paying fuller attention to question (*b*) would be an important element in an attempt to enlarge on Waltz's study.

We should add that Waltz does not fully examine problems associated with (*c*). 'How did this particular war come about?' will be answered in different ways depending on what 'this particular war' is. This gives rise to important questions regarding the variety of war origins. But, as we noted, Waltz only mentions two scenarios, and his reference to them is very brief. He does not investigate in any detail the variety of the ways in which war comes about.

A recognition that questions (*a*), (*b*), and (*c*) should be given a separate, and fuller, treatment, then, is an appropriate starting-point for a more coherent and thorough treatment of how to reason about the causes of war than was achieved by Waltz in his pioneering work.

1.2 HISTORY, THEORY, AND IDEOLOGY

We should move on to another important work in the genre,
Nelson and Olin's *Why War?* This appeared twenty years after
Man, the State and War. Like the latter, the former analyses the
structure of ideas about the causes of war, but, unlike the latter,
the former concentrates on works on the origins of *particular*
wars.

Nelson and Olin's Main Contentions

Nelson and Olin's primary objective is to show that historians, in
giving an account of the origins of a particular war, use causal
theories of war; that a historian's theory is likely to reflect his or
her ideology; and that therefore we can better understand, compare, and evaluate what historians are saying when we compre-
hend their ideological and theoretical perspectives (Nelson and
Olin 1979: 92).

By 'ideology' Nelson and Olin mean fundamental assumptions
about human beings and society, such as conservativism, liberalism, and radicalism (Nelson and Olin 1979: 5). A 'theory', unlike
a 'historical explanation' of a single event, they claim, 'must be
able to account for two or more comparable events' (1979: 2).
They examine historical writings on the First World War and the
Second World War to illustrate their contentions.

With respect to these wars, Nelson and Olin (1979: 102, 145)
acknowledge that the conservative perspective is rare among historians. However, there are some causal theories of war which,
according to the authors, reflect conservativism; and these theories, they claim (1979: 102 ff., 141 ff.), are used by some historians in giving an account of the origins of these wars.

According to the two authors, 'there are at least two distinct
strains of conservative thought about the subject: one which presupposes that individuals and nations are basically aggressive in
behavior' (1979: 16), and the other 'which suggests that wars
result when nations lose their discipline and order, or when international hierarchies break down' (1979: 16).

The contention that wars occur because of the basically aggressive behaviour of individuals corresponds to Waltz's first image.

The argument that wars result when nations lose their discipline and order is somewhat vague, but the two authors seem to have in mind here the contention, for example, that a democratic (and other non-aristocratic) national leadership is inexperienced in the traditional skills of diplomacy, and thereby contributes to international disorder (Nelson and Olin 1979: 27–8). The argument that a given war was caused by the breakdown of an international hierarchy is an application to the international sphere of the central tenet of conservativism, that order presupposes the defence of a status quo by the hitherto superior class.

As the two authors show (1979: 106 ff., 147 ff.), the theories of war which stem from liberalism are diverse, and much more common among historians of the two world wars than are conservative theories.

According to one liberal theory, liberal nation-states behave rationally and cooperatively under normal circumstances. However, for a variety of identifiable reasons, such as stress or frustration, their leaders and citizens fall victim to misperception and stereotypes. It is such abnormal and undesirable states of mind which account for war. Another version of liberal theory holds that war results from the relative lack of social integration at the international level compared to what is normally the case within the domestic sphere. Liberalism may also lead a historian to point to a conspiratorial motive on the part of the ruling élite or a particular interest group. For example, a government may resort to an aggressive action against other states in order to bolster its position in the face of domestic discontent; or a particular pressure group, such as a military-industrial complex, in pursuit of its own parochial interest, may push the government to follow an aggressive foreign policy, ending in war (Nelson and Olin 1979: ch. 2, 106 ff., 147 ff.).

The explanation of war in terms of a military-industrial complex, as Nelson and Olin (1979: 177) acknowledge, is close to a version of radical theory. However, according to them (1979: ch. 3, 123 ff., 168 ff.), whether Marxist–Leninist or revisionist, radicalism sees in the capitalist system as such the cause of imperialism and war.

Revisionists (unlike Marxist–Leninists), the authors say, 'are not absolutely confident that a maturing capitalism inevitably produces international conflict' (1979: 87). However, according to the authors

(1979: 177), revisionists hold that capitalist institutions severely limit the options available to decision-makers, and that it is 'far more likely under capitalism than under socialism, that leading economic interests will have the need and ability to persuade decision-makers to engage in imperialist aggression and war' (1979: 87). The authors (1979: 123 ff., 168 ff.) illustrate these claims skilfully with respect to a large number of mainly historical writings on the origins of the two world wars.

It may be observed at this stage that the distinction among the three kinds of question regarding the causes of war, which, as we saw, is not consistently or fully employed by Waltz, is not used by Nelson and Olin either.

For example, consider the following three propositions: (1) 'that war occurs because of aggressive human nature'; (2) 'that capitalist states are more war-prone than socialist states'; and (3) 'that misperception largely accounts for a given war'. Nelson and Olin distinguish these three propositions primarily on the ground that they represent different ideologies: conservativism, radicalism, and liberalism, respectively. However, we must note that (1) relates to any war, that (2) concerns the relative frequency of involvement in war, and that (3) is about a specific instance of war. Thus (1), (2), and (3) are distinguishable also because they constitute possible answers to different kinds of question: (*a*), (*b*), and (*c*), respectively, as formulated above.

Nelson and Olin (1979: 33) are aware that the argument from human nature is weak when explaining why a particular war occurred at a given time, but the distinction among the three kinds of question, (*a*), (*b*), and (*c*), is hardly noted in their discussion. The effect of this neglect upon their main conclusion will be noted in the next subsection.

Before we proceed, one important observation must be added: because (1), (2), and (3), as noted above, are answers to different categories of question regarding the causes of war, they are not in fact mutually incompatible even though they may reflect different ideologies. This point is worth stressing, because there is an understandable tendency to suppose that remarks stemming from different ideologies must necessarily be mutually incompatible. However, different remarks cannot be mutually incompatible if they are not answers to the same question. To put it another way, mutual incompatibility of different answers presupposes that they be directed at the same question. If they are not, each of them can be right, or wrong, independently.

Therefore, it is by no means inconsistent to suggest, in line with (1), (2), and (3) at the same time, that aggressive human nature partly explains why war is possible; that capitalist states, because of their structural characteristics, are more war-prone than socialist states; but that this particular war has resulted largely from misperception. Of course, one or more of these suggestions may in fact be mistaken, but at least they are not mutually inconsistent, despite the difference in their respective ideological underpinnings as suggested by Nelson and Olin.

This shows that, in analysing different ideas about the causes of war, a classification of suggested answers in terms of the types of question they aim at is more fundamental than the classification of the same in the light of their ideological grounding. Only after we have classified various remarks regarding the causes of war in terms of the types of question to which they are directed might it become useful to introduce an ideology-based classification. This reinforces our conclusion reached earlier in connection with Waltz's tripartite classification.

The Central Weakness of Nelson and Olin

There is no need here to criticize Nelson and Olin's work in detail. There are some points at which a fuller explanation may be called for, but there is little doubt that the method of analysis employed in their book is useful in clarifying the structure of historical controversies regarding the origins of wars. One important weakness of the two authors, however, is that they do not give sufficient weight to the fact that wars come about in different ways.

To clarify this point, it is necessary to summarize the assumptions which underlie the two authors' own view about how best to explain the causes of war. The following summary is based on their book as a whole, but its Introduction and Epilogue are particularly helpful in clarifying the authors' assumptions.

According to them, the outbreak of a particular war is 'an event'. A historical explanation of such an event gives an account of the event itself, and no other events. However, such an explanation is impossible without a causal theory. It is a distinguishing feature of such a theory that it is capable of explaining a plurality of comparable events. One theory may point to one type of cause, and another to another type. In general, a multi-causal explanation is to be preferred. By combining a number of mutually consistent theories, we should be able to formulate a more satisfactory causal account of war.

The position summarized above may seem innocuous, even commendable, because of its eclecticism and the air of impartiality which accompanies it. In order to give an account of the origins of a particular war, it is certainly desirable to be aware of a number of possible explanations or theories, and it is plausible that a more satisfactory explanation of the war's outbreak can be formulated by combining some of them rather than taking note of only one.

However, Nelson and Olin are apparently in search of a best-fitting theory which goes beyond explaining one specific instance of war. Recall that, according to them, a theory is capable of explaining a plurality of similar events. They appear also to suppose that there must in principle be one theory which is best fitting in the sense that it explains, if not literally all outbreaks of war, at least the largest number of them, or, failing that, the most significant outbreaks (determined by some independent criterion of 'significance'). They do not suppose that such a theory can be literally singled out from their list. But they appear to think that such a theory can be constructed—subject, of course, to supersession by an even better theory when one is found—by combining some selected ones in a consistent manner.

Their preferred theory (or model) depicts the process and effects of war as well as how it begins. It is built round the left-liberal and revisionist perspectives, and portrays the phase leading up to the outbreak of war roughly as follows: a society suffers economic depression, or a noticeable disparity of wealth develops among its citizens; frustration deepens on the part of the relatively deprived class, which seeks reform; but this is resisted by the conservative force within; this upsets domestic stability, and the conservative force, anxious to maintain its position, attempts to unite the nation by resorting to an aggressive foreign policy resulting in war (Nelson and Olin 1979: 188–91).

Undoubtedly, this is a plausible scenario of how a war (or a type of war) might come about (see further Levy 1989*b*; and Sect. 3.1). However, the following remarks with which the authors end their discussion betray, through a conspicuous omission, their belief that what they have constructed is potentially a 'best-fitting theory' in the sense just specified.

The crucial questions for the reader, of course, are these: Does such an ambitious vision [i.e. their model] violate your own ideological predilections? Does it flow logically from its own ideological foundations? Is it, or can it be, internally consistent? Can it be tested, and if and when it is, does it accord with historical reality? (1979: 191)

The most pertinent question which is conspicuously absent from the above list is this: 'With respect to which particular war or wars is this model a best-fitting one?'

What combination of causes best explains the outbreak of a particular war is a question relevant to that war specifically, and not necessarily to other wars which have taken place. Although another war like that one must naturally be explained well by the same set of causes, there is no guarantee that any other wars which have taken place are like that one. There is no assurance, therefore, that Nelson and Olin's preferred model, although it may be best fitting with respect to some specific wars, is also best fitting in the sense that it explains all outbreaks of war, the largest number of them, or even the most significant of them.

The major weakness of the authors' conclusion is that they do not give sufficient weight to the fact that wars come about in different ways, and fail thereby to specify the range of wars which they expect their favoured theory to encompass. They would have avoided this error if they had taken seriously the distinction noted above among the three kinds of question (*a*), (*b*), and (*c*), regarding 'all wars', 'many wars', and 'this particular war', respectively. Indeed, they would have conceded that their model did not contain an answer to (*a*) or even to (*b*), although it might explain some particular instances of war; and this might in turn have led them to take seriously the idea that other models would be needed to cover other kinds of war.

CONCLUSION

In this chapter, we have examined in detail the main contentions of *Man, the State and War*, and outlined the central thesis of *Why War?* Their respective frameworks for analysing existing ideas about the causes of war are very useful in bringing some order to the plethora of answers which have so far been suggested. However, one of the primary reasons why there is such a bewildering variety of answers to what causes war is that there are different kinds of question which are commonly asked with respect to the subject. Separating these questions is thus the most vital first step in sorting out how to reason about the causes of war. In particular, the following types must be distinguished: (*a*) 'What are the conditions which must be present for wars to occur?'; (*b*) 'Under what sorts of circumstances have wars occurred more frequently?'; and (*c*) 'How did this particular war come about?'

It should be noted that both Waltz, and Nelson and Olin, go beyond merely classifying various answers to what are the major causes of war. They advance their own views on this subject. Waltz's answer is that international anarchy is the most fundamental cause of all wars. Nelson and Olin, by contrast, suggest that the most important cause of war is socio-economic, and that the most significant source of war is found in domestic political instability resulting from an inability, which they regard as typical of capitalism, to solve socio-economic problems effectively.

However, Waltz's argument in favour of the third image contains a number of conceptual or logical errors, which have been exposed in detail. It has been suggested that he might have avoided some of these errors if he had adhered more consistently to the distinction which he himself draws between questions (*a*) and (*c*) in particular. Nelson and Olin, too, might have avoided the error of not specifying the range of wars their preferred model is supposed to explain, and they might have constructed some other models to cover the untouched range, if they had fully taken note of the distinction among questions (*a*), (*b*), and (*c*).

Enough critical remarks have been made with respect to the two existing analyses of ideas about the causes of war. We must now move on, more constructively, to see how the new framework of analysis, based on the distinction among the three kinds of question, can deliver the goods. We shall begin by examining question (*a*) in the next chapter.

2

PREREQUISITES

Rousseau's answer is really that war occurs because there is nothing to prevent it.

(Waltz 1959: 188)

The results just reported strongly support the proposition that positive expected utility is necessary—though not sufficient—for a leader to initiate a serious international dispute, including a war.

(Bueno de Mesquita 1981: 129)

THE first of our three questions regarding the causes of war concerns those conditions which must be present for war to occur. These conditions may be called 'prerequisites' or 'necessary conditions' of war—not of any particular war, but of war as such, and hence of any war, and therefore of all wars.

If such conditions do exist, we may be able to identify them, and perhaps even remove them. It is in the nature of necessary conditions of war that, if we were to have succeeded in removing any one of them, we would necessarily have eliminated all future wars. The absence of any one of them would veto the very possibility of war. It is therefore such conditions that the seekers of world peace would wish ideally to be able to identify. At the very least, it is worth considering whether or not such conditions exist.

There are, however, two main ways of identifying a 'necessary condition', which it is important to distinguish at the outset. A couple of examples will illustrate the basic distinction.

Suppose I have been invited to give a paper at a conference. Unless I have written a paper, or someone has written one for me, and, in any case, unless I am in possession of a paper, I will not be able to give one at the conference. Having my paper ready, therefore, is a necessary condition for my presenting it.

Suppose at the conference I became seriously distressed about the reception of the paper. In an exaggerated gesture of self-pity, I might decide to burn the remaining copies. Clearly, if oxygen were not present, I would be unable to do this. Indeed, I would be unable even to survive. The presence of oxygen, therefore, is a necessary condition for both these things.

These contrasting examples seem to show that there are two quite different paths to identifying a necessary condition. It is necessary for me 'to have' a paper in order for me to be able 'to give' it, and to see this quite obvious point it is sufficient to notice what logical relationship obtains between the concepts expressed by the words 'to give' and 'to have'. The competence required here may therefore be labelled 'logical', 'conceptual', or 'semantic'. By contrast, no amount of logical, conceptual, or semantic reasoning alone is sufficient to establish that the existence of oxygen is necessary for my burning paper or keeping alive: here a scientific investigation has been required (Leicester 1956).

Correspondingly, when in search of a condition which must be present for war to occur, we need to know which of the two kinds of thing we are after. Are we in search of those things whose necessity for the possibility of war is implicit in the meanings of relevant words, and can therefore be understood by simply analysing and seeing the relationship between them? Or are we in pursuit of those factors whose necessity for the same can only be understood by a scientific enquiry into international relations?

The first kind of enquiry will remind us of those conditions in whose absence war, logically, could not take place: it follows logically from a counterfactual supposition that these conditions were absent that, in such circumstances, war could not possibly occur. We may call these 'logically necessary conditions', or 'logical prerequisites' of war: in the absence of any one of these conditions, war would be a *logical impossibility*, as would be a conference presentation without anything to present.

The second type of investigation, if successful, will yield, as part of a wider system of knowledge, an empirically well-confirmed hypothesis stating a factor or factors in whose absence war does not occur, and a plausible theoretical explanation showing that this has to be so. We may call these factors 'scientifically necessary conditions' of war: in the absence of any one of these conditions, war would be a *scientific impossibility*, as would be a fire without oxygen.

There are, however, some qualifying observations to make about the distinction just drawn between the two modes of enquiry, and the corresponding one between the two types of necessary condition, logical and scientific. The problem is that the distinction is not quite so absolute as is apparently suggested by the two contrasting sets of examples noted above.

To illustrate this point, consider the following example: 'For our bodies to remain alive it is necessary that they take in life-sustaining substances.' It might perhaps be thought that anyone who understood what was meant by 'to remain alive' and 'life-sustaining substances' could see the truth of this statement. Clearly, there is a close connection between the two key terms here.

Yet we also need to notice a few other things to arrive at the statement in question: that our bodies continue to live until they die; that this process is irreversible; that one's body's (as opposed to someone else's) taking in something (as opposed to nothing) is related to its remaining alive; that some of the things (as opposed to everything) that one's body takes in are related to its keeping alive; and that these things have a life-sustaining property.

Of course, just an intelligent guess might enable us to come so far, but when we do the guessing we do not remain in the world of meanings: we base our assertions on observation and reasoning about conditions of our bodies and what they absorb. This example shows that a statement of a necessary condition may not always fall neatly into one or the other category, logical or scientific: there are hybrid cases, partly definitional and, though in a very rudimentary way, partly scientific.

It will have been noticed that characterizing some substance as 'life-sustaining' is to point to its causal power without spelling out what constitutes that particular faculty. From the viewpoint of science, it is only a provisional description. As science progresses, it becomes possible to specify in more and more detail the 'life-sustaining' property of this substance. Science progressively localizes causes. For example, it may be that the substance is rich in 'essential amino acids'. It is further possible to remove a residual definitional element from this term by showing what about such amino acids is 'essential' to sustaining life. In other words, a statement of a necessary condition, currently heavily dependent on a definitional connection, may have a more scientific future.

These observations suggest that the distinction between the two modes of enquiry, and the corresponding distinction between logically and scientifically necessary conditions, must be treated with caution.[1] Yet a significant gap does exist between, on the one hand, an attempt to identify necessary conditions of war by analysing the relationship between the meanings of relevant words, and, on the other, an attempt to do the same by applying to the field of International Relations a mode of enquiry and explanation practised in modern natural science.

In Section 2.1 we identify a number of factors whose status as necessary conditions of war derives from the meanings of the words employed. However, it may be that like the statement concerning 'life-sustaining substances' some of the statements discussed in Section 2.1 can in principle be superseded by scientific statements. In Section 2.2, we examine this question first. We then move on to an assessment of some researchers' claims to have identified necessary conditions of war through a scientific path.

2.1 LOGICALLY NECESSARY CONDITIONS OF WAR

One necessary condition of war is said to be found in the structure of the international environment. As we saw in Chapter 1, 'international anarchy', or the fact that there is nothing in the international system to prevent war, is said by Waltz to be 'the permissive cause' of war. Waltz's 'permissive cause' is treated here as equivalent to what we are calling a 'necessary condition'. Such conditions, however, are found also at the human and societal/state levels. In the following, we shall deal with necessary conditions of war at the three levels in turn, and explore whether any one of them can be said to be more important or fundamental than the others.

International Anarchy

When Waltz asserts that there is 'nothing' in the international system to prevent war, and refers to this condition as the permissive

---

[1] Those statements which are true by virtue of the meanings of the words they employ are called 'analytic', and are distinguished from 'synthetic' statements which require empirical substantiation. The philosopher W. V. O. Quine (1961*b*) has argued, however, that the analytic–synthetic distinction cannot be explicated satisfactorily. See Suppe (1977: 67 ff.) and Hollis (1994: 77–8) for an effective summary and critical discussion of Quine's controversial paper.

TABLE 2.1. *Perfectly/imperfectly effective anti-war device*

	When absent?	When present?	Absence necessary for war?
Imperfectly effective anti-war device	War possible	War possible	No
Perfectly effective anti-war device	War possible	War impossible	Yes

cause of war among states, what he has in mind as missing from the system must be some kind of anti-war device. This much is obvious. We should ask what sort of anti-war device it must be in order that its absence from the international system can count as a *necessary* condition of international war.

The meaning of 'anarchy'

It becomes clear that no ordinary sort of anti-war device would satisfy such a stringent requirement. The League of Nations was an anti-war device, and so, currently, is the United Nations. But the former failed to prevent the Second World War, above all, and there have been a number of wars under the latter. These are, therefore, instances of an *imperfectly* effective anti-war device. This much is also quite obvious.

Now, clearly, it is in the nature of an imperfectly effective anti-war device that war is possible not only in its absence, but also in its presence: this is what 'imperfectly effective' means. Since this is so, it is easy to see that the absence of such a device is not in fact a necessary condition of war: it is not necessary that such a device be absent, for even in its presence war can still occur. For the absence of something to qualify as a necessary condition of war, it needs to be the case that, in its presence, war simply could not happen at all. This reveals that only if we have in mind a *perfectly* effective anti-war device, in whose presence war would be a sheer impossibility, can we in fact say that its absence is a *necessary* condition of war. The argument here is summarized in Table 2.1 (see also Waltz 1979: 103; Welch 1993: 13).

There is no need as yet to consider what a perfectly effective anti-war device might look like, or whether in reality there could be such a thing. What needs to be asked first is what kind of remark is being made when the absence of such a device from the international system is said to be a necessary condition of war among states.

In considering this, we cannot fail to notice that if there were such a device in the international system (or anywhere else for that matter), logically, there could be no international war: that is what 'a perfectly effective anti-war device' means. This shows that in asserting that there is nothing in the international system to prevent war, and in referring to this particular condition as a permissive cause of war, Waltz is in fact stating a logical pre-requisite of war among states and not a scientifically necessary condition of it. As we noted in Chapter 1, this is conceded even by Waltz himself at one point (1959: 228–9).

In another context, A. W. MacRae remarks:

> Anyone is free to object that a particular question is trivial because the answer is obvious, or uninteresting because the answer makes no important difference to our view of the world, but it is not, in any absolute sense, a mistake to ask it. The only mistake is to ask one question but interpret the answer as though it related to a different question. (1988: 164)

This observation is pertinent to assessing Waltz's answer: it is a mistake to treat his answer as though it were an answer to the question asking for a scientifically necessary condition of war.

Anarchy in international theory

Some further comments are in order relating to this perhaps somewhat idiosyncratic interpretation of Waltz's position. First of all, the argument advanced above relates exclusively to Waltz's assertion that international anarchy is the *permissive* cause (or *necessary* condition) of international war. This is not in fact the only thing he has said about the influence of the structure of the international environment upon the behaviour of states. In particular, he is well known for his claim that a bipolar system is, other things being equal, more stable than a multipolar one (Waltz 1964; 1979: ch. 8; 1989: 44 ff.; see also Bueno de Mesquita 1978). Waltz's view of the relative stability of the bipolar world, however, is clearly not a simple logical claim, but involves empirical reasoning. It is by no means the intention of the foregoing discussion, therefore, to suggest that every aspect of Waltz's structural theory of international politics is reducible to a logical thesis.

Secondly, the term 'international anarchy' is used above as a substitute for a more cumbersome formula, 'the fact that there is nothing in the international system to prevent war', and this, in turn, is understood to mean 'the absence from the international system of a perfectly effective anti-war device'. It will rightly be objected that 'international anarchy' does not usually mean anything so artificially (and even senselessly) narrow as this, but that it points to a relatively decentralized institutional structure of, or the absence of government from, the international environment (Waltz 1959: 159; 1979: 88, ch. 6; 1989: 42). Nevertheless, it is only under this narrow definition that 'international anarchy' can be said to be a necessary condition of war at all. It is only under this definition, extremely artificial though it is, that Waltz's thesis that 'international anarchy' is a permissive cause (or necessary condition) of war can be treated as a valid claim.[2]

Thirdly, however, we must also acknowledge the importance of 'international anarchy' in the more usual sense of the absence of government from the international system. This is held by many, including Waltz himself, to *promote* competition and dispute among the units (Waltz 1959: ch. 6–8; 1979: ch. 6). There is no doubt that we observe in international relations much competition for security, mutual mistrust, and even, in some cases, pre-emptive and preventive motivations. But such tendencies, said to follow from the anarchical (or relatively decentralized) structure of the international system are not *evenly* distributed among its units. In fact, this supposed 'logic of anarchy'—according to which anarchy *entails* disorder—is not even pervasive. There are certain zones of

---

[2] On the ambiguity of the term 'anarchy', and on the appropriateness or otherwise of characterizing the international system as 'anarchical', see Milner (1991). While critical of the tendency to treat anarchy as though it were an exclusive and distinctive structural characteristic of the international environment, Milner concedes that 'anarchy [defined as an absence of central authority] is an important condition of world politics' (1991: 85). Similar views to Milner's main contentions were advanced earlier by Hedley Bull (1966) and Alan James (1964). A very helpful analysis of the concept of (de)centralization is found in Kelsen (1961: 303 ff.).

peace, for example, the so-called pluralistic security communities, such as North America or Scandinavia, where the 'logic' is defied, or fails to operate fully (Deutsch *et al.* 1957; Buzan 1991: 175–81).

The point here needs to be explicated further in the light of Waltz's remarks about the so-called 'security dilemma'. He writes:

> John Herz coined the term 'security dilemma' to describe the condition in which states, unsure of one anothers' [*sic*] intentions, arm for the sake of security and in doing so set a vicious circle in motion. Having armed for the sake of security, states feel less secure and buy more arms because the means to anyone's security is a threat to someone else who in turn responds by arming ... Whatever the weaponry and however many states in the system, states have to live with their security dilemma, which is produced not by their wills but by their situations. A dilemma cannot be solved; it can more or less readily be dealt with. (1979: 186–7)

Clearly, the security dilemma is not something we can neglect in the theory or practice of international relations. Yet, as Waltz himself notices, the dilemma is faced only where states are unsure of one another's intentions. Admittedly, most states are not entirely sure of most other states' intentions most of the time: they are not even sure of their own at times. However, some states are practically certain of one another's *non-belligerent* intentions in their mutual dealings. Such states, like any other state, will still have security problems to solve, but not all problems are dilemmas. In short, the security dilemma does not *always* arise. International anarchy, in the sense of the absence of central authority from the international environment, is not sufficient by itself to necessitate the security dilemma.

Fourthly, the idea that international anarchy (or absence of government), unlike domestic anarchy, does not necessarily entail disorder among the units has long been the central tenet of the so-called 'English School of International Relations', represented by such writers as C. A. W. Manning and Hedley Bull (Manning 1975; Bull 1977; Suganami 1983; 1989a; Wilson 1989). Waltz appears to be opposed to this idea, based on the rejection of the domestic analogy, since he states, 'Among men as among states, anarchy, or the absence of government, is associated with the occurrence of violence' (1979: 102). However, the argument that cooperation is possible under anarchy, and is a significant feature of international relations, is now increasingly familiar across the Atlantic.[3]

Thus, according to Robert Jervis (1978), international anarchy does not necessarily entail the security dilemma, but the effects of anarchy would vary depending on the types of military strategic postures on the part of the units involved. In Alexander Wendt's apt formula, 'anarchy is what states make of it', and thus there is no single inescapable 'logic' of anarchy in the international system (1992). John Vasquez concurs when he remarks that the 'great mistake of realism has been to assume that a struggle for power is a constant verité [*sic*] of history' (1993: 148). Further, Robert Axelrod (1990) argues that cooperation can emerge and spread *even* among egoistic units under anarchy if, among other things, a small cluster of interacting units adopt an extremely simple strategy called 'tit for tat' recommended by Anatol Rapoport.[4]

In any case, as Robert Keohane (1989) rightly notes, the international system, though anarchical, is institutionalized in various ways, making cooperation a significant feature of interactions among the units. Partly because of this, Helen Milner (1991) thinks that treating 'anarchy' as the starting point for theorizing about international relations is heuristically counter-productive. This view is shared by John Vasquez (1993: 267-8), who refers favourably in this context to Bull's *Anarchical Society*.

Even Waltz, acknowledging that 'peace has prevailed much more reliably among democratic states than elsewhere', has recently expressed his hope '[o]n external as well as internal grounds . . . that more countries will become democratic' (1991: 670). By this remark, Waltz must be said implicitly to have conceded that the

---

[3] See, in this connection, Buzan (1993), which attempts to relate the English school's central contentions to those of mainly North American structural realists and regime theorists. Buzan's non-historical, functional reconstruction of the origins of international society is anticipated by the idea of the 'minimum content of Natural Law' formulated by H. L. A. Hart, who influenced Hedley Bull (Hart 1961: chs. 9-10; Bull 1977: ix). It is also very close to the position taken by Alan James, another member of the English School (James 1986; 1992: esp. 390; 1993a: esp. 95-6; 1993b: esp. 277).

[4] Briefly, a unit following this strategy would act cooperatively at the beginning, and would only act non-cooperatively immediately in response to the partner's non-cooperative act, returning to cooperative behaviour as soon as the partner switches to cooperation. See Axelrod (1990) for details. See, however, Wendt's criticism (1992: 416-7) of the essentially behavioural orientation of Axelrod's approach.

so-called 'logic of anarchy' may be overcome among certain kinds of units, particularly among democratic states (see Sect. 3.3).

Fifthly, even if the 'logic of anarchy' were to be universally operative, which it is not, it would not necessarily follow that international anarchy was by itself sufficient to produce *war* among states: anarchy may promote competition and dispute, but these do not necessarily end in war. This reminds us that 'international anarchy' in the sense of the absence of government from the international sphere is not a sufficient condition of war: it does not make war 'inevitable'.

It is essential to stress this last point because the assertion to the contrary is very popular, and carelessly endorsed by some seasoned commentators and authoritative writers on international affairs (see Waltz 1959: 159, 182). We only need to note, however, that a statement of the form 'given x, war is inevitable' is straightforwardly false unless x is a sufficient condition of war, which 'international anarchy', in the sense of the absence of central authority from the international sphere, transparently is not.

This is also true with respect to 'international anarchy' in the sense of the absence from the international system of a perfectly effective anti-war device, which, as we saw, is only *a* necessary condition of war among states. Given this condition alone, there-fore, war is not yet possible, let alone inevitable. In order for war to become possible among states, all the other conjointly necessary conditions, whatever they might be, must be satisfied.

Sixthly, because 'international anarchy' may mean a number of things, it is worthwhile to explore whether there is any sense in which it is a sufficient condition of war at all. The answer must be in the negative. Even if 'international anarchy' were to be taken to mean a highly war-conducive international circumstance, as, for example, in the period leading to the outbreak of the First World War, it would still require 'a spark to set fire to the heap', as it is proverbially said of that war. Even in a continuously tense and unstable international situation where war is effectively part of states' everyday expectations, no war could break out without the relevant governments' deliberate decision to resort to war, however limited their freedom of action might be owing to domestic, international, and other circumstances (see Chapter 5). This shows that 'international anarchy' even in a highly war-conducive sense is not by itself a sufficient condition of war.

Finally, it may perhaps be objected that, given international anarchy, whatever its definition, war is inevitable in the sense that it will come about somewhere, sometime (Waltz 1979: 102). This may be a good bet to make because, when challenged, we can always say that we have not waited long enough to prove us right in our prediction. But this assertion in effect concedes that war will come about only when conditions other than international anarchy have been fulfilled: that would be the whole point of waiting. It therefore admits that international anarchy, whatever its definition, does not by itself make war inevitable.

This most obvious fact should be acknowledged more openly. A fatalistic suggestion to the contrary, when made in the context of a serious dispute or crisis, is likely to be self-fulfilling. When made in a more general context, it forecloses potential avenues of progress towards a more peaceful world. As John Vasquez suggests, 'the arbitrariness of power politics social construction' (1993: 118) ought to be recognized for 'when power politics is a way of life, war is more likely to occur' (1993: 115).

Human Nature

'War is inevitable, human nature being what it is.' This belief is also quite common, but just as erroneous and pernicious as the view that international anarchy makes war inevitable among states (Bateson 1989; Goldstein 1989). There are, however, a few things about human nature which constitute necessary conditions of war, understood as an organized inter-societal armed conflict, of which international war is a major category and the main concern of this book. Some of these conditions are identified in this section.

Sociability and anti-social qualities

When human characteristics are said to be responsible for war, they are usually depicted as negative qualities. Selfishness and callousness are examples. These qualities are negative in the sense that they are anti-social characteristics.

However, it is because human beings as a species are not solitary animals, but have sociability, that it makes sense to characterize a particular act, disposition, or personality as selfish or callous at all. Indeed, we may suggest, categories such as 'selfishness' and 'callousness' presuppose an ethical standard. But if human beings were entirely asocial in the first place, no ethical standard could meaningfully be applied to them. The sociability of human beings, as a species, is thus logically prior to anti-social tendencies which they may exhibit in their (social) life.

Another point to note is that selfishness and callousness are not absolute qualities: they vary in degree. They do so not only from one type of person to another, but also with respect to each person from one kind of occasion to another. A person who is selfish or callous to another with respect to a given issue may not be so to the same extent with respect to another issue, or to someone else. For example, one may be more selfish about time than about money, and may be more so about time to one's parents than to one's own children.

This ability of human beings to differentiate their attitudes towards others contextually, and so vary the degree of their anti-socialness (and hence also their loyalty), has remained a key element of human nature (Reynolds, Falger, and Vine 1987). Without this differentiating ability, it would be impossible for the human race to continue to be divided among a plurality of particularistic societies: their continued existence presupposes that the members of one society be on the whole less anti-social (or more loyal) among themselves than towards those of another. Further, without the existence of a plurality of particularistic societies, there could be no war, since, by definition, 'war' is an inter-societal conflict.

Thomas Hobbes was terminologically inexact when he equated the state of nature with a state of 'war of every man, against every man' (1651: 145). Inasmuch as 'war' is, by definition, fought between groups, and not amongst atomistic individuals, a better term for Hobbes's imagined state of nature would be 'chaos'. 'War', by contrast, presupposes at least two cohesive societies within each of which anti-social tendencies are controlled, disciplined, and punished to a considerable degree. Otherwise, it would not be even plausible to claim, as is done by some bellicist thinkers, that war was a necessary condition of certain heroic virtues, such as self-denial.[5]

---

[5] Concerning Hobbes's concept of war, however, we must note that, for him, it was not actual fighting that constituted 'war', but 'the known disposition thereto, during all the time there is no assurance to the contrary' (1651: 143). On bellicism, see Field Marshal Helmuth von Moltke's letter to Professor Johann Caspar Bluntschli, reprinted in Bluntschli (1879–91: ii. 271–4, at 271). See also Ceadel (1987: ch. 3).

On these grounds, it is misleading to say, as is often suggested, that the wickedness of human nature (e.g. human selfishness) is a necessary condition of war. More fundamentally, human beings have a sociability. To the extent that they have anti-social traits, they also have a capacity to control them. The end result is the continued division of the human race into a plurality of particularistic societies. And it is this division that is crucial to the possibility of war. It is therefore more accurate to say that a human ability to sustain a plurality of particularistic societies is a necessary condition of war.

Such an ability may be called a 'discriminatory sociability' in contrast to a 'universal sociability', defined as an ability to form and sustain an undivided and indivisible society, embracing the entire human race. It may perhaps be that humanity has a latent potential to attain a universal sociability as history unfolds itself (Linklater 1982). But it remains the case that the possibility of war, conceived as a form of inter-societal conflict, presupposes the division of the human race into particularistic societies; and that the human ability to sustain this division through what is referred to here as a discriminatory sociability is a necessary condition of war.

Human and other animals

The remark that a discriminatory sociability of human beings is a necessary condition of war is a statement of one of war's logical prerequisites. It is in the end trivially true. None the less, it is interesting to notice the presence of this particular condition in human beings because it is largely absent from non-human animals.

Those species of animal which do not form groups, such as snakes or spiders, obviously do not engage in inter-group conflict: they do not have the requisite degree of sociability. Indeed, the human race is almost unique in its ability to organize its separate societies so effectively as to make it possible for them to engage in a sustained military conflict, which war is. Thus, in the vast majority of cases, animal fights take place between individuals and not between organized groups (Rapoport 1974: 114; Huntingford 1989: 30).

Of course, some animals do form groups. But interestingly, according to F. A. Huntingford, 'in many highly successful species, groups (whether they be schools of minnows, flocks of starlings or herds of wildebeeste) *form, merge and break up* to the mutual benefit of all concerned and without any aggression at all' (Huntingford 1989: 30; emphasis added). Such fluid sociability seems much less conspicuous among the humans.

Like the humans, however, some 'social' animals are known to engage in inter-group conflict. For example, Anatol Rapoport (1974: 114) mentions fighting between two 'armies' of ants. He is right to note, however, that 'an ant's responses to another ant seems to be rigidly mechanical and can be analysed into stereotyped components, precluding any basis for assuming a planned course of action characteristic of human behavior' (1974: 255 n. 7; see further Wallis 1962).

Huntingford confirms that 'in a small minority of species of non-human animals ... groups do sometimes defend territories and they use coordinated and occasionally injurious fighting to do so' (1989: 33). In particular, non-human primates, such as chimpanzees, are well known for their almost human ability to engage in inter-group violence. But this is said to be relatively uncommon, and, unlike human warfare, not to involve the use of weapons or specialized individual roles (Huntingford 1989: 33; *Science News* 1978).

Inhibition against intra-specific violence

A comparison with certain other species of animal points to another necessary condition of war in the nature of human beings. It is their ability to kill their own kind.

It may be objected that an absolute pacifist would be unable to do this. However, a person with an absolute pacifist conviction and immaculate record so far might perhaps change his or her attitude when confronted with a radically new situation, for example, if a member of his or her family became an innocent victim of an unprovoked military attack against their country. More fundamentally, an absolute pacifist is not someone who is incapable of killing other human beings, but who tries out of his or her conviction to avoid killing them even in self-defence, individual or collective. It is his or her capacity to kill other human beings that he or she finds it imperative to control: without this capacity he or she would not be a 'pacifist', but merely 'unable to kill'. An infant, it may further be objected, would be unable to kill other human beings. However, he or she may be said to possess an as yet not fully developed capacity to kill other human beings. In any case, the following points may be made on the subject of human ability to kill their own kind.

Certain species of animal are reported by ethologists to be apparently equipped with inhibition against escalating intra-specific violence beyond a certain range. Because of this, when two members of the same species of this sort engage in a violent conflict between themselves, the dominant contestant almost mechanically refrains from further attacks when the opponent resorts to a 'ritualized' appeasement gesture, signalling, as it were, an intent to submit. This renders intra-specific killing rare among such species (Lorenz 1961: ch. 12; Ewer 1968: chs. 6 and 7).

However, this type of inhibition is apparently either absent or insufficiently effective in the case of human beings. It follows that, even though killings may in fact be relatively uncommon amongst human beings (Atkinson *et al.* 1987: 375), they do take place in various contexts, such as one-to-one combat, mob violence, or conflict between groups. Where the weaker party indicates readiness to submit, this does not, in the case of conflict among humans, so effectively result in the de-escalation or cessation of hostilities as in the case of certain other animals.

The consequent ability of human beings to kill other human beings is a necessary condition of war. This necessary condition, too, is of a logical kind, since the link between it and the possibility of war derives from the meanings of the relevant words: 'war', by definition, involves 'killings'.

It is important to add here that a human capacity to kill other human beings is not the same as 'aggressiveness'. 'Aggressiveness' may be understood either as a general tendency to be easily provoked into the type of behaviour labelled 'aggressive', or as a momentary disposition which, if uncontrolled, produces that kind of behaviour. Aggressiveness in the first sense, like the level of intelligence, varies in degree from one person to another, and in the second sense it varies with respect to each person from one moment to another. Aggressiveness, in either sense, of some key individuals might form part of the explanation of some wars. Here, however, we are pointing to a human capacity, as opposed to incapacity, to kill members of the same species as a logical prerequisite of all wars.

War and mistakes

War is sometimes said to result not so much from the wickedness of human beings, but from their fallibility. As Robert Jervis notes, '[i]f every war has a loser, it would seem to stand to reason that the defeated state made serious miscalculations when it decided to fight' (1989: 103). It is often the case, moreover, that the length and bloodiness of war was not anticipated even by the victor (Blainey 1988: 292). If would-be belligerents could know in advance the cost and outcome of the forthcoming war, they might never start it. Too often, it is the war itself that slowly and in agony teaches them the lesson of reality (Stoessinger 1985: 211). It thus seems very likely that serious miscalculations are committed by some key officials of at least one party when the decision to go to war is made.

However, war without miscalculation is not impossible. A classic example of such a war is found in Thucydides' *History of the Peloponnesian War*, in one of its best-known chapters, 'The Melian Dialogue', outlined below (Thucydides 1954 edn.: Book V, The Melian Dialogue).

The island of Melos was ruled by colonists from Sparta. The Melians, originally neutral in the war between Athens and Sparta, were forced by Athenian attacks on their land to become open enemies of Athens. The Athenians, now encamped in the Melian territory, demanded surrender without a fight. The Melians, knowing that surrender would mean enslavement, argued that the Athenians should accept Melian neutrality: the Melians would be friends of the Athenians without being allies of either side. This the Athenians would not accept, for fear of being seen to be too weak to control the islanders. As a sea power, they claimed, they must not be seen to be incapable of subjugating relatively weak islanders such as the Melians. The Melians retorted that God was on their side, and that they sincerely believed that Sparta would not abandon its own colonists. The Athenians insisted that, on the contrary, God was on *their* side, and mocked the naïve optimism of the Melians.

The reader is left with the impression, however, that it was not the overly optimistic calculations on the part of the Melians that made them so fatefully stubborn. Rather, it was a desperate choice between dishonourable enslavement without resistance and honourable defeat that made them fight. The outcome, as was predictable undoubtedly even to the Melians, was devastating. After a long siege, the Melians were forced to surrender unconditionally to the Athenians, who put to death all the men of military age whom they took, and sold the women and children as slaves. The Melians fought the Athenians not because of optimistic miscalculations, but because honour mattered in the face of a severe injustice about to be inflicted upon them by an overwhelming military power.

Robert Jervis, in defending his thesis that war without miscalculation is possible, agrees that, strange though it may sound to modern ears, a potentially suicidal war in defence of honour is conceivable (Jervis 1989: 103). The Belgian decision in 1914 to reject the German ultimatum, which demanded passage through Belgium to attack France, may be one modern example (Bell 1986: 10). Jervis adds that an international reputation for having the resolve to fight even under ostensibly unfavourable conditions would be a national asset in the long run, and that this might also motivate states to resist rather than surrender (Jervis 1989: 104). If, under these circumstances, a resisting state is beaten as predicted even by itself, its defeat must be said to have been a calculated one.

Jervis also makes an important observation that leaders can rarely be certain of a war's outcome. They may believe that the chances of victory are small and yet rationally decide to fight 'if the gains of victory are large and the costs of losing are not much greater than those of making the concessions necessary to avoid war' (Jervis 1989: 104). If under these circumstances a state fights and loses, it cannot be said to have miscalculated: it acted rationally (to be technical, in terms of its 'expected utility'), but it lost the gamble, on this occasion. Japan's attack on Pearl Harbor in December 1941 may be explained in this way (Sagan 1989).

These considerations show that war without miscalculation is conceivable, and that it certainly does not follow from the concept of war that every war involves miscalculation by at least one party. Human fallibility, understood as a human capacity or tendency to make errors of judgement on the basis of information available, is not therefore a necessary condition of war (see Quester 1984: 45).

War-Fighting Societies

Human beings form societies of all kinds, but not all kinds of society engage in war. Societies which engage in war are of a specific sort to which human beings attach particular significance. They differentiate their societies into a war-fighting type and a non-war-fighting type.

The demarcation line is conventional, and not rigid. Yet a society of the kind which no one regards as a war-fighting type would be unable to engage in war. Of course, if perceptions change and a hitherto non-war-fighting type of society, say a religious community, has come to be seen as a war-fighting one, such a society will now be able to engage in war, especially when, concomitantly with the change in perceptions, the society is now equipped with a capacity to participate in a sustained military conflict. But then it can no longer be said that no one regards this kind of society as a war-fighting type.

This line of reasoning points to another logical prerequisite of war: sufficient prevalence of the belief among a number of societies that there are circumstances under which it is their function to resort to arms against one another, and in so doing to demand the cooperation of society members. In the modern international system, the sovereign state is a primary example of this type of society; and a sufficiently prevalent belief that one of the proper functions of sovereign states is under certain circumstances to resort to arms in their mutual dealings is a condition without which war would be impossible amongst them.

Indeed, sovereign states have become so privileged that we nowadays tend to think of war as something that takes place almost by definition only between them. However, an inter-group conflict involving the use of physical force occurs not only between sovereign states, but also within them: for example, between criminal gangs, ethnic groups, and political factions. As was noted, this book's main concern is international wars. But it would be erroneous to say that other kinds of inter-societal armed conflict are definitely not wars. The most we can say perhaps is that, the less state-like the groups, the more metaphorical, we feel, the term becomes. A gang war is war by courtesy, and war between political factions seeking control of the state is normally called 'civil' war.

The point here, therefore, is not that the coexistence of sovereign states is logically necessary for war, which of course is true if war is defined as a form of conflict between sovereign states. The point rather is that the possibility of war between *them* presupposes a prevailing conception of the sovereign state as a warfighting entity (just as much as the possibility of war between other kinds of society presupposes a prevalent assumption that *they* are war-fighting ones). What degree of prevalence is required for war to be possible is a question to which only a circular answer could be given: sufficient not to rule out the possibility of war.

What kind of society, whether or not organized as a sovereign state, is likely to see itself as a war-fighting type? One plausible answer is to point to those societies which are polarized internally between two correlative life-styles, one subservient, the other combative. Among such societies we would expect to see prevail the belief that it is their function under appropriate circumstances to resort to arms against one another, and in so doing to demand the cooperation of society members.

Patriarchal societies, socializing women into subservience and men into combativeness, have historically been a predominant example of this kind of society. As Virginia Woolf (1938) stressed on the eve of the Second World War, patriarchy is a historically significant force for war (see also Yudkin 1982: 263; Enloe 1983: esp. ch. 8; Strange 1983; Reardon 1985). It cannot be said, however, that patriarchy is by itself a sufficient condition of war. Nor is it plausible to argue that patriarchy is a necessary condition of war, that is, that between non-patriarchal societies war would be impossible.

The Question of Priority

As summarized in Table 2.2, we have identified some logical prerequisites of war, and international war in particular, at the levels of human beings, societies, and the international system.

Clearly, each of these conditions is necessary for war among states. Since each of them is absolutely, and hence equally, necessary, their contributions towards war among states must be said to be of equal weight. In this sense, it is impossible to say that a necessary condition of international war at any one level is more important than those at other levels.

TABLE 2.2. *Logical prerequisites of war at the three levels*

Human beings	(i) The 'discriminatory sociability' of human beings, and their capacity to kill members of their own species (without either of which no organized inter-societal armed conflict could take place, including war among states).
Societies/states	(ii) Sufficient prevalence of the belief among a number of societies, in particular the states, that there are circumstances under which it is their function to resort to arms against one another, and in so doing to demand the cooperation of society members (without which no organized armed conflict could take place between societies of that kind, in particular the states).
The international system	(iii) The absence from the international system of a perfectly effective anti-war device (in whose presence there could be no international war).

However, a necessary condition at one level may perhaps be more fundamental than those at the other levels in the sense that the former explains the latter. For example, if a prevailing conception of the state as a war-fighting entity is a necessary condition of war among states, is there a case for suggesting that such a conception is in turn explained by the element of anarchy in international relations? If so, priority may perhaps be given to (iii) over (ii) in Table 2.2; Waltz's third-image view might be defended in this way (Waltz 1959: 230).

Back to the meanings of 'anarchy'

In dealing with this issue, we should begin by reminding ourselves that 'international anarchy' may mean a number of things. In particular, the following three meanings have been isolated in our discussion:

(1) 'the absence from the international system of a perfectly effective anti-war device';
(2) 'the relatively decentralized institutional structure of the international system'; and
(3) 'a continuously tense and unstable international situation where war is effectively part of states' everyday expectations'.

We may refer to 'international anarchy' in these senses as anarchy$_1$, anarchy$_2$, and anarchy$_3$, respectively. Anarchy$_2$ is the most usual sense of 'international anarchy', and some see anarchy$_3$ as its universal consequence. This view is challenged by those who see in anarchy$_2$ a possibility of orderly coexistence among some states. Anarchy$_1$, admittedly, is not a natural meaning of 'international anarchy', but it is only under this definition that, as we saw, it can be said to be a necessary condition of international war at all.

International anarchy and war-fighting states

Now, whichever sense of 'international anarchy' is adopted, it is not implausible to suggest that, because of 'international anarchy', states continue to conceive of themselves as a war-fighting type. Given anarchy$_1$ or anarchy$_2$, it is understandable that states should consider that it is *their* function to resort to arms under certain circumstances. Now, contrary to some exaggerated claims, it is not true that anarchy$_3$ is a universal consequence of anarchy$_1$ or anarchy$_2$. However, to the extent that anarchy$_3$ prevails among any particular set of states, again it is understandable that these states should be prepared to fight at any moment.

None the less, this is only one side of the story. It is also likely that the explanation in fact runs in the opposite direction. Thus, it may be because the conception of the state as a war-fighting kind of society prevails that the institution of self-help persists in the international system, rendering it the kind of place where an effective anti-war device, whether perfectly so or not, is desirable but absent. In other words, anarchy$_1$ and anarchy$_2$ are the consequences. Furthermore, where the conception of the state as a war-fighting entity is given priority over other more peace-oriented conceptions, militarism strengthens, and this may stimulate a similar orientation among the neighbouring states, leading eventually to anarchy$_3$ (see Sect. 5.3).

Since there is no evidence to suggest that the direction of causation is exclusively from 'international anarchy', in whichever sense, to the conception of the state as a war-fighting type, it is not plausible to argue that 'international anarchy' is definitely the more fundamental of the two among the causes of war.

In any case, neither anarchy$_1$ nor anarchy$_2$ is sufficient by itself to produce a prevailing conception of the state as a war-fighting type. The fact of international anarchy in either of these senses needs to be *perceived* and *interpreted* as implying the need to be prepared to fight external wars. That this interpretation is not necessarily automatic can be surmised from the phenomenon of the so-called pluralistic security communities where war has become effectively ruled out as a means of intra-communal interactions. Anarchy$_3$, by contrast, is sufficient to make states see themselves as a war-fighting kind of entity. But, of course, unless states saw themselves in this way there would be no anarchy$_3$.

International anarchy and human nature

Moving back to those aspects of human nature which are responsible for the possibility of war, it is clear that a human ability to kill its own kind is not a function either of the nature of the state or of the international environment. Killing takes place within and across the boundaries of states, and even without the state, let alone the international system. The political organization of the world, therefore, does not explain this particular human trait.

But, what of discriminatory sociability? Is there a case for suggesting that the nature of the state or of the international environment (or of both) is responsible for this?

In answering this, it is imperative to return to the intended meaning of the term 'discriminatory sociability'. It refers to a human ability to sustain a plurality of particularistic societies. Such an ability is absent from those species of animal which do not form groups. It is also absent from those which have 'fluid sociability' whereby groups regularly form, merge, and break up without any conflict.

Underlying the ability of human beings to sustain a plurality of particularistic societies is their more general ability to differentiate their attitudes towards others contextually, and so vary the degree of their anti-socialness and hence loyalty. To be able to differentiate their attitudes towards others contextually, however, human beings must have a notion of social contexts. And it is indubitably the case that a very strong sense of social context is supplied by the political division of the world into sovereign states. This has institutionalized the distinction between the inside and the outside, the context of the domestic and the context of the international, turning each domestic society into a highly particularistic community in its relations with others.

Nevertheless, the general ability of human beings to differentiate their attitudes towards others contextually is not a function exclusively of the world political order. We do things to members of our family, or those whom we love, which we would not do to others. And this has nothing to do with whether we live as citizens of a particular state among a number coexisting in the world.

It appears therefore that, even though the political organization of the world is a very important element in concretizing the discriminatory sociability of human beings, the political organization of the world does not offer a sufficient explanation of it. Furthermore, there is also a case for suggesting that it is the human ability to sustain particularistic societies which is partly responsible for the continued division of the world into sovereign states.

Priority, then, could not be given one-sidedly to the nature of the international system over the war-enabling nature of the state, or of human beings. This particular path to resurrecting the third image therefore appears to fail.

2.2 SCIENTIFICALLY NECESSARY CONDITIONS OF WAR

Earlier, we noted that a statement of a necessary condition which depends heavily on a definitional connection between the key words used may be replaced by a more scientific one. We illustrated this by the following statement: 'For our bodies to remain alive it is necessary that they take in life-sustaining substances.' Another example is a statement such as the following: 'A necessary condition of my seeing an object is that it be visible.'

Of course, the object's visibility is not a sufficient condition of my seeing it: I may be blind or it may be obstructed from my view. But the statement correctly points to a necessary condition of my seeing an object. The statement moreover is true by virtue of the link in the meanings of the two key words, 'seeing' and 'visible'. It may, therefore, be classified perhaps as a statement of a logical prerequisite. However, this can be replaced or superseded by a statement of a scientifically necessary condition such as the following: 'A necessary condition of my seeing an object with the naked eye is that the wavelengths of the rays of light emitted or reflected by it be within a given range, roughly between 380×10^{-9} metres and 800×10^{-9} metres.'

As we move on to investigate whether there are scientifically necessary conditions of war, we should first ask if any proposition which we have so far classified as a statement of a logical pre-requisite of war can similarly be replaced by a scientific statement. This is followed by an assessment of certain researchers' claims to have identified a necessary condition of war by applying a scientific method to the field of International Relations.

From Words to Science?

The three logical theses which emerged in Section 2.1 are now examined in turn. These are 'the international-anarchy thesis', 'the human-nature thesis', and 'the prevailing-conception thesis'.

The international-anarchy thesis

What we shall now call 'the international-anarchy thesis' states that international anarchy (or anarchy$_1$) is a necessary condition of war between states. Can this thesis find a scientific reformulation?

The answer is negative. The problem with this thesis is that it is impossible to substitute a more informative description for 'international anarchy'. If we are asked to describe what sort of anti-war device it is whose absence from the international environment makes the system an 'anarchical' one *in the required sense*, we cannot do any better than reply that it is a device which could prevent war perfectly effectively.

It is not for the want of trying that we can do no better: any attempt to give a concrete structural description of the device would be met by a challenge that it might not always work. Crucially, we can see the validity of this challenge because we know that an institutional device, such as collective security, would not work unless supported by a human will to make it work, and that the will is not always present.

Given that the international anarchy thesis as such cannot therefore be made non-trivial, there seems very little point in advancing it. Indeed, the thesis appears senseless in that there can never be such a thing as a 'perfectly effective anti-war device' anyway. As Waltz (1979: 103) rightly observes, '[n]o human order is proof against violence'. But, of course, what cannot possibly exist cannot meaningfully be said to be missing. Why then insist on saying that its absence is a, or even *the*, necessary condition of war? We might as well say that the absence *from my bedroom* of a perfectly effective anti-war device is a necessary condition of war, which, just as absurdly, it is.

Yet it is easy to see why the view that a major cause of war is found in the structure of the international environment continues to be very popular. In the first place, we tend to believe that some wars might have been avoided after all if the international system had been equipped with an anti-war device of some sort. We may disagree about the requisite shape of such a device, but we can certainly think of several candidates: compulsory arbitration, for example. In the presence of such a device, it is possible to speculate, this or that war might have been avoided, though certainly not all wars.

More generally, it is quite commonly assumed that to create a more peaceful world it is necessary to equip the international system with a more centralized legal order as in the domestic sphere (Suganami 1989a). This prescriptive prejudgement, known as the domestic analogy, is likely to be the main source of the continued popularity of the view that a major cause of war is located in the anarchical structure of the international environment.

This belief, as is often pointed out, cannot be accepted uncritically (Bull 1966; Suganami 1989a). But, more importantly, the 'international-anarchy thesis' points to 'the absence from the international sphere of a perfectly effective anti-war device' (or 'anarchy$_1$,' in our notation) as a necessary condition of international war. The logical validity of this thesis is sealed off from any attempt empirically to demonstrate that the relatively decentralized structure of the international system (or 'anarchy$_2$') is responsible for the relative frequency of violent conflict in that environment. The popular assumption that the decentralized structure of the international system is a major cause of war, therefore, is not only unacceptable without qualifications, but entirely irrelevant to what is called here the international-anarchy thesis.

The human-nature thesis

Do the other statements of a logical prerequisite of war share the fate of the international-anarchy thesis in being unable to transcend the realm of words into that of science? Can the human-nature thesis (that the discriminatory sociability of human beings, or their ability to kill their own kind, is a necessary condition of war) be superseded by a scientific reformulation?

To examine this, consider the following statement: 'A necessary condition of my seeing an object is that I have sight.' This is trivially true, but it can be replaced by a more informative one in terms of the relevant features of my eyes, optic nerve, and brain. Make an imaginative leap and suppose for the sake of argument that, in a parallel fashion, we succeed in identifying whatever features of our brain or body account for our discriminatory sociability or our ability to kill other human beings. We could then replace a human-nature thesis with a more informative one, stating a scientifically necessary condition of war.

Such an eventuality may be in the realm of science fiction rather than that of science proper (see, for the current state of knowledge regarding human brain and 'aggressive' behaviour, Herbert 1989). But, unlike the case of the international-anarchy thesis, perhaps we cannot claim to know in advance that the path to discovery is irresistibly blocked.

The problem here, however, is that there may not be an exclusive one-to-one correspondence between given features of our brain and body, on the one hand, and our discriminatory sociability or our ability to kill other human beings, on the other. Some aspects of these features may be partly responsible for our other capacities —for example, our ability to defend ourselves against a variety of dangers. By removing those features of our brain and body necessary for war (supposing for the sake of argument that this could be done at all), we might make war impossible, but in all likelihood in conjunction with a wide variety of human activity mostly unrelated to war. And, of course, those persons who do the removing would not have those features removed from themselves, and thus a possibility of war would remain amongst them—provided, among other things, that there remained a sufficient number of them to form at least two societies.

The prevailing-conception thesis

There remains another thesis to examine, which we may now call 'the prevailing-conception thesis'. This identifies a logical prerequisite of war in the sufficient prevalence of the belief among a number of societies that there are circumstances under which it is their function to resort to arms against one another, and in so doing to demand the cooperation of society members.

An attempt to substitute a scientifically viable term for the prevalence of a given belief is likely to face insurmountable difficulties. But even more damaging is the fact that the thesis refers to 'sufficient prevalence' of the stated belief. When asked how prevalent the belief must be, we can only repeat what we have already said: 'sufficient not to rule out the possibility of war'. The requisite degree of prevalence cannot be identified without reference to the possibility of war itself, and any claim to have identified it independently of this would be defeated by a valid challenge that war might still occur with a somewhat smaller degree of prevalence. Like the international-anarchy thesis, then, the prevailing-conception thesis seems condemned to remain a purely semantic statement.

However, it can be said in defence of the prevailing-conception thesis that what is generally believed to be the function of the state in international relations may significantly affect the quality of life in the international arena. If the general belief is that there is a wide range of circumstances under which it is the function of the state to resort to arms against other states, then there may be many occasions for war. When the range narrows down, at least some types of war may no longer be fought so often (Luard 1986). Further, when the belief that it is a function of the state to resort to arms against other states under a given range of circumstances weakens among a particular class of states (say, among liberal states), then interstate wars within that class may diminish in frequency. But these remarks do not alter the fact that the prevailing-conception thesis as such, stating a necessary condition of all wars in the way explained, cannot be reformulated as a scientific statement.

A Direct Approach

Can we not apply a scientific mode of enquiry to the field of International Relations directly, and identify scientifically necessary conditions of war without, as we attempted in the previous sub-section, first going through a semantic path? This approach, how-ever, does not appear to have succeeded in establishing any condition literally as a *sine qua non* of war. An exception might perhaps be thought to be implicit in Michael Doyle's contention (1983; 1986; 1993) that there has not been a single instance of 'war' between any two 'liberal states'.

'War' and 'peace' among 'liberal states'

Of course, this contention would depend on how 'war' and 'lib-eral states' are defined. As for 'war', Doyle lists 118 of them chronologically, from the British–Maharattan War (1817–1818) to the Iran–Iraqi War (1980–) (Doyle 1983: 214–15, table 2; the latter war was ongoing at the time of Doyle's writing). This table, reprinted with some minor alterations from Melvin Small and J. David Singer's *Resort to Arms* (1982: 79–80), is a list of all 'inter-state' and 'extra-systemic' wars of the period 1816–1980, which they identified in their well-known Correlates of War Project.

In this Project, an 'interstate war' is defined as '[c]onflict involv-ing at least one member of interstate system on each side of the war, resulting in a total of 1,000 or more battle deaths' (Singer and Small 1972: 381).[6] An 'extra-systemic war', by contrast, is an '[i]nternational war in which there was a member of the interstate system on only one side of the war, resulting in an average of 1000 battle deaths per year for system member participants' (Singer and Small 1972: 382). For a member of the interstate system to count as being involved in an interstate or extra-systemic war, it must incur at least 100 battle deaths, or engage at least 1,000 troops in active combat (Singer and Small 1972: 381).[7]

---

[6] In the Falklands/Malvinas War (1982), there were, according to Middlebrook (1989: 282–3), 655 Argentinian and 255 British war dead. If the Correlates of War criteria were to be applied strictly, therefore, this conflict would not count as an interstate 'war'. Bruce Russett, who also believes that there were about 950 battle deaths in this war, suggests, however, that 'not to count it would be splitting hairs' (1993: 12).

[7] Members of the 'interstate system' are, for 1816–1919, '[n]ational entities, with independent control over own foreign policy, population of at least 500,000, and diplomatic recognition from Great Britain and France'; and, for 1920–65, '[n]ational entities, with independent control over own foreign policy, and either (a) membership in League of Nations or United Nations, or (b) population of at least 500,000 and diplomatic recognition from any two major powers' (Singer and Small 1972: 381). The membership criteria for 1920–65 are extended in Small and

Doyle's criteria of a 'liberal state' are explained in the detailed footnotes to one of his tables; the table lists an increasing number of liberal states chronologically from the late eighteenth century onwards, with forty-nine of them named in the period since 1945 (Doyle 1983: 212, nn. *a*, *b*, and *c* to table 1). In one of these footnotes, he writes (1983: 212 n. *a*):

I have drawn up this approximate list of 'Liberal Regimes' according to the four institutions described as essential: market and private property economies; polities that are externally sovereign; citizens who possess juridical rights; and 'republican' (whether republican or monarchical), representative, government. This latter includes the requirement that the legislative branch have an effective role in public policy and be formally and competitively, either potentially or actually, elected. Furthermore, I have taken into account whether male suffrage is wide (that is, 30 per cent) or open to 'achievement' by inhabitants (for example, to poll-tax payers or householders) of the national or metropolitan territory. Female suffrage is granted within a generation of its being demanded; and representative government is internally sovereign (for example, including and especially over military and foreign affairs) as well as stable (in existence for at least three years).

Naturally, on slightly different criteria, a few 'wars' may turn out to have taken place between 'liberal states' after all. For example, the Anglo-American War (1812–14) may count as a war between liberal states (Levy 1989*a*: 270, 311 n. 99; Waltz 1991: 670; Mann 1993: 767). According to Doyle (1983, 209, table 1), however, Britain was not a liberal state until 1832, and this war therefore fails to provide a clear counter-example. We can debate about such marginal cases at length, and, cognizant of this, Doyle (1983: 213) adds one relevant qualification: it is between 'constitutionally secure' liberal states that war has not yet taken place. Still, counter-examples which led Doyle to add this qualifying

Singer's 1982 publication to cover the 1965–80 period (Small and Singer 1982: 41–3). 'Major powers', as identified by Singer and Small, are: Great Britain, 1816–1980; France, 1816–1940, 1945–80; Italy, 1860–1943, Russia, 1816–1917, 1922–80; Japan, 1895–1945; Austria-Hungary, 1816–1918; United States, 1899–1980; Germany/Prussia, 1816–1918, 1925–45; China, 1950–1980 (Singer and Small 1972: 381; Small and Singer 1982: 45). There are three types of 'extra-systemic war', although only the first two appear in Small and Singer's table used by Doyle: 'imperial wars', 'colonial wars', and 'internationalized civil wars' (Small and Singer 1982: 52). On the Correlates of War Project's definition of war, see also Vasquez (1993: 25–9).

Prerequisites

phrase are in turn very few. After a detailed study, James Lee Ray has concluded that '[m]ost of the supposed exceptions are international wars between democratic states only if very minor conflicts are counted as wars, and/or if states displaying democratic characteristics of an uncertain, tenuous nature are categorized nevertheless as "democratic"' (Ray 1993: 269; Russett 1993: 11–20).[8]

Let us therefore assume, with Doyle, that there has not been a single instance of war between any two (constitutionally secure) liberal states. Even this perfect regularity, however, is insufficient by itself to make us say that war between (such) liberal states is a scientific impossibility (or, by implication, that the absence of liberalism from at least one party is a scientifically necessary condition of war). To add credibility to such a claim, we need a plausible theory showing that war could not occur between any two (constitutionally secure) liberal states.

Doyle's theory of inter-liberal peace

According to Doyle's favoured theory (1983: 225–32; 1986: 1156–62; 1993: 186 ff.), three main conditions have together contributed to peace among liberal states. Briefly, these are: domestic constraints which liberal institutions impose upon governments' freedom of action in foreign policy; mutual respect among liberal states based on shared liberal values; and vested interest in peace resulting from transnational commercial interdependence among the citizens of liberal states.

On the first of these three explanatory factors, Bruce Russett and William Antholis have offered an important observation. They write:

So long as this explanation focuses on the characteristics of single states, it cannot explain the consistent evidence that democracies are about as war-prone in general (not toward other democracies) as other kinds of states. The argument is more persuasive when it becomes complex, and

---

[8] Waltz (1991: 669–70) maintains that Germany in 1914 was a democracy. If so, the First World War will constitute a serious exception to the rule. However, Doyle (1983: 222) is right to exclude Imperial Germany from the list of liberal states. On this issue, Russett offers a succinct explanation (1993: 18–19): 'In Prussia/Germany the emperor appointed and could dismiss the chancellor; a defeat in the Reichstag did not remove the chancellor from office. The emperor's direct authority over the army and foreign policy deprives the state of the democratic criterion of "responsible executive" on war and peace matters; Berghahn (1973, 9) calls the constitutional position of the monarchy "almost absolutist."'

strategic. If democratic leaders generally regard other democracies as reluctant to fight, bound by institutional constraints, they will not fear being attacked by another democracy. Also, they will know that the institutional constraints, and the need for public debate in the other democracy, will prevent a surprise attack and so eliminate any of their own incentives to launch a pre-emptive strike. Two democratic states—each constrained from going to war and anticipating the other to be so inhibited—likely will settle their conflicts short of war (1992, 417)'.[9]

However, the conditions identified by Doyle, with or without the modification introduced above, do not *guarantee* peace even where all of them combine. Doyle is himself careful enough, therefore, to warn that no one should argue that wars between liberal states are *impossible*, and acknowledges thereby what must after all be conceded: the absence of liberalism from at least one party is *not* a scientifically necessary condition of war. The most we can say, according to Doyle (1983: 213), is that the impressive record constitutes preliminary evidence indicating that there exists a significant predisposition against warfare between liberal states. This point will be investigated further in the next chapter.

Rummel's claims

Independently of Doyle's study, Rudolph Rummel (1983) reports that there is no 'violence' between 'libertarian' states in his data period 1976–80. On the basis of certain other investigators' data as well as his own, Rummel also maintains that *'we have not had a real war between democracies over a century and a half, from 1816 to 1980'* (1983: 48; emphasis in original).[10] However, he appears to go beyond Doyle when he claims that a *'necessary condition'* of violence between two states is that at least one of them be partially or completely nonlibertarian' (1983: 67; emphasis added). Nevertheless, the theory Rummel briefly presents (1983: 27–8) to explain inter-libertarian peace is substantially the same as Doyle's, and we cannot therefore expect Rummel's theory to perform what Doyle's does not: to point to a scientifically *necessary* condition of war.

In fact, according to Rummel, the theory leads us to expect that '[between libertarian states] violence may occur only in the most

---

[9] See also Bueno de Mesquita and Lalman (1992: ch. 5, esp. 145–64).
[10] 'War' is a narrower category than 'violence' in Rummel's definitions. See Rummel (1983: 30–9).

extraordinary and unusual circumstances' (1983: 28). But this wording is significant: it explicitly, and rightly, concedes that, *according to the theory*, there are unspecified circumstances under which violence occurs between libertarian states. In short, the theory is not about a *necessary* condition of war; it is not meant to show that violence is *impossible* between libertarian states.

Furthermore, despite his impressive finding with respect to the data period 1976–80, the assertion that there is no violence between libertarian states has not been tested by Rummel with respect to other historical periods. Thus Rummel's strong claim that a '*necessary condition* of violence between two states is that at least one of them be partially or completely nonlibertarian' (1983: 67; emphasis added) is an exaggeration, if it was meant to be taken literally at all.

Bueno de Mesquita's claims

Another notable analyst, who has very self-consciously followed a scientific path in his attempt to identify a necessary condition of war, is Bruce Bueno de Mesquita. In his book *The War Trap* (1981) he claims that his empirical investigations with respect to the period 1816–1974 strongly support a theoretically derived proposition that 'positive expected utility' is a necessary condition for a state to initiate a war. This means that, in his view, states will never initiate a war if in so doing they expect probably to suffer a net loss in value, or 'utility', and that this universal hypothesis is strongly confirmed by his empirical investigations (Bueno de Mesquita 1981: esp. 29; 1985: esp. 163).

Curiously, in his reply to one of his critics, Bueno de Mesquita maintains that the heart of his 1981 book 'is *not* that positive expected utility is necessary for conflict [and war] initiation' (Bueno de Mesquita 1984a: 74; emphasis added). The critic concerned is right, however, to insist that he is unable to agree with this disclaimer because the book is replete with statements suggesting the contrary (Khong 1984b: 77). We should also note that, in his 1981 book, Bueno de Mesquita is concerned with *initiation* of war and other forms of conflict, and 'third-party decisions to join an ongoing war' are excluded from his analysis (Bueno de Mesquita 1981: 99–100). In his list of interstate wars, therefore, we find (in the place of the First World War) a war of 1914 initiated by Austria–Hungary against Yugoslavia (Serbia). Similarly, in the place of the Second World War in Europe, we find an interstate war of 1939 initiated by Germany against Poland. No war is listed as having begun in 1941, the year in which Germany attacked the Soviet Union, and Japan the United States (Bueno de Mesquita 1981: 209).

Bueno de Mesquita's book has attracted considerable attention and praise, but has also been subjected to serious criticisms by a number of able specialists.[11] Since Bueno de Mesquita's works and those of his critics are too technically complex to be dealt with here in any detail, we shall concentrate on one point which cannot go unnoticed from the viewpoint of the present chapter. It concerns the fact that the results of Bueno de Mesquita's empirical investigations reveal that there were some initiators of war which actually had negative expected utility. Of the total of seventy-six war initiators which Bueno de Mesquita counted with respect to the entire period, eleven (amounting to about 14 per cent of the total) in fact had negative expected utility as defined and estimated by him (Bueno de Mesquita 1981: 129, table 5.1).

Given this, Bueno de Mesquita has two alternatives: either to insist that the results of his empirical investigations 'strongly support' the theoretically derived proposition that positive expected utility is a necessary condition for a state to initiate a war; or to abandon the language of necessity altogether and simply report the impressive strength of statistical association between whether a state's expected utility (as defined and estimated by him) is positive or negative, on the one hand, and whether the state becomes an 'initiator' or a 'victim' of war, on the other (as shown in Bueno de Mesquita 1981: 129, table 5.1). However, he favours the first alternative (1981: 129), apparently attributing disconfirming instances to inevitable measurement error (1981: 94, 126, 130).

Of course, at least some of the eleven disconfirming instances may be due to error of measurement. Clearly, however, such error must have affected confirming instances as well as disconfirming ones. There seems no compelling reason to suppose that the disconfirming instances are consistently due to measurement error so large that we must discount them all; but that measurement error which may also have affected confirming instances is small

---

[11] See Khong (1984*a*, 1984*b*); Majeski and Sylvan (1984); Nicholson (1987*a*, 1987*b*); Wagner (1984). See, for his own defence, Bueno de Mesquita (1984*a*, 1984*b*, 1987). See also Bueno de Mesquita (1985).

enough to be ignored in every instance. The net result may be that there are after all some genuine disconfirming instances unexplained by the theory.[12]

Since counter-examples amounting even approximately to 14 per cent are not insubstantial, some critics have felt that Bueno de Mesquita's empirical evidence cannot in fact be said strongly to support the universal (necessary condition) hypothesis being tested (Khong 1984a: 50–53; 1984b: 77; Majeski and Sylvan 1984: 339 n. 17; Nicholson 1987b: 367–8). In any case, since it is impossible to be certain about the effects of measurement error in Bueno de Mesquita's estimation, it would have been more prudent for him not to insist on the first (necessary-condition) alternative, but to be content with the more defensible, and still very impressive, second (statistical) alternative, noted above.

Furthermore, as Michael Nicholson (1987a: 361) notes, the proposition concerning war initiation which is actually defended by Bueno de Mesquita empirically is 'that initiation in war is positively correlated [strongly] with relative power, distance, and the congruence of alliance configurations in a particular nonlinear functional form'. As pointed out by Nicholson, among others, there are some serious uncertainties as to how this relates to the 'expected-utility' theory to which Bueno de Mesquita claims to subscribe (see Wagner 1984; Nicholson 1987a).

Bueno de Mesquita is right to accept the proposition that war is a means to an end. This proposition seems so exceptionless that it almost appears true by definition: 'aimless violence' is just that, not 'war', we may be tempted to say. In any case, it is quite plausible that no state would ever go to war *entirely purposelessly*. Perhaps it is true, therefore, that a state would not initiate a war if it (or whoever was in charge) believed that doing so served no purpose whatsoever. For a state to initiate a war at all there must be some purpose to it.

In short, whenever there is war, there must also be some war aims. But this is not necessarily the same as saying that a state would not initiate a war if it (or whoever was in charge) believed that the net expected benefits of initiating a war was smaller than the net expected benefits of refraining from doing so. This involves

---

[12] See Chalmers (1982: 52) for an amusing story highlighting the problematic nature of the kind of move made by Bueno de Mesquita in defending his position.

an altogether more complicated thought process. In any case, contrary to Bueno de Mesquita's assumption, there seems no overwhelming reason to suppose that a state would *never* initiate a war if it (or whoever was in charge) believed that the net expected benefits of initiating a war were smaller than the net expected benefits of refraining from doing so. A state may simply fail to pay attention to the latter item.

Furthermore, according to Bueno de Mesquita himself, the leaders' choices of war or peace 'depend on their estimation of costs and benefits *and* their comprehension of right and wrong' (1981: 5; emphasis added). If, however, moral values are acknowledged to be part of the leaders' decision schemes, then it is unclear why their assessment of the expected costs and benefits in purely non-moral terms can be said to constitute a necessary condition for war initiation.

Given such considerations, Bueno de Mesquita's claim to have identified a (scientifically) necessary condition of war initiation must be rejected.

CONCLUSION

In the main body of this chapter, three paths have been suggested as a way of identifying necessary conditions of war. One is to formulate a statement of a necessary condition of war which is sustained by the meanings of the words it employs. This method has led to three theses: 'international anarchy', 'human nature', and 'prevailing conception', each pointing to a logical prerequisite of (international) war.[13] A second method was introduced when we examined whether it is possible to substitute a statement of a scientifically necessary condition for each of these theses. The international-anarchy and prevailing-conception theses failed. By contrast, we may perhaps concede that scientific reformulation is not in principle impossible in the case of the human-nature thesis. A third approach was to apply a scientific mode of enquiry directly to international relations.

The third approach does not appear so far to have succeeded in

[13] The latter two theses in fact point to logical prerequisites of war in a wider sense, of which war between states is a major example.

identifying a necessary condition of war. This may not, however, be due to the lack of effort on the part of the scientists involved. It seems more likely that there are no scientifically necessary conditions of war other than those which we might conceivably identify through the second approach with respect to the human-nature thesis. However, as we saw, these conditions may not be 'localized' to war, but may also be necessary for a wide variety of human activity of which inter-societal armed conflict is only a part.

These results seem to reflect an important fact about war. There is a reasonably clear agreement as to what the term 'war' means. It is therefore relatively easy to formulate some of the logical prerequisites of war. However, actual instances of war are varied, and they may not fruitfully be subsumed under a single scientific theory, even under a more modest one pointing only to a necessary condition of war (as opposed to the necessary and sufficient condition of it).

It needs to be noted that the reason for this judgement here is not that 'war', *being a social phenomenon*, could not fruitfully be subjected to a natural scientific enquiry, although this case could also be made. The key point here is rather that 'war'—like 'illness' or 'crime'—*being an ordinary-language term*, need not itself be a causally unified category. Two instances of war may be like two cases of 'stomach pain', perhaps outwardly similar but causally distinct, like 'ulcer' and 'cancer'. To suppose the contrary may well be methodologically unwise.

This judgement is shared by John Vasquez, who states: 'the hope that there are a few necessary conditions that must always be present in order for war to occur is probably not going to be fulfilled' (1993: 48). Vasquez, however, goes on to attempt to identify necessary conditions of 'world war', defined as 'a large-scale severe war among major states that involves the leading states at some point in the war and most other major states in a struggle to resolve the most fundamental issues on the global political agenda' (1993: 227; see also Vasquez 1993: 342–3 n. 1 for examples of 'world war'). Vasquez suggests:

A careful analysis of statistical findings on interstate wars from 1816 to 1965 reveals that world wars are associated with three [conjointly] necessary conditions: (1) a multipolar distribution of capability in the system; (2) an alliance system that reduces this multipolarity to two hostile blocs;

and (3) the creation of two blocs in which one does not have a clear preponderance of capability over the other. (1993: 248)

As Vasquez acknowledges, however, this empirical generalization would need to be backed by further research showing 'that these three conditions also preceded world wars prior to 1816' (1993: 262). But, contrary to Vasquez's own suggestion (1993: 262), even that would be insufficient to make us say that the three conditions are conjointly necessary for the outbreak of world war. In the first place, the category of 'world war' as defined by him is flexible enough for a candidate perhaps to emerge which is not preceded by the three conditions but which arguably counts as a world war. Secondly, and more importantly, there is no theoretical reason why a world war may not break out, for example, against the background of a bipolar, as opposed to a multipolar, distribution of capability. The most we can say about the three conditions identified by Vasquez appears to be that they have frequently formed part of the cause of world war.

It was noted at the outset that an urge to identify necessary conditions of war may arise from a desire to prevent *all* future wars. The discussion of this chapter suggests that such a desire is not likely to be satisfied. Yet it is quite likely that there are ways of avoiding *some* future wars or lessening the frequency of war. For example, a realistic calculation of the cost of embarking on a war in the circumstances faced may deter many wars. A new institutional device at the international level may succeed in preventing some wars. Narrowing down the range of circumstances under which it is conventionally thought appropriate to go to war could not be without some positive impact. And above all, the fact that there has not been a single instance of war between any two liberal states may indicate a type of international relations which is less war-prone than other types. These speculations lead us to consider our second question about the causes of war: under what sorts of circumstances have wars occurred more frequently? This forms the subject of the next chapter.

3

CORRELATES

Nearly everyone knows that correlation is not causation.

(Haas 1974: 59)

The numbers must be used carefully for interpretation, not mechanically.

(Russett 1993: 54)

A NUMBER of distinct questions arise under the rubric of the causes of war. 'What are the necessary conditions of *all* wars?' is one. To this, however, a conceptual enquiry produces relatively trivial answers, and a scientific investigation is likely not to yield any positive answer at all. Historians would urge us to ask a more modest, but to them more meaningful, question: 'What caused *this* war?' If one's aim is to reduce the frequency of future wars, however, this question is perhaps less useful to explore than a more general question, 'What have been the *relatively common* causes of war?'.

Historians would suggest that this general question—call this (*b'*) —could only arise after a series of particular ones: we study many wars, identify the causes of each, and then make a list of those causes, if any, which appear relatively frequently. J. G. Stoessinger follows this path in his *Why Nations Go to War* (1985). If, however, each war studied yields several plausible interpretations regarding its causes, as can be expected from Nelson and Olin's survey (1979), it cannot be a very easy task to make a reliable list of frequent causes by comparing many wars.

Another possible route is statistical. This leads us to investigate a cluster of questions such as our question (*b*): 'Under what sorts of circumstances have wars occurred more frequently?' Exploring this question may be a valuable first step towards answering (*b'*): 'What have been the relatively common causes of war?' Moreover, war-related conditions may be useful to identify regardless of whether they are also causally significant factors: the correlational knowledge, though not necessarily a causal knowledge, may be used as a basis for prediction and control, and may perhaps contribute to the reduction in the frequency of future wars (Haas 1974: 4; Singer 1979*a*: 170–1).

Out of such a rationale has grown a vast body of writings, almost exclusively North American in origin. The main aim of this chapter is to select and interpret certain important findings located in this literature. To this end, the chapter is divided into three sections in the light of the three kinds of situation which we encounter as we survey the field. These are:

(1) where we suspect a causal link between a given type of condition and the occurrence of war (or, more broadly, 'international conflict' or 'foreign violence'), but where no correlation is clearly seen between the variables examined;

(2) where, on the basis of a very strong association identified between a given type of condition and the occurrence of war over a long period, the former is said to be at least a valuable early warning indicator of war, if not necessarily a cause of it; and

(3) where a number of researchers have uncovered an exceptionally regular pattern on a war/peace issue, and where they also offer a plausible causal theory to explain the pattern.

In the following, the first case is illustrated by Rudolph Rummel's classic study reporting negative findings regarding the relationship between national attributes and the foreign conflict behaviour of states; the second case by Michael Wallace's much-debated investigation into the statistical association between arms races and war; and the third by Michael Doyle's well-known works, which show that liberal states hardly ever engage in war among themselves.

Only a negligible fraction of the vast amount of existing findings is discussed below. A more extensive treatment is found in a number of recent works, among which the following are particularly helpful: Vasquez (1987), Levy (1989*a*), Midlarsky (1989), Vasquez and Henehan (1992), and Vasquez (1993). The studies examined in this chapter are such paradigmatic ones, however, that they raise fundamental conceptual issues of wider relevance to the correlational study of war.

3.1 THE ABSENCE OF A STRONG CORRELATION

Is there any correlation between what a given state is like and what it tends to do? Or, as Rummel, the author of some of the

best-known studies on this subject puts it: 'Is the magnitude of a
nation's position on the attribute dimensions, say economic development, related to its magnitude on the behavior dimensions, such
as conflict?' (1968: 187). More specifically, does the degree of foreign conflict behaviour shown by a state over a period vary in proportion to its other quantified national characteristics?

Rummel on National Attributes and International Conflict

Under the rubric of what Rummel calls foreign-conflict behaviour
are thirteen statistically interrelated variables, such as 'anti-foreign
demonstrations, severance of diplomatic relations, ambassadors
expelled or recalled, other diplomatic officials expelled or recalled,
accusations, threats, mobilizations, military action, and wars' (1968:
200–1; the definitions of these terms are found in Rummel 1963:
26–7, and Rummel 1972: 133–4). The data for these variables
were collected on seventy-seven nations for the period 1955–7
from such sources as *The New York Times Index*, *Keesing's Contemporary Archives*, *Facts on File*, *Britannica Book of the Year*,
and *New International Yearbook* (Rummel 1968: 201 n. 6; on the
adequacy of these sources and related issues, see Scolnik 1974:
486–93).

On the national-attributes side, over 200 variables were taken
into consideration, encompassing a wide variety of items such as
a country's GNP, average rainfall, cancer deaths per population,
and the legitimacy of the existing government. Such national-
attribute variables, however, exhibit a statistically discernible pattern: certain national attributes tend to go hand in hand, forming
a bundle so to speak, and these are not so closely associated with
members of any other bundle. For example, the number of tele-
phones per capita, GNP per capita, the amount of energy consumption per capita, and the percentage of non-agricultural
population are closely associated among themselves, but not with
other national attributes. This particular bundle is interpreted, not
unreasonably, as indicating a country's 'economic development'
(Rummel 1968: 204).

The next move Rummel makes is to see, bundle by bundle,
whether there is a statistical relationship between any member of
a given set on the national-attributes side, and any of the thirteen

variables on the foreign-conflict-behaviour side. For example, Rummel asks, is there any indication that the larger the proportion of agricultural workers within the national population, the more (or the less) belligerent a state is measured in terms, for instance, of the number of military actions it undertakes? By subjecting his empirical data to a wide range of questions of this sort, Rummel examines the several statistical hypotheses regarding the relationship between a country's national characteristics and its propensity to engage in international conflict.

Rummel finds hardly any strong linear relationship, however. For example, with respect to the hypothesis that the level of economic development or technical development of a country is highly related to its foreign conflict behaviour, the strongest correlation is found between GNP per capita and the severance of diplomatic relations; and also between energy consumption per capita and diplomatic officials of lesser than ambassadorial rank expelled or recalled. Even in these two cases, correlation is relatively weak, the coefficient in both cases scoring only +0.35 (Rummel 1968: 204). According to Rummel, the correlation coefficients of the economic-development variables with the thirteen foreign-conflict variables are almost all less than the absolute value of 0.30 (i.e. between −0.30 and +0.30). Rummel also reports that his negative conclusion here accords with those of a few other comparable works (1968: 204–5).[1]

Similar observations are made by Rummel with respect to nearly all the other hypotheses he examines. Thus, he concludes, the available empirical evidence seems to suggest that a country's foreign conflict behaviour is not highly related (either positively or negatively) to the amount of its international communications, transactions, or cooperation; the degree of totalitarianism of its government; its power, economic or technological development, or military capabilities; its domestic instability; psychological motivations of its

---

[1] That a 'strong positive, or negative, linear correlation' exists between two variables ('independent' and 'dependent') means roughly that there is a conspicuous tendency for the dependent variable to increase, or decrease, in direct proportion to the increase in the independent variable. A 'correlation coefficient' is used to measure how conspicuous this tendency is, and can in principle range from −1.00 to +1.00. The coefficient of +1.00 means perfect positive linear correlation, and −1.00 perfect negative linear correlation. The coefficient of 0.00 means no linear correlation. Rummel considers a coefficient smaller than the absolute value of 0.30 as suggesting the absence of a linear relationship between the variables concerned.

citizens, or the values upheld in the society. The evidence is said to be ambiguous as to whether there is a relationship between the number of a country's borders and its foreign conflict behaviour (Rummel 1968: 211–12).[2] As to whether combinations of these national attributes might be related to foreign conflict behaviour, Rummel's conclusion is again negative (1968: 212–13).

Exceptionally, a few national-attribute variables show rather strong correlation with some variables indicative of a country's involvement in international conflict. For example, the ratio of foreign titles translated to domestic books shows a comparatively strong (negative) correlation with anti-foreign demonstrations, the coefficient scoring –0.46 (Rummel 1968: 206). The number of military personnel shows an even stronger (positive) correlation with troop movements, and also with accusations, the coefficient reaching +0.55 in both cases (Rummel 1968: 208). But these are treated as insufficient, in the face of the overall pattern uncovered, to substantiate the statistical hypotheses concerned.

Such negative conclusions, though undoubtedly frustrating to the researchers, are said none the less to be valuable: it is partly through the elimination of popularly entertained, but empirically unsubstantiated, suppositions that our scientific knowledge can make progress. Reflecting on his almost entirely negative findings, Rummel thus makes one final observation: what should be investigated next is not the relationship between what a state is like individually and what it tends to do to others, but the relationship between the characteristics of a pair of states and the relative degree of conflict between them (Rummel 1968: 213–14; see further Most and Starr 1983).

This is an important insight, which, as we shall see in Section 3.3 has led to an interesting correlational discovery. Here, however, some critical observations are in order regarding the type of approach Rummel took in his investigation, and the resultant negative findings. The discussion below, though of wider relevance, focuses on the relationship between domestic instability and international conflict.[3]

---

[2] Correlation between territorial contiguity and war-proneness appears to have become well established (Vasquez 1993: ch. 4).

[3] The discussion below follows in outline Jack Levy's excellent critique of the literature on this subject (1989b). Other noteworthy critical surveys include Scolnik (1974); Mack (1975); Zinnes (1976: 160–75, 180–2); Stohl (1980).

Domestic Instability and International Conflict: A Complex Relationship

It is difficult to doubt that a country's involvement in international conflict of some kind is in some cases caused partly by internal instability of some type. For example, the leaders, insecure in an unstable polity, may resort to a diversionary foreign policy, and this, because of its aggressiveness towards the outside world, may result in international conflict of some kind, including war, whether such a result had actually been intended by them from the start or, which is perhaps more likely, was brought about by miscalculations. The First World War is said by some historians to be a good illustration of this—as is, more recently, the Falklands/Malvinas War.[4]

This type of causal scenario is what Rummel had in mind when he tested his statistical hypothesis that the instability of a nation is highly related to its foreign conflict behaviour (Rummel 1963: 208). Rummel's negative findings on this particular relationship were first reported in Rummel (1963), and were supported in a similar study by Tanter (1966) with respect to the period 1958–60. The assumption underlying such an investigation is that a *causal* relationship between domestic instability and international conflict will be found reflected in their *statistical* relationship. This is analogous to a popular assumption, for example, that if smoking causes cancer then smoking and cancer will be found to be statistically correlated. However, it is uncertain whether we should suppose in the first place, as Rummel has done, that the *more* unstable a state is internally, the *more* aggressive it will be externally.

On the one hand, it may be suggested that it is precisely when domestic turmoil gets seriously out of hand that the leadership resorts to such drastic measures as foreign expeditions for diversionary purposes (Mayer 1969: 295–6). As Levy notes, there is even some social-psychological evidence to suggest that, 'the greater the internal threat, the less elites have to lose from risky measures and the more likely they are to gamble' (1989*b*: 274; see also Levy 1992:

---

[4] On the First World War, see Mayer (1967); Berghahn (1973); Gordon (1974); and Fischer (1975). Regarding the Falklands/Malvinas War, Levy and Vakili (1992) stress Argentina's intra-regime conflict as a key factor. This agrees with Mayer's observation (1977: 230) that 'not pre-revolutionary pressures but cleavages in the hegemonic bloc and unsettlement or stalemate of government are the womb of crisis and of crisis-generated war'. For a similar argument with respect to Germany and the First World War, see Mommsen (1973).

286–7), although the gamble need not necessarily take the form of external diversion. On the other hand, it also makes sense to suppose that, when a country suffers more than a certain degree of internal instability, its leadership becomes too preoccupied with domestic problems to be able to allocate resources for an aggressive foreign policy (Mayer 1969: 295, 299; 1977: 230–1; Blainey 1988: 81).

Thus, in a carefully formulated passage, Arno Mayer synthesizes these two potentially incompatible scenarios as follows:

> It appears, then, that the calculus of the internal political effects of intensified external conflict or war is more likely either to deter or to encourage recourse to war in a revolutionary era and under conditions of internal instability than in times of domestic and international equipoise. (1969: 296)

This is an altogether different hypothesis from the one which interested Rummel.

To complicate the matter further, a country undergoing serious internal instability may become a target for interference from outside. For example, a neighbouring state or states may take advantage of the current weakness of the unstable state, and resort to aggressive foreign policy against it, as illustrated by Iraq's attack on Iran in 1980. Or an outside state or states may try to influence the course of domestic turmoil in the target state and intervene accordingly, as shown by several cases of hegemonic intervention by great powers, such as the US intervention in the Dominican Republic in 1965, and cases involving lesser powers, such as the Israeli and Syrian interventions in Lebanon in the 1980s. The target state may of course anticipate such moves, and act against external threats in genuine pre-emptive self-defence, or exploit the threats to justify what is partly or primarily a diversionary response to an internal crisis, as illustrated by such cases as France in 1792, Russia in 1918, and Iran in 1980.[5]

It is already clear from this sketch that the statistical relationship between domestic instability and international conflict is likely to be a complex one. The relationship may not be linear, and

---

[5] All these illustrations are from Levy (1989b: 269–70). In addition to such standard scenarios, where domestic instability leads to international conflict, Levy (1989b, 267–71) discusses cases where international conflict leads to domestic instability, and also where domestic instability leads to international conflict which in turn exacerbates domestic instability. As he notes (1989b: 269, 271), these various scenarios cannot appropriately be tested without paying attention to the nature and direction of the relevant causal mechanisms at work.

some plausible 'contextual variables' should be taken into account in searching for a pattern (Hazlewood 1975). We should ask in what sorts of context what type of internal instability is likely to be related in what way to what kind of international conflict. On this kind of subject we cannot realistically expect to arrive at a simple, exact, and well-confirmed formula familiar in physics, but may test some plausible hypotheses with a view to obtaining broad generalizations with which to facilitate a rough forecast, and perhaps also a measure of control (for a succinct statement of the rationale here, see Rapoport 1968: 40–6).

According to Wilkenfeld (1973b), for example, there is some indication that the type of regime ('personalist', 'centrist', or 'polyarchic') may be an important contextual variable, and Russett (1990) also notes, among other things, the potential relevance of regime type ('democratic' or 'non-democratic'). Other plausibly relevant contextual variables include: the relative military capability of the unstable state; the rate of change thereof; the unstable state's economic conditions; the key leaders' personality characteristics, for example, their risk-taking propensities; availability of a convenient external scapegoat; other countries' responses in the immediate past; and the strength of normative constraints in the international system; and so on. Given the likely relevance of a number of such variables, it is unsurprising that Rummel has found no strong correlation simply between domestic instability and foreign conflict behaviour, and that we have not reached the stage where we can with sufficient confidence forecast a probable international outcome of a country's internal instability.

In this regard Russett (1990) is an insightful work. Interestingly, he offers a conclusion apparently contrary to Rummel's: whether democratic or undemocratic, 'domestic political unrest, whether or not stemming from economic deprivation, often results in involvement in militarized disputes' (Russett 1990: 136). Disappointingly, Russett does not say *how* often, which renders his remark somewhat vacuous.[6]

---

[6] We may also note Russett's acknowledgement (1990: 140 n. 7) that his data do not distinguish between initiating a dispute and becoming a target of one. More technically, though this point cannot be elaborated here, the appropriateness of Russett's use of significance tests would appear to be questionable since his variables are not random. On significance tests, see Galtung (1967: 358–89); Morrison and Henkel (1970).

As we noted at the beginning of this section, it is difficult to doubt that a country's involvement in international conflict of some kind is in some cases caused partly by internal instability of some type. It is also clear, however, that such a non-straightforward or complex causal relationship is unlikely to manifest itself in a simple statistical correlation such that the *more* unstable a state is internally, the *more* it will be involved in foreign conflict behaviour *whatever* its other circumstances.

It follows that a negative finding on this issue resulting from the kind of approach Rummel took—one which tests a linear hypothesis without paying sufficient attention to contextual variables—does not show that there is no complex causal relationship between domestic instability and international conflict. To generalize from this observation, Rummel's negative findings do not show that there is no complex causal relationship between any of his national attributes and foreign conflict behaviour.

Rummel's (1968) article is a first-generation product in quantitative international studies, and its relatively crude character is understandable. It should be added in this connection that, in a more recent and also much-debated article (1983), Rummel has suggested that there is a strong negative correlation between the libertarianism of a state and its foreign violence. This new finding is based on conflict data from the period 1976–80. Since Rummel's new sample period differs from that of his earlier study, there is no necessary contradiction in the two findings. Nevertheless, the new conclusion has been seen to be contrary to a scholarly consensus, and has attracted much critical attention.

According to Erich Weede (1984) and Steven Chan (1984), for example, the alleged correlation with respect to the period 1976–80 is not supported when similar hypotheses are tested against a longer historical period (1960–80 in the case of Weede, and 1816–1980 in the case of Chan): Rummel's sample period (1976–80) seems, therefore, to be a statistical aberration. Moreover, when 'extra-systemic' (mainly colonial and imperialist) wars are included in the analysis (together with wars between sovereign states within the international system), Rummel's proposition that the more libertarian a state, the less its foreign violence cannot be supported (Chan 1984). Chan suggests, however, that, although freer countries are not less war-prone than their less free *contemporaries*, there is some evidence to suggest that when a country *becomes* freer it also tends to *become* less war-prone (1984: 639 ff.).

Further research is worthwhile on this subject, and Rummel can be praised for having stimulated many investigations in this field, the most striking outcome of which so far will be discussed in Section 3.3. But now we turn to the second kind of situation encountered in correlational studies, represented by Michael Wallace's important work (1979).

3.2 AN EARLY WARNING INDICATOR OF WAR

Using the data collected by the Correlates of War Project, Wallace has identified 99 'serious disputes' between 'great powers' in the period 1816–1965, and found that they resulted in the 'outbreak of full-scale war' in 26 cases. Of these 26 cases, however, as many as 23 were accompanied by a 'runaway arms race'. By contrast, according to Wallace, of the 73 cases in which 'serious disputes' did not end in 'full-scale war', as many as 68 were not accompanied by such an arms race. He concludes, 'rapid competitive military growth is *strongly associated* with the escalation of military confrontations into war' (1979: 15; emphasis Wallace's); and he asserts that the former constitutes at least 'a valuable "early warning indicator"' of the latter (1979: 15).

Definitions

Since any correlational finding is shaped by what is counted or measured, it is imperative to keep in mind Wallace's scope of investigation and how he defines his basic terms.[7] In the first place, his study relates exclusively to serious disputes between great powers in the 1816–1965 period. The 'great powers' are: Britain (1815–1965), France (1816–1940; 1945–65), the USA (1898–1965), Germany (1816–1918; 1923–45), Austria–Hungary (1816–1917), Russia (1816–1917; 1920–65), Japan (1904–45), and China (1950–1965). A 'serious dispute' is a military confrontation between any two great powers in which at least one of the following acts was committed by at least one party: 'the act of blockade, declaration of war, seizure or occupation of territory, the use of military forces, the mobilization of armed forces, and the seizure of foreign personnel or materiel'.

---

[7] The following summary is based on Wallace (1979: 7–13).

Some serious disputes of the period escalated into 'war'. 'A great power war' is defined as: a military clash in which at least one great power participated on each side, and which resulted in at least 1,000 battle-related fatalities. Where more than two great powers participated in a war (or a dispute), Wallace considers every pair of great powers at war (or in dispute) with each other as being engaged in a *separate* war (or dispute). A serious dispute (or war) between a great power and a minor power bound in a military alliance to another great power is included in the analysis.

A pair of great powers are considered by Wallace to be engaged in 'a runaway arms race' where an 'arms race index value', which he calculates for every pair of disputing states in his list, is above 90.00.[8] The complex mathematical formula Wallace has used in calculating the index value embodies an attempt to distinguish 'a runaway arms race' from 'normal' arms competition, and to ensure that 'only long-term, intense, bilateral growth in arms expenditures will score high' on the arms race scale (Wallace 1979: 13).

Each arms race index value is a product of two numbers, each number representing the estimated degree of acceleration in a disputing country's arms-spending in the year prior to the dispute; and this estimate is based on extrapolation from the record of the country's arms-spending for the ten years prior to the dispute, and calculated in such a way that the estimate is relatively more sensitive to the final phase of the ten-year span (Wallace 1979: 11–13).[9]

Arms Races as an Early Warning Indicator of War

Three questions arise regarding Wallace's contentions: (1) Is his correlational finding well substantiated *with respect to his sample period 1816–1965*? (2) If so, can a runaway arms race be treated, *in future*, as an early warning indicator of the escalation of a

---

[8] This important point is made explicit in Wallace (1982: 45), where it is said that an index value equal to or exceeding 90.00 means 'an average annual bilateral predispute growth rate of 10%' or above in the arms build-up. On the appropriateness of this threshold, see Altfeld (1983); Wallace (1983).

[9] See, however, Diehl (1983: 207), who rightly notes that, since an arms race index calculated by Wallace for each pair of disputing states is a *product* of each side's estimated military spending, it fails to distinguish unilateral arms build-ups from bilateral arms races. For example, if Country *A* had a score of 100 and Country *B* a score of 1, the index value would still be 100, which, by Wallace's criterion, would be classified as a runaway arms race.

serious dispute into war? (3) If so, does it constitute a *valuable* early warning indicator? These questions are examined below in the reverse order.

How valuable is the indicator?

Suppose (1) and (2) have been affirmed. To simplify the argument, suppose also that your country (a great power), of which you are the leader, and my country (another great power), of which I am your counterpart, have been engaged in an ever-intensifying arms race over the last ten years, and that the race now qualifies as a 'runaway' variety by Wallace's criterion. Suppose further that our two countries are now engaged in a serious dispute as defined by Wallace. This situation may or may not result in war, but we are warned that, statistically, the probability of escalation is high in such circumstances.

On the basis of this warning, what could be done at this stage to avoid war? Not much by us, in fact, if we only take heed of Wallace's warning late in our confrontation. It may be noticed that, by Wallace's definition, we may, in the most extreme case, already have declared war, and even incurred several hundred battle-related deaths. How are we to stop the next few bombs and bullets killing a few hundred more soldiers, and thereby prevent our 'serious dispute' from escalating into a 'war' as defined?[10]

If I had taken Wallace's warning seriously into account at an earlier stage of conflict escalation, I might have been more willing to consider taking such steps as are likely to prevent war. However, since our two countries are now engaged in a serious dispute accompanied by a runaway arms race, tensions are already high and mutual suspicions paramount. In such circumstances, my subjective freedom of action is severely restricted for a number of familiar reasons.

Even if, fearing war, I am willing to de-escalate, crucially I may not be reasonably certain that you are reasonably certain about my dovish intentions. If so, fearing your first strike, I may be tempted to pre-empt you.[11] To avoid this, it is vital to show evidence of my

---

[10] Wallace does not say that 'arms race' is an early warning indicator of 'war', but that 'a runaway arms race' is one when combined with a 'serious dispute'. See further Diehl and Kingston (1987).

[11] The incentive to pre-empt is strengthened where 'the cult of the offensive' prevails. See Snyder (1984); Van Evera (1984).

dovishness by taking some suggestive measures early on. However, this is easier said than done, since I may not be reasonably certain that you will yourself take Wallace's warning seriously. If I feel you may soon escalate, I may not find it very sensible to de-escalate now. Further, even if I wish to take some de-escalatory measures, I may feel the need to appease hawkish rivals within (supposing, of course, that some of my colleagues do not take Wallace's warning seriously), and they may stress the need not to modify existing contingency plans geared towards escalation (Levy 1986). If I act according to such needs, my own dovish intentions will not be made credible to you. Worse still, my position in the decision-making hierarchy may be precarious, and a more militant leader may soon gain influence; and I may not be reasonably certain that you consider this to be a sufficiently unlikely eventuality. All this presupposes that I am initially willing to de-escalate, but, of course, I may consider war as a tolerably rational means to obtain my country's aims at least in the present instance.

All these arguments work with respect to you in relation to me. Further, neither you nor I may know what to do next: hesitancy may not be so uncommon among decision-makers. If so, neither you nor I can even begin to be reasonably certain about each other's intentions, unless, of course, we misjudge: and the misjudgement we most want to avoid is to assume peaceful intent on the part of the adversary where none in fact exists.

Thus, at this stage, where a runaway arms race has already begun and our two countries are engaged in a serious dispute, a warning that war is highly likely to come is of limited value to war avoidance by ourselves. Perhaps the indicator is valuable in revealing an urgent need for mediation. The value of the indicator for a third-party settlement, however, is contingent on the existence, aims, and abilities of a would-be mediator. If the mediator's resources are limited, he or she can achieve very little, particularly if in addition either of us considers escalatory measures as a tolerably rational response to the situation.

These familiar doubts arise even if we assume that questions (1) and (2), noted above, have been affirmed. We must now turn to them. Suppose, therefore, that (1) has been affirmed, that is, that Wallace's correlational finding is reasonably well substantiated with respect to his sample period 1816–1965. Can we then affirm (2), and suggest that a runaway arms race, when combined with a serious dispute, predicts a *future* great power war?

How safe is extrapolation?

There is no doubt that in some future cases a runaway arms race, combined with a serious dispute, will result in war not only between great powers, but also between lesser powers. But the frequency ratio of such an eventuality between great powers cannot be inferred mechanically from Wallace's findings. The impressive length of Wallace's sample period (1816–1965) may appear reassuring. Still, we may predict that a runaway arms race combined with a serious dispute between great powers is highly likely to result in war *only if* we are willing to presume that relevant conditions of the sample period will remain largely unchanged in the future period to which we apply our prediction: this is a key qualification necessary to any attempt at probabilistic extrapolation from a past statistical record. The possession of nuclear weapons by great powers since about the middle of the twentieth century (and the change in the meaning of 'great power war' dramatically brought home by the presence of these weapons) is one of the features which would make us doubt the appropriateness of extrapolating from Wallace's study.

We see from Wallace's table 1 (1979: 9–11) that between 1945 and 1965 there was just one instance which satisfies his definition of a 'serious dispute between great powers engaged in a runaway arms race'. This was in 1962, and must therefore be the Cuban Missile Crisis, which, fortunately, did not end in war (see Wallace's comment on this case in Wallace 1979: 14). Of course, we cannot extrapolate from just one example, but this case does illustrate the ground for doubting the appropriateness of extrapolating from a largely pre-nuclear experience: nuclear powers *may* behave more cautiously than did great powers in the past.

Interestingly, the main reason why war was avoided in the Cuban case was the key leaders' belief in the overwhelming costs in the event of a nuclear war, combined with the high probability in their minds of that horrific eventuality in the absence of control and compromise (Trachtenberg 1991c). Thus, to the extent that these leaders can be depicted as having acted as though they had taken something like Wallace's warning seriously into account, the case may of course be used to illustrate the importance of heeding his type of warning.[12] But to argue in this way is to shift the ground. Wallace's own move in advancing his warning is to extrapolate from the past record of dangers into the future on the assumption that the pre-nuclear/nuclear divide is not crucial to the argument (Wallace 1990: 122).

Wallace is entirely right to warn against nuclear complacency (1990: 122). Given the devastating effects even of a small-scale nuclear war, doubting the validity of his statistical extrapolation may be academic. We should add here that the dangers of a major nuclear war might have receded with the end of the Cold War, but that those of a nuclear accident most certainly have not (Wallace 1994). But if we want to argue probabilistically, as does Wallace, from the past statistical record to the future (rather than stress the virtual irrelevance of probability considerations in the face of the magnitude of a *possible* disaster), then the problem of extrapolation cannot be circumvented; and, to this end, the record of peace among nuclear powers for nearly half a century may be as relevant as Wallace's findings based largely on the pre-nuclear age.[13]

How solid are the findings?

Extrapolation from a past statistical record cannot be trusted without qualification even where the initial correlational finding is reasonably well established. Where this is itself contentious, it

[12] It is worth recalling here that President Kennedy had recently read Barbara Tuchman's *The Guns of August* (Kennedy 1969: 62–3), a well-known work on the origins of the First World War which stresses the extent to which the war's outbreak was attributable to the key governments' careless loss of control over the rapid development of events in the summer of 1914. President Kennedy remarked during the crisis: 'I am not going to follow a course which will allow anyone to write a comparable book about this time, *The Missiles of October*' (Kennedy 1969: 127).
[13] To refer to 'the record of peace among nuclear powers' is *not* to suggest that in the absence of such weapons another world war would have occurred. To assume this, as John Mueller rightly points out in an article originally published in 1988, would be to ignore 'several other important war-discouraging factors in the postwar world' (1990: 4). Mueller does accept, however, that nuclear weapons 'compound and dramatize a military reality that by 1945 had already become appalling' (1990: 5). In any case, if, as Mueller suggests, a great power war, for various reasons, is now 'spectacularly unlikely' (1990: 26), then extrapolation from the period in a substantial part of which such a remark, for whatever reasons, could not have been made is still precarious. A similar view to Mueller's is stated briefly in Luard (1986: 395–9); see also Jervis (1990) for a succinct and well-considered critique of Mueller.

becomes difficult to choose between incompatible predictions emanating from diverse findings. This is to some extent the case with
Wallace's 1979 findings, which Paul Diehl has scrutinized and
contradicted (Diehl 1983).[14]

Some of the key moves Diehl makes in arriving at his main
conclusion are worth recounting to illustrate potential sources of
dispute among statistical analysts.

First of all, whereas Wallace had relied on a preliminary draft
of the Correlates of War Project compilations, Diehl takes advantage of a more recent and complete version, which corrected some
errors in the draft, added new information, and extended the data
period by five years, to 1970 (Diehl 1983: 207). Diehl considers
that his data are, therefore, a little more accurate and informative
than Wallace's. However, the differences in the two sets of raw
data are said by Diehl (1983: 210) to be too small to be the main
source of conspicuous divergence in the findings obtained. This
view is shared by Wallace, who subsequently shows that the new
data leave the basic relationship essentially unaltered (1990: 119).

Secondly, Wallace and Diehl resort to different methods of calculating the arms race index (Diehl 1983: 208). However, this too
is said by Diehl (1983: 209–10) to be an unlikely source of large
discrepancies in their findings. This point also is subsequently
confirmed by Wallace (1990: 120–1).

The most important source of difference turns out to be quite
elementary: *how what counts is counted*. It will be remembered
that Wallace's method of counting wars and serious disputes is
'state-dyadic': where more than two great powers participated in
a war or a dispute, he considers every pair (or 'dyad') of great
powers at war or in dispute with each other as being engaged in
a *separate* war or dispute.

To see the impact of this counting decision, compare the following two cases. In one, State *A* and State *B* are engaged in a serious
dispute, which is genuinely bilateral. In the other, State *C* and
State *D* are in a serious dispute in coalition against State *E* and
State *F* also in coalition. The first case is unproblematic. In the
second, however, four serious disputes are counted: *C* versus *E*;

---

[14] The controversy surrounding Wallace's investigations is usefully summarized
in Siverson and Diehl (1989). See also a brief summary in Nicholson (1992: 180–
3), and comments in Vasquez and Henehan (1992: 88–92, 103–8); Vasquez (1993:
177–84). The most recent reply by Wallace is in Wallace (1990).

C versus *F*; *D* versus *E*; and *D* versus *F*. It follows that, by this
method of counting, Wallace automatically accords to the second
case four times more confirmatory potential with respect to his
statistical hypothesis than he gives to the first case.

However, given that in the second type of situation the fact of
coalition, formal or informal, is likely to have had some influence
on the development of events, it may not constitute an uncontam-
inated test case for Wallace's purposes. If so, it is perhaps more
sensible not to accord so much power of confirmation to cases like
this. At any rate, it is worth investigating whether Wallace's correlational finding is supported even when we decide to count the
second type of situation as constituting one case, not many. And
this is a major part of what Diehl has done in his reanalysis. Thus,
for example, the dispute leading to the Crimean War is now coded:
Russia versus Great Britain and France (Diehl 1983: 206, 207);
and not Russia versus Great Britain, *and* Russia versus France.

Another adjustment Diehl makes in the counting procedure
concerns war-related disputes, namely those which are linked to
ongoing wars. The problem here can be explained with reference
to one key example. According to Wallace, there was, in 1945, a
'serious dispute' between Russia and Japan, and this escalated into
a 'war' immediately. We cannot ignore, however, that for the few
years prior to the onset (in 1945, according to Wallace) of the
serious dispute between the two contestants, one had been engaged in the Second World War in Europe, and the other in Asia
and the Pacific. Where, as in this case, *at least* one member of a
disputing dyad was already at war elsewhere at the onset of the
dispute, Wallace noted that the arms race index calculated according to his standard procedures may be artificially inflated.

This stands to reason. Remember that, according to Wallace's
standard procedures, an arms race index is a product of two
numbers, each number representing the estimated degree of acceleration in a disputing country's arms-spending in the year prior
to the dispute; and this estimate is based on extrapolation from
the record of the country's arms-spending for the ten years prior
to the dispute, and calculated in such a way that the estimate is
relatively more sensitive to the final phase of the ten-year span.
Therefore, even if there had been no runaway arms race *between*
Russia and Japan themselves in the ten-year period up to 1945,
Wallace's index might well suggest otherwise, since it would reflect

vastly increased arms-spending resulting from the two disputants' mutually independent engagement in the Second World War. An arms race index calculated in the standard manner by Wallace would be insensitive to this.

To avoid this potential error, therefore, Wallace modified his procedures in such cases. His remedy was to base an arms race index on a ten-year period immediately prior to 'the first *war* entry' (Wallace 1983: 233–4; emphasis added). This means that, in the case of the Russo-Japanese dyad, the arms race index was calculated with reference to the period prior to 1941, the year in which Russia, and subsequently Japan, entered the Second World War.

Diehl, however, considers this adjustment as in turn problematic. In his view, this modified procedure may result in estimating the intensity of the arms race between the disputants several years prior to the onset of *their* dispute, and this may not be a relevant factor in its escalation (Diehl 1983: 206; see also Siverson and Diehl 1989: 209). In any case, according to Diehl, the dispute, followed by war, between Russia and Japan in 1945 is highly unlikely to be a suitable test case: 'it is difficult to believe that this brief war was anything but a result of the hostilities associated with World War II' (1983: 206).

This line of reasoning has led Diehl to make a rather drastic move: any dispute which was related to an ongoing major power war is to be excluded from calculation (Diehl 1983: 207, 211 n. 3). Diehl also suggests that it is almost impossible accurately to estimate wartime military expenditures for a country whose whole economy is devoted to the war effort. Accordingly, another radical move is made: serious disputes belonging to the two periods 1915–20 and 1940–7 are also eliminated from the list *even where* independent of ongoing wars (Diehl 1983: 208, 211 n. 4).

Finally, Diehl (1983: 208) states that he has chosen to designate as a 'mutual military build-up' any instance where both sides in a dispute (whether states or coalitions, formal or informal) were increasing their military expenditures at a rate of 8 per cent or more for the three years before the initiation of the dispute.[15]

---

[15] Diehl (1983: 207) prefers the term 'mutual military (or arms) buildup' to 'arms race' because his method does not establish the presence or otherwise of the latter, 'a more sensitive test of military spending decisions' being required for that end: an 'arms race' is an *intentional* activity.

TABLE 3.1. *Wallace's 1979 findings*

	Escalation into war	No escalation into war	Total
Runaway arms race	23	5	28
No runaway arms race	3	68	71
TOTAL	26	73	99

TABLE 3.2. *Diehl's 1983 reanalysis*

	Escalation into war	No escalation into war	Total
Mutual arms build-up	3	9	12
No mutual arms build-up	10	64	74
TOTAL	13	73	86

By this criterion, and with a new set of cases outlined above, Diehl reaches a finding radically different from Wallace's: of the 86 cases of 'serious disputes', 13 resulted in 'war'; of these 13, however, 'mutual military build-up' preceded only 3; and of the 12 cases where a 'mutual military build-up' preceded a 'serious dispute', as many as 9 did not end in 'war' (Diehl 1983: 208, table II). The two investigators' findings are summarized in Tables 3.1 and 3.2.

It is particularly important to note that Diehl's non-'state-dyadic' coding method has resulted in the collapse of 10 cases, which, in Wallace's study, fit the 'arms race–escalation' sequence, into 3 integrated disputes; and that another 10 cases of serious disputes which, according to Wallace, also fit the sequence were eliminated because they were not independent of ongoing wars (Diehl 1983: 210). Clearly, the discrepancy in the findings is largely due to different initial decisions on how to count what counts.

On reflection, as he subsequently acknowledges, Diehl may have been too puritanical in his concern to eliminate *potentially* contaminated cases from his study, and his procedures may have artificially deflated the degree of association between a mutual military build-up and escalation.[16] However, even if Diehl's counting procedures are therefore to be rejected in favour of Wallace's, the latter's contention that a runaway arms race constitutes 'a valuable early warning indicator' will require serious reservations given the considerations noted in the previous two subsections.

Findings by Wallace, Diehl, and others on arms races and escalation appear to have caused much discussion among the interpreters of correlational works. Some of the most constructive remarks come from Vasquez. According to him (1993: 177–84), military build-ups do appear to make it more likely that a serious dispute will escalate to war, but only *in certain circumstances*. He suggests that, where the contestants are contiguous, and are roughly equal major powers or power blocs which have been engaged in a series of crises, escalation to war is highly likely (1993: 183–4). This seems a sensible conclusion to reach. Under such critical circumstances, however, Wallace's early warning would almost certainly be too late.

Clearly, the value (understood as utility for war avoidance) of an identified correlate as an early warning indicator must be carefully assessed case by case, and the strength of correlation, while relevant, is not by itself a sufficient guarantee.

The notion of an early warning indicator

One important observation may be added here concerning the notion of 'an early warning indicator' itself. Where a condition strongly associated with the occurrence of war has been identified, the analyst may characterize it as 'at least an early warning indicator of war' to avoid confusing correlation for causation (e.g. Wallace 1990: 116). But this notion, if it is to form part of a scientific enquiry, cannot be severed from the idea of causality, as was noted briefly in this volume's Introduction, and explained more fully below.

---

[16] See Siverson and Diehl (1989: 209–10), where they concede, 'just because a nation joins an ongoing war on the side of a prewar ally does not necessarily remove the contribution of an arms race to the decision to begin fighting'. They also state (1989: 211), 'although alliances may well be responsible for the spread of war, it is by no means correct to assume that there is no relationship between the arms acquisition policies of allies and their entry into war'. On the appropriateness or otherwise of Wallace's counting methods, see further Wallace (1980: 290); Weede (1980: 286); Wallace (1982: 46–7); Vasquez (1987: 136 n. 85); Wallace (1990: 117, 119–20).

Three ideal-type relationships are conceivable between 'an early warning indicator of war' and 'war'. These are:

(1) An early warning indicator of war is an effect of an early portion of a process which, if not effectively responded to, is likely to eventuate in war.

(2) An early warning indicator of war is a condition such that (*a*) it is not itself an effect of an early portion of a process which, if not effectively responded to, is likely to eventuate in war; but (*b*) it still occurs quite often at an early stage of such a process; and (*c*) when it does occur, it is known to make the situation more war-prone.

(3) An early warning indicator of war is a condition whose occurrence some time before the outbreak of war is statistically regular, but without any plausible reason known to us.

We may call an early warning indicator in the first category 'a symptom'; in the second category 'a common intervening cause'; and the most appropriate term for the third category would be 'an omen'. A hybrid of the first two is also conceivable. For example, an arms race may be a symptom of the gradually deteriorating conditions, but may in turn contribute to their further worsening (Wallace 1990: 115, 117–18).

Of the three categories, the first two involve causal notions. Without at least implicitly entering the causal realm it is impossible to talk of anything as being an *effect* of a process as in (1), or to suggest, as in (2), that it *makes* the situation more war-prone; it is also impossible to talk of the process as being likely to result in war unless *effectively responded to*.

Thus, in characterizing a given correlate of war as at least an early warning indicator, correlational analysts are introducing causal notions unless they are to concede merely to be referring to war's 'omen'. This they are unlikely in fact to do. To characterize a given correlate as at least an early warning indicator seems, therefore, to be a way of suggesting that a causal mechanism may underlie the identified pattern, and yet acknowledging that the mechanism may not be responsible for *all* instances confirming the pattern. The idea that a plausible causal mechanism may be responsible only for a portion of a regular pattern uncovered is discussed further in Section 3.3.

3.3 EXPLAINING A STRONG CORRELATION

Many findings resulting from statistical investigations into war or international conflict are negative, incompatible, or incommensurate (Scolnik 1974: 502–3; Siverson and Sullivan 1983; Levy 1989*a*; Dessler 1991). One notable exception so far is a consensus among leading researchers that war rarely, if ever, occurs between liberal or democratic states (Babst 1972; Small and Singer 1976: 67; Doyle 1983; Rummel 1983: 38–52; Chan 1984: 620; Rummel 1985; Doyle 1986; Garnham 1986: 283–4; Maoz and Abdolali 1989; Levy 1989*c*: 87–8; Doyle 1993; Russett 1993: ch. 1). As Russett remarks, '[t]his research result is extremely robust, in that by various measures of war and militarized diplomatic disputes, and various measures of democracy, the relative rarity of violent conflict between democracies still holds up' (1993: 10). The key terms used by these researchers—'liberal', 'libertarian', 'democratic', 'republican', 'free', and 'elective', and so on—are, however, sufficiently similar in meaning to warrant the use of 'liberal' to represent all (Ray 1993: 252). According to Levy, this regular conjunction of dyadic liberalism and peace—the term 'dyadic liberalism' is used here to denote cases where two countries concerned *both* qualify as liberal states—'comes as close as anything we have to an empirical law in international relations' (1989*c*: 88). In answer to our question (*b*), 'Under what sorts of circumstances have wars occurred more frequently?', therefore, one of the most reliable responses so far is to suggest: 'Where at least one party in contest was non-liberal.' This correlational discovery thus deserves a very special treatment.

Of course, there may be some exceptions to the regular pattern, depending on how 'war' and 'liberal states' are defined (Waltz 1993: 78; Cohen 1994). Nevertheless, as we noted in Chapter 2, convincing counter-examples are few or even perhaps non-existent (Ray 1993; Russett 1993: 11–20). Given also the plausibility of a number of causal links suggested between dyadic liberalism and inter-liberal peace, it is tempting to say that dyadic liberalism must have had something causally to do with the phenomenon of inter-liberal peace overall. In this final part, we examine this issue with reference to Doyle's theoretical contribution.

Doyle's Reasoning

According to Michael Doyle's favoured theory, as we saw, peace between liberal states has resulted from a combination of three main conditions which, he says, are associated with dyadic liberalism. Briefly, these are: domestic constraints which liberal institutions impose upon the governments' freedom of action in foreign policy; mutual respect between liberal states based on shared liberal values; and a vested interest in peace resulting from transnational commercial interdependence among the citizens of liberal states (Doyle 1983: 225–32, 324–5; 1986: 1156–62; 1993: 186 ff.).

What is Doyle suggesting, however, when he offers his theory as the most plausible alternative? Does he mean that his theory explains *all instances of* inter-liberal peace? It is unlikely that it does, and Doyle (1986: 1156) acknowledges this when he remarks that the impressive record of inter-liberal peace does not prove liberalism to be the sole valid explanation of it.

Does he mean perhaps that his theory explains *by far the largest proportion of* inter-liberal peace? He might be thinking along these lines, but he does not show this to be the case, nor does he discuss how such a claim might be substantiated.

Does he perhaps mean then that his theory explains *some historically significant instances of* inter-liberal peace? If so, he does not discuss how we may determine which cases are historically significant. Besides, where he refers to historical examples, some of which we may agree to be significant in some sense, he uses them merely as illustrations of the regular pattern (1983: 215–16). He does not investigate whether dyadic liberalism was part of the cause of inter-liberal peace in such cases.

Doyle's claim, it turns out, is that his theory is better than other likely theories—Realist ones, in particular. The main thrust of his argument against these theories is (1) that even in the presence of those conditions which they point to as peace-conducive there may not be a very long period of peace; and further (2) that even where those conditions were absent a relatively long period of peace existed among liberal states (Doyle 1983: 220–4; see also Doyle 1986: 1157, and Doyle 1993: 185, where Marxist theory, too, is rejected in favour of his own).

For example, 'prudent diplomacy' or 'the balance of power' is said by some Realists to be peace-conducive. Such things, however, do not sustain a long period of peace, since they are also capable of producing war, at times even necessitating a preventive war (Doyle 1983: 220 ff.). These things therefore cannot be expected to account for 'more than a century and a half of peace among independent liberal states' (Doyle 1983: 220). Conversely, the presence of a hegemonic power is said by some Realists to be conducive to peace, but even in the absence of such a power peace could be sustained: 'the liberal peace persisted in the interwar period when international society lacked a predominant hegemonic power' (Doyle 1983: 223).

In short, Doyle's main grounds for rejecting alternative (Realist) theories are that those conditions which, according to them, are peace-conducive are (1) neither sufficient (2) nor necessary for a relatively long period of peace among states.

However, point (1) regarding 'sufficiency' applies to some extent also to Doyle's own theory inasmuch as the three conditions suggested by him as joint causes of peace between liberal states may not in fact be sufficient to guarantee it. Even where two liberal states satisfy the three conditions identified by Doyle to be causally significant, the two states may still go to war in the long run, as Doyle himself acknowledges when he remarks that 'no one should argue that such wars are impossible' (1983: 213).

Furthermore, point (2) regarding 'necessity' can also be made against Doyle's own theory. For example, we learn from Doyle's list of wars (1983: 214–15) that Russia and the USA never fought a war with each other during the period 1816–1980. Based on the Correlates of War Project findings, this list excludes the US participation (1918–20) in the Allied Intervention in Russia.[17] In addition, there was no war between the two countries before 1816, nor after 1980. Therefore, Russia and the USA have never fought a war with each other since American independence, either before or after the Russian Revolution, even though Russia has never been, and the USA has always been, a liberal state (Doyle 1983:

[17] The Project recognized the intervention against Russia during the Civil War of 1917–21 in principle as an interstate war, but decided to exclude it from their list of interstate wars for a number of reasons. Most importantly, the intervening powers are said not to have been fighting a war against a common enemy, but each was engaged in a different region for its own peculiar reasons, seldom engaging Red forces in more than a brief skirmish. It is also said that the US forces lost perhaps 500 men, more by disease and freezing than by combat. See Singer and Small (1972: 34).

209–12, table 1). The duration of this Russo-US peace coincides with that of inter-liberal peace as studied by Doyle. Clearly, therefore, dyadic liberalism is not a 'necessary' condition of sustained peace.

Doyle's rejection of other (Realist) theories on the grounds that the conditions they suppose to be conducive to peace are neither sufficient nor necessary for sustained peace thus backfires: dyadic liberalism, too, appears to be in the same boat.[18] This most certainly does not mean that Doyle's theory is no better than Realist alternatives, or that dyadic liberalism and Realist-recommended conditions are equally efficacious in producing peace. But Doyle's stated grounds in favour of his own theory are somewhat precarious.

What is also noteworthy about Doyle's method of selecting a better theory is that he rejects alternative theories by saying that they cannot plausibly explain 150 years or more of peace among liberal states, that is, the phenomenon of inter-liberal peace *in its entirety*. It seems unrealistic, however, to expect any single theory —including Doyle's own—to be able to do this. A number of different explanations can coexist for the phenomenon of inter-liberal peace as a whole, but this point seems mostly unnoticed by Doyle, his supporters, and critics. Instead, there is a marked tendency to regard various theories as *competing* explanations for the phenomenon.[19]

However, it is unwise to start our causal enquiry on this subject by assuming that there must necessarily be *one* causal scenario which consistently represents the entire phenomenon of inter-liberal peace, by far the largest proportion of it, or even a major portion of its more significant instances. On the contrary, it is methodologically more prudent to take seriously the possibility that there may be different paths to inter-liberal peace, and at least initially to conjecture a variety of possible interpretations with respect to separate instances of the phenomenon. In the following, therefore, such interpretations are outlined.

[18] A type of condition which is neither necessary nor sufficient for sustained peace may still be causally associated with it. See Mackie (1980); Most and Starr (1983); Quester (1984); and Dessler (1991).

[19] See e.g. Layne (1994). Cohen (1994) is perhaps an exception in this regard. See also Russett and Ray, and Cohen (1995: 323–5).

Plausible Scenarios of Inter-Liberal Peace

It is important to stress here that none of the 'theses' below is presumed to apply to all instances of inter-liberal peace. They are no more than possible scenarios, each of which may represent a relevant subset of all the instances of the regular phenomenon, and they can thus coexist without contradiction. Therefore, they are not in competition with one another.

A variety of theses

First of all, there is what we may call the 'dyadic-causality thesis', which holds: 'the circumstances were such that some aspects or consequences of the fact that the two states concerned were both liberal (or perceived to be so by themselves) were part of the cause of peace between them'. To use Doyle's own example (1983: 216), this thesis may fit liberal Italy's decision, despite its membership of the Triple Alliance, to fight on the side of France and Britain in the First World War against illiberal Germany and Austria. Disappointingly, Doyle's sole evidence here is no more than a book review in which it is said that the book's author depicts the life of an Italian historian and political activist who stressed the importance of liberal Italy's cooperation with other liberal states, France and Britain in particular (Doyle 1983: 217 n. 8; see also Babst 1972: 56; Vivarelli 1980). Obviously, more substantial historical evidence is needed to argue that the 'dyadic-causality thesis' applies to the Italian choice of its allies in the war. For the present purpose, it is sufficient to note that some such case as the Italian decision exemplifies this thesis.[20]

In some cases, however, the liberalism of only one of the two liberal states concerned may have been causally relevant to the peace between them. For example, the 'Cod War' in the earlier part of the 1970s between Iceland, liberal since 1944 (Doyle 1983: 211), and Britain, also liberal, did not develop into a hot war perhaps because Britain was too liberal to fight, and because Iceland assessed that it could not achieve its aims by war with Britain. It is possible further that Iceland's realistic calculations were

---

[20] See Owen (1994) for important case studies confirming the thesis, which, however, do not include the Italian decision.

causally independent of its liberalism. If so, the 'monadic-causality thesis' applies to this case, which says: 'the circumstances were such that some aspects or consequences of the fact that one of the two states was liberal were part of the cause of peace between them (although the fact that the other state was also liberal was, in this case, causally irrelevant)'.

It is also possible in some cases that causation is in the opposite direction. For example, the USA and Japan have jointly been liberal since 1951 (Doyle 1983: 211). It is conceivable that Japan, having been liberalized by the USA as a result of the Second World War, managed to remain liberal, and did not resume an illiberal path, partly because of a peaceful relationship which it began to enjoy with the USA (and other major liberal countries). If so, the 'reverse-causality thesis' applies to the case: 'the circumstances were such that peace between this pair of states was part of the cause of the adoption and maintenance of at least some aspects of liberalism at least on one side'.[21]

Of course, as is suggested by Doyle's central thesis, the fact that since 1951 the USA and Japan have both been liberal may in turn have reinforced their peaceful relationship. In that case, the 'reciprocal-causality thesis' applies: 'the circumstances were such that peace contributed to dyadic liberalism, and this in turn reinforced peace'.

Then there is what we may call the 'collateral-effects thesis'. For example, Australia has been liberal since 1901, and New Zealand since 1907 (Doyle 1983: 210). Certainly, this may have contributed to peace between them. However, they owe their liberalism partly to their inheritance of political culture and institutions from Britain (Doyle 1983: 333). It is also likely that their common ancestry, their co-membership of the Commonwealth, and perhaps the British hegemony at an earlier stage have contributed to their peaceful relationship (Cohen 1994: 215). If, for the sake of illustration, we also suppose that in this case there has been no causal relationship between their liberalism as such and their peace, we have the 'collateral-effects thesis' in operation: 'the circumstances were such that certain common factors (e.g. the two countries'

---

[21] Layne believes that this thesis may contain 'a more useful approach' (1994: 45) than the dyadic causality thesis to 'investigating the links between domestic structure and foreign policy' (ibid.) But, it is contended here, the two theses can coexist without contradiction.

common origins) are part of the cause of their liberalism as well as their peace, but there is no causal relationship in either direction between their liberalism and peace'. In any case, an early phase of the Australian–New Zealand relations may perhaps be explained by the 'collateral-effects thesis'.

Finally, dyadic liberalism and peace may in some cases be purely coincidental. For example, Latvia and Chile were both liberal from 1922 to 1924, and once again in 1932 (Doyle 1983: 210). In these four years, it is highly unlikely that their liberalism played any causal part in the absence of war between them. It is not even remotely plausible that peace between them played any causal part in the development of liberalism in either of them (as in the 'reverse-causality' case); or that the cause of their liberalism and the cause of peace between them overlapped (as in the 'collateral-effects' case). If so, the 'coincidence thesis' applies: 'the circumstances were such that liberalism of the two countries and the absence of war between them are a pure coincidence, unrelated to each other either as cause and effect in either direction, or even as collateral effects of the same cause'.[22]

The division of inter-liberal peace into subsets

The point of all this is to show that there is no guarantee that only one of the above theses will hold true consistently with respect to *all* instances of inter-liberal peace. Indeed, there is no guarantee even that the cause of peace between any two liberal states remains the same throughout different historical periods (Layne 1994: 27).

It is quite plausible that the 'dyadic-causality thesis' applies to some cases of inter-liberal peace; but that in some instances the 'reverse-causality thesis' holds; that there are a few examples which show the 'collateral-effects thesis' to be true; and further that the 'coincidence thesis' finds its application in a number of cases. Some variants of these theses may also apply, such as the 'monadic-causality' and 'reciprocal-causality' theses. When a given theory is under attack, Imre Lakatos's contention (1970) that only a better theory can replace a theory is frequently invoked (e.g. Bueno de Mesquita 1984b: 343). It is, however, unlikely to be any *single* theory that will replace Doyle's theory.

It follows from the foregoing discussion that, even though we

---

[22] Cohen (1994) seems to attach much importance to this thesis.

may be reasonably certain that the causal link running from dyadic liberalism towards peace is one of the legs upon which the overall phenomenon of inter-liberal peace rests, it is difficult to measure the degree of contribution made by this particular causal link, or the strength of this leg. The question which remains is: does this matter? In the next subsection, some comments are offered on this issue.

Contribution of Dyadic Liberalism towards Peace

It seems clear that a bundle of peace-conducive mechanisms, such as the ones—though not necessarily identical to the ones—thought by Doyle to distinguish inter-liberal relations, are at least potentially associated with dyadic liberalism. There is no guarantee with respect to a given pair of liberal states that any such mechanism necessarily operates. Further, even where some such mechanisms do operate, they do not guarantee peace: they are only conducive to it. However, this conduciveness to peace is an important factor.

Where the 'dyadic-causality thesis' applies, some peace-conducive mechanisms potentially associated with dyadic liberalism actually operate, perhaps in conjunction with certain other factors, to balance out those which are war-conducive, such as the absence of a hegemon or a common enemy. In addition, where the 'reciprocal-causality thesis' applies, the 'dyadic-causality thesis', by definition, already applies. Further, where 'monadic-causality', 'reverse-causality', 'collateral-effects', or 'coincidence' thesis applies, the parties concerned *ex hypothesi* already form a liberal dyad, and thus 'dyadic-causality thesis' may come to apply there also: there is nothing in the logic of any of these theses to exclude this possibility.

Thus, not only do certain peace-conducive mechanisms already operate in those cases which substantiate the 'dyadic-causality' and 'reciprocal-causality' theses, but they can also become operative in other kinds of inter-liberal relations. They can come to operate where hitherto non-liberal states turn liberal, as may be the case in some parts of Eastern Europe, and join the existing set of liberal dyads. In this sense, dyadic liberalism is a constant potential force for peace even though it may not always overwhelm contending forces.

However, it is difficult to say, even despite the unbroken or nearly unbroken record of inter-liberal peace, that dyadic liberalism constitutes *the most effective* mechanism against war. This is partly because we do not know for certain that the impressive record has itself resulted mainly from the operation of this particular mechanism. It is also because there may be other kinds of relatively sustained peace, perhaps less impressive in outward consistency than the inter-liberal variety, but actually resulting mainly from the operation of certain other relevant mechanisms.

None the less, it is plausible that where, for example, the three peace-conducive conditions thought by Doyle to distinguish inter-liberal relations are met, they will work with considerable (if not necessarily overwhelming) effectiveness. Interestingly, we would hesitate to make a comparable remark with the same degree of conviction about certain other suggested remedies for war: prudent diplomacy, or the balance of power, for example. When we hesitate to do this, and thereby distinguish the inter-liberal mechanism from certain other suggested cures for war, we seem to base our judgement partly on qualitative, as opposed to quantitative, considerations, as explained below.

In the first place, the peace-conducive factors potentially associated with dyadic liberalism are linked with peace much less tenuously than are the Realist ones considered here. That is to say, the conditions under which the inter-liberal mechanisms can operate to secure peace seem less complex or numerous than in the case of Realist mechanisms. Indeed, the more optimistic would suggest that the only requisite condition, in the inter-liberal case, was a sufficient intensity of interaction between the liberal states concerned. By contrast, it is more difficult to specify the conditions under which 'prudent diplomacy' or the 'balance of power' will lead to peace rather than to war. In this sense, the inter-liberal mechanisms for peace are more readily intelligible than the Realist mechanisms.[23]

Further, liberal states can fortify themselves not with a single, but with multiple layers of peace-conducive mechanisms in their mutual relations. According to Doyle's interpretation, derived from Immanuel Kant, these mechanisms comprise *domestic* constraints, *international* respect, and *transnational* ties. These three dimensions are conjointly exhaustive of global human relations. It is

[23] The relationship between 'intelligibility' and 'causality' is discussed in Ch. 4. The concept of 'mechanism' and its relation to 'intelligibility' are discussed in Ch. 5.3.

therefore easy to suppose that the inter-liberal mechanisms must be quite powerful: they can work on all the three fronts. The same cannot be said of the Realist mechanisms noted here.

Our judgement in favour of the inter-liberal mechanisms appears to be grounded partly in the relative plausibility we, for such qualitative reasons, acknowledge in the mechanisms linking dyadic liberalism and inter-liberal peace. Charles A. Kupchan and Clifford A. Kupchan appear to think along the same lines when they remark, '[t]he *deductive* case for the claim that the spread of democracy should lead to a more peaceful international setting is . . . quite compelling' (1991: 149 n. 100; emphasis added).[24]

It is not suggested here that quantitative aspects of inter-liberal peace are unimportant. Of course, the impressive record of inter-liberal peace, the qualifying observation that liberal states have fought (sometimes aggressive) wars against non-liberal states, and the record of wars between non-liberal states are interesting and thought-provoking.[25] This has alerted theorists such as Doyle to work out in some detail what plausible mechanisms there may be which operate to contribute to peace in the inter-liberal context, but not in others.

Furthermore, some researchers are determined to gather statistical evidence with which they hope to identify, however tentatively, which particular peace-conducive condition, potentially associated with dyadic liberalism, is likely to have contributed most to peaceful interactions of liberal states (Russett 1993: ch. 4). However, even in those cases which fit a statistically dominant pattern, a correlate identified may or may not be part of the cause of inter-liberal peace in particular instances. As Russett rightly

---

[24] There are some sceptics who would not find the claim at all compelling. John Mearsheimer (1990) is one. His criticisms (1990: 49–51) are effective against those who exaggerate the power of peace-conducive inter-liberal mechanisms, but are ineffective against those who simply hold, as is suggested here, that there are circumstances in which inter-liberal mechanisms work to counterbalance war-conducive tendencies. The same point can be made about Layne (1994), which builds on Mearsheimer (1990). See also Hoffmann, Keohane, and Mearsheimer (1990); Russett, Risse-Kappen and Mearsheimer (1990–1).

[25] Spiro (1994) points out that, given the vast number of state dyads, the relatively small number of liberal dyads, and the extreme infrequency of war, it is probabilistically unsurprising to find no or very few inter-liberal wars. Still, the fact that liberal states have never or hardly ever been found opposed in war is interesting, and quite unexpected if it is assumed that the choice of sides in war is totally at random. See further Russet, Layne, Spiro, and Doyle (1995).

acknowledges, '[s]tatistical analysis of many cases rarely can provide a fully satisfying explanation of underlying political processes' (1993: 92). Unfortunately, historical case studies which examine the influence of dyadic liberalism upon the quality of particular inter-liberal relations are still rare.[26]

Explaining particular cases

Supposing that dyadic liberalism potentially contains a mechanism of some considerable strength against war, can we perhaps say that its absence has been a contributory cause of wars? It certainly seems likely that the absence of domestic constraints, the lack of mutual respect, and/or the weakness of transnational interdependence contributed to the occurrence of some wars. One of the central contests in the First World War, that between Germany and Russia, is a striking example (Joll 1984).

However, this sort of assertion obviously needs to be backed by historical enquiry, and this in turn requires us to learn, among other things, the key figures' perceptions and motives.[27] We cannot move mechanically from the theory that dyadic liberalism is a good medicine against war to the assertion that its absence must necessarily be part of the cause of war in given instances. Such a mechanical move would be 'ideological' in a stronger sense than Nelson and Olin (1979) intended. What the theory does is to suggest a cluster of causal hypotheses which may be worth examining in explaining the occurrence of particular wars. We must also note in qualification, however, that the absence of liberalism is a fact of doubtful relevance in explaining the occurrence of any war which historically predated the emergence of liberalism in the late eighteenth century: we would not explain the Great Fire of London (1666) in terms of the absence of automatic water sprinklers.

---

[26] Layne (1994) and Owen (1994) are recent exceptions. John Macmillan's forthcoming work, provisionally entitled *On Liberal Peace*, will be an important contribution in this respect. Macmillan, however, is critical of the currently dominant view that there must be a peace-conducive mechanism which operates exclusively in the relations of liberal states, and argues instead that liberalism as a creed contains a 'pacificistic' tendency in the sense defined by Ceadel (1987). This interpretation is compatible with the fact that liberal states engage in war with non-liberal states and perhaps among themselves in some cases.

[27] The nature of historical enquiry is discussed in Chs. 4 and 5. It is interesting to note here that Russett and Antholis stress the causal importance of the leaders' perceptions and motives in accounting for an imperfect democratic peace in Ancient Greece (Russett and Antholis 1992; Russett 1993: ch. 3). See also Owen (1994).

CONCLUSION

Our question (*b*) asks: 'Under what sorts of circumstances have wars occurred more frequently?' This question may be thought to be of interest partly because it may assist us in suggesting a plausible answer to question (*b'*): 'What have been the relatively common causes of war?' Since correlation is not necessarily causation, however, an answer to (*b*) may not be found to be a satisfactory answer for (*b'*). Still, (*b*) is worth asking because in some cases the correlational information obtained may be used for prediction and control.

One approach to (*b*) is to test a series of statistical hypotheses regarding the relationship between national attributes and international conflict. In a classic study of this kind, Rummel reached negative conclusions. This might partly be an unlucky result attributable to the characteristics of the sample period (Rummel 1963: 7–8; 1968: 207 n. 27; Hazlewood 1975: esp. 240). However, Rummel's negative conclusions are not entirely unexpected after all: in retrospect, it would have been somewhat surprising to see an approximately linear relationship between, say, a country's internal instability and its conflict-proneness. On this particular issue, a well-substantiated generalization seems yet to be found. This is not surprising given the variety of potentially relevant contextual variables.

Occasionally, an unusually strong association is noted between a particular variable and war, facilitating a very simple generalization. Wallace's finding regarding 'a runaway arms race' and 'the escalation of a serious dispute into war' is one such example.

However, it was noted that Wallace's finding is a function of the particular counting procedures he adopted. This may be inevitable, but even on the basis of his findings, extrapolation into the future may not be warranted. Further, in the particular case of Wallace's investigation, the value for war avoidance of the predictor variable studied was doubted. Thus, even where we are lucky enough to identify a condition which has been strongly associated with the occurrence of war, we must be cautious in treating it as a *useful* early warning indicator of war.

In the light of many negative or inconclusive findings, the consensus among the leading analysts that there has been hardly any instance of war between liberal states is striking. Besides, there are certain plausible causal mechanisms explaining this. The idea that such mechanisms constitute a good remedy for war, however, stems partly from a qualitative judgement regarding their operation. The impressive record of inter-liberal peace adds some credibility to this judgement. To strengthen the case, a careful historical analysis is required with respect to a number of critical instances.

The foregoing discussion points implicitly to the importance of historical enquiry, and of familiarity with causal processes in various historical situations ending in war, or not, as the case may be. Such familiarity will assist us in hypothesis formulation by alerting us to certain potentially relevant contextual variables. It will help us evaluate the usefulness of a given early warning indicator by reminding us of the complexity of circumstances leading to the outbreaks of war. And without historical substantiation, even a well-supported answer to the statistical question (*b*), backed by a plausible causal theory, cannot be said to offer a satisfactory answer to the causal question (*b'*). This is because without historical studies it is difficult to know which, and how many significant, confirming instances of the regularity identified are plausibly explained by the causal theory in hand.

We should move on, therefore, to discuss the outcomes of various historical investigations into the causes of particular wars. Before this, in the next chapter, we take a philosophical interlude, and offer an analysis of the concept of causation.

4

CAUSATION

> One issue deserving further analysis is the topic of causation itself.
>
> (Dessler 1991: 351)

> the 'causes' of the war between Octavius and Antony are the events preceding that war, exactly as the causes of what happens in Act IV of *Antony and Cleopatra* are what happened in the first three acts.
>
> (Veyne 1984: 91)

HAVING considered necessary conditions of war, and correlates of war, we should move on to discuss the outcomes of various historical investigations into the causes of particular wars. Before this, in this chapter, we offer an analysis of the concept of causation. This detour is necessary for a number of reasons.

In the first place, if we do not understand what it means to say that something 'caused' something else, we cannot hope to find what 'caused' a particular war. Secondly, even though '[n]early everyone knows that correlation is not causation' (Haas 1974: 59), it cannot be said with the same degree of confidence that nearly everyone knows what it means to say that something 'caused' something else, and, in particular, whether a causal statement of this type necessarily involves correlational knowledge. Thirdly, if it were to be found that this last question should be answered in the affirmative, that is to say, if 'the establishment of covariation— while not *sufficient*—is indeed *necessary* to the search for causation' (Singer 1979b: 181; emphasis in original), then we could not simply 'move on' from the correlational to the historical enquiry. If, as Rummel states, '[o]bserved concurrence of phenomena is a *necessary* . . . condition for the assertion of causality' (1972: 32; emphasis added), then it may be that, even when in search of the causes of particular wars, we could not in fact move away from our correlational question (*b*). We need some reassurance that this is not in fact so.

Philosophers have produced a vast amount of writing on this and other related issues, but mostly in a highly technical language which even for the more philosophically minded reader is exceedingly difficult to follow (see e.g. Brand 1976). Unfortunately, there seems no easily comprehensible work available which, without oversimplifying, summarizes the pros and cons of various positions advanced by philosophers on the issue, gets us out of the maze, and provides us with a plausible answer. This chapter is intended as a remedy, and is necessary groundwork for the next chapter, which deals with the outcomes of historical investigations into the origins of wars.

It appears sometimes to be felt that the wording of this phrase— 'historical investigations into the *origins* of wars'—is highly significant. It is occasionally heard that a historian can say something about the *origins* of a war, but not about its *causes*; or, more generally, that the aim of history is 'to describe and narrate', and that 'it is simply not the historian's business to give explanations' (Dray 1957: 14; this is not Dray's own view, however). Such a position is rejected in this chapter, which argues that answering the causal question, 'What caused this war?'—call this (*c′*)—is essentially the same as, or at least requires, answering our question (*c*), 'How did this particular war come about?'; and that neither (*c*) nor (*c′*) requires us to answer our question (*b*), 'Under what sorts of circumstances have wars occurred more frequently?'

This chapter is divided into four sections. The first three sections examine three common theories of the concept of causation in turn. Briefly, the first theory attaches central importance to 'regularity' in explicating 'causality'. The second analyses the meaning of 'causality' in terms of the idea that, without 'the cause', 'the effect' would not have occurred. And the third treats 'explanation' as integral to the concept of 'causation', and considers 'a cause' intrinsically as 'an explanatory factor'. The differences among these three positions will become clear as the discussion progresses.

Of the three views of causality just mentioned, the first view is probably the one most commonly entertained. The second view is also relatively common. In the following discussion, however, the first view, despite its considerable popularity, is shown to be inadequate. The second view, despite its merits, is still shown to require many extra qualifications to sustain it. And the relatively unnoticed third view emerges as the most plausible of the three.

Section 4.4 builds on this tentative conclusion, and analyses the nature and structure of a causal account of particular wars as a basis for a more detailed, substantive discussion in Chapter 5.

SECTION 4.1 CAUSAL EXPLANATION AS INVOLVING GENERAL LAWS

An appropriate starting-point for discussing philosophical theories of the concept of causation is the very influential view stated in Carl Hempel's analysis of a causal explanation of singular events.

Hempel on Causal Explanation

Hempel wrote as follows in a well-known article, entitled 'The Function of General Laws in History', originally published in 1942:

The explanation of the occurrence of an event of some specific kind E at a certain place and time consists, as it is usually expressed, in indicating the causes or determining factors of E. Now the assertion that a set of events—say, of the kinds C_1, C_2, . . . , C_n—have caused the event to be explained, amounts to the statement that, according to certain general laws, a set of events of the kinds mentioned is regularly accompanied by an event of kind E. Thus, the scientific explanation of the event in question consists of (1) a set of statements asserting the occurrence of certain events C_1 . . . C_n at certain times and places, [and] (2) a set of universal hypotheses, such that (a) the statements of both groups are reasonably well confirmed by empirical evidence, [and] (b) from the two groups of statements the sentence asserting the occurrence of event E can be logically deduced. (1965b: 232)

An example may be helpful in explicating a key point of this complicated paragraph. There is a well-known law (i) that, if the volume is kept constant, the pressure of a gas increases as its temperature rises. Now suppose (ii) that a gas was placed in a firm container with its volume kept constant, and was heated up; and that we observed (iii) that the pressure of the gas increased. Notice that given (i) and (ii), (iii) follows logically. One of Hempel's central contentions, applied to this example, is that it is this demonstration of logical deducibility of (iii) from (i) and (ii) combined that constitutes a causal explanation of the event stated in (iii).

To the above-cited passage, Hempel adds that 'a set of events can be said to have caused the event to be explained *only if* general laws can be indicated which connect "causes" and "effect" in the manner characterized above' (1965*b*: 233; emphasis added). Thus, according to Hempel, the rise in the temperature of the gas can be said to have 'caused' the increase in its pressure only to the extent that there is a well-confirmed law connecting the two phenomena in the relevant way.

Another philosopher who holds a similar view to Hempel on the nature of causal explanation is Karl Popper. He summarizes his position succinctly as follows: 'To give a *causal explanation* of an event means to deduce a statement which describes it, using as premises of the deduction one or more *universal laws*, together with certain singular statements, the *initial conditions*' (1972: 59; emphasis in original). He adds: 'The initial conditions describe what is usually called the "*cause*" of the event in question' (1972: 60, emphasis in original).

The two philosophers' views on the subject are so close that some commentators (e.g. Donagan 1964) talk of 'the Popper–Hempel theory' of explanation. This theory, however, is more commonly known as the 'covering-law theory of explanation' because it holds that to explain a particular case a law or laws 'covering' it must be invoked (Dray 1957: ch. I). To simplify our exposition, we shall focus on Hempel's works below.

Hempel on Hempel

In explicating the paragraph cited at the beginning of this section, Hempel remarks that the symbols C_1, C_2, and so on, and E have been chosen to suggest the terms 'cause' and 'effect' (1965*b*: 232); but that these symbols 'stand for kinds or properties of events, not for what is sometimes called individual events' (1965*b*: 233). Hempel's remark here can be explained with the help of the following example.

Suppose I suffer from an ulcerated condition of the stomach, but last Monday night I ate a large amount of curry at my favourite Indian restaurant called 'Koh-I-Noor' with a philosopher who is writing a book on 'Time'. Suppose that the next morning I woke up with pains in my stomach, and that we are to explain this event by pointing to Monday night's event as its cause.

To do this, according to Hempel, the law involved must in principle be stated. But the law thereby invoked would not describe the events in the ways we have just done. That I ate curry, that I did so on Monday night, that this was at my favourite Indian restaurant called 'Koh-I-Noor', that I was with a philosopher who is writing a book on 'Time', that I felt pains as I was waking up on Tuesday morning are all facts about these events. But these facts would not (so we may safely presume) form part of the law to be invoked. The law will refer to the events by their *relevant features*, and will state, for example, that, if those who suffer from an ulcerated condition of the stomach eat more than a certain amount of hot food (not necessarily curry), they will develop stomach pains within several hours.

In short, Hempel's point here is this: we explain the occurrence of a particular event by pointing to certain other events as its cause; but our reference to the cause-events and the effect-event obviously involves *descriptions* of all these events; the laws which, according to Hempel, necessarily form part of our explanation, however, hold between the cause-events and the effect-event *only under certain relevant descriptions of them* (see also Danto 1965: esp. 218).

In a more extensive work (1965c), Hempel adds another important observation: laws, which form part of our explanation, have, in turn, their conditions of applicability. Thus, when we invoke laws as part of our explanation, we are of course assuming that the circumstances were suitable for the laws to operate. To use Hempel's own, admittedly rather artificial, illustration, a law (or general statement) invoked may be that in a mammal, stoppage of the heart will lead to death. Where we explain someone's death in terms of this law and his heart failure, we are assuming that, for example, a heart–lung machine was not used, and that therefore the law was operative in the circumstances (1965c: 348).

Thus Hempel now amplifies his analysis of a singular causal statement as follows. The expression 'a singular causal statement' is used here to denote a statement of the form '*a* caused *b*' where *a* and *b* are understood to be descriptions of particular events, where 'events' are, in turn, understood not necessarily to exclude 'actions' and 'states'.

When an individual event *b* is said to have been caused by another individual event *a* . . . *a* and *b* must be viewed as particular events of certain kinds (such as heating or cooling of a gas, expansion or shrinking of a gas) of which there may be further instances. And the law tacitly implied by the assertion that *b*, as an event of kind *B*, was caused by *a* as an event of kind *A* is a general statement of causal connection to the effect that, under suitable circumstances, an instance of *A* is invariably accompanied by an instance of *B*. (1965c: 349)

Hempel's questions and answers

In discussing Hempel's view of causation, it is imperative to notice that, in the few passages cited above, he is not dealing with just one, but three separate questions in fact. These are:

(1) what a singular causal statement *amounts to*;
(2) what *evidence* is required to make such a statement; and
(3) how it is that stating the cause of an event also *explains* its occurrence.

The first of these questions concerns the meaning of a singular causal statement. Hempel's position on this issue may be called 'a regularity theory of the meaning of singular causal statements'.[1] The second question noted above relates to how a singular causal statement is arrived at. On this issue, Hempel advances the view that a general statement (or law) must come before a singular causal statement. The third question has to do with the linkage between causation and explanation. Hempel answers this question by joining together the regularity theory of the meaning of singular causal statements, just mentioned, and the covering-law theory of explanation, touched on earlier.

The idea of laws or regularities is thus essential to Hempel's treatment of all three questions. However, a close examination reveals that his regularity-based answers are only plausible if diluted considerably. Hempel's response to each of the three questions is examined in turn below, followed by a brief discussion of one of the implications of discarding the Hempelian views.

Are Laws Implied by a Singular Causal Statement?

As regards question (1) noted above, Hempel maintains that a singular causal remark 'amounts to' the assertion that, according to certain general laws, cause-type events are regularly accompanied by an effect-type event. But this response is ambiguous. Is

[1] This terms derives from Mackie (1980: 20, 77).

he saying that when we make a singular causal assertion, we are also claiming to *know* the relevant laws, or claiming merely that some laws *exist* which underlie the assertion even though we may be unable to state them exactly? We may refer to these alternatives as the stronger and the weaker theses, respectively.

The stronger thesis is dubious, however. As is often noted (e.g. by Mackie 1980: 77), we commonly make a singular causal assertion even though we are unable to state, and therefore do not claim to know, what laws underlie the assertion.

We say, for example, that my having been in contact with someone who had a cold caused me to develop one even though we do not thereby claim to know what laws underlie the assertion. Indeed, we freely admit that there is no law known even to the medical experts specifying the exact circumstances under which our being in contact with a sufferer of a cold is followed by our catching it. Similarly, historians offer causal accounts of the outbreaks of wars, even though they would not thereby claim to know what laws relating to the outbreak of war underlie their assertions.

Hempel in fact accepts the force of this argument, but suggests that, where we concede not to know the laws in detail, we cannot claim to be giving a *full* explanation of the occurrence of the event concerned: we can claim only to be giving a *sketch* of its explanation, something which we may hope eventually to develop into a full explanation (1965c: 349–50). Hempel's idea of 'explanation sketch' is familiar to those interested in the analytical philosophy of history.

Whether a singular causal statement we offer constitutes a full explanation or only an explanation sketch by Hempel's criterion, however, it remains the case that when we make such a statement we do not necessarily claim to know the content of the law or laws supposed by Hempel to be associated with such a statement. The stronger thesis must therefore be rejected.[2]

---

[2] A somewhat technical issue needs to be clarified here concerning Hempel's notion of an explanation sketch. Hempel (1965c: 350–1) distinguishes an approximation to a supposedly existent universal law currently available only as a *statistical generalization* (e.g. pertaining to the connection between smoking and lung cancer) from *a genuine law of an unimprovably statistical form* (e.g. pertaining to radioactive decay). According to Hempel (1965c: 417–18), whereas the former, being an incomplete law, produces only an explanation sketch, the latter, being a genuine law, yields a full explanation. Hempel's above-noted concession that even

As for the weaker thesis, the suggestion is that when we make a singular causal remark, our doing so logically commits us to the view that there *is* a law (or *are* laws) underlying the assertion even though we may be unable to state it (or them). This finds support among some philosophers (e.g. Davidson 1980c: 160; see, for a parallel view with respect to 'explanation', M. White 1965: 56–61). Hempel himself states that at least this weaker interpretation cannot be treated as inappropriate (1965c: 363).

It is tempting to suggest, however, that the weaker thesis amounts to a statement of faith protected by the fact that it is impossible to produce evidence *against* the existence of a law whose content is not specified (Scriven 1975: 9; Mink 1967–8: 679). In any case, this weaker thesis comes close to admitting that the knowledge of causality in specific instances is prior to the knowledge of corresponding causal laws: causal laws are not known in advance of singular causal judgements that we make (Scriven 1959: 456; Ducasse 1975: 118–20).

Hempel is opposed to this view, however. He maintains that 'a set of events can be said to have caused the event to be explained *only if* general laws can be indicated which connect "causes" and "effect"' (1965b: 233; emphasis added). This can be taken to constitute his response to question (2) formulated above: 'what evidence is required to make a singular causal statement?'

Is the Knowledge of Regularity Required as Evidence?

The idea that the knowledge of regularity is vital in our search for causation is prevalent among certain social scientists. Thus, according to Rummel, as we noted, 'Observed concurrence of phenomena is a necessary but not sufficient condition for the assertion of causality' (1972: 32). Haas agrees: 'Nearly everyone knows that correlation is not causation; instead, a correlation enables us to see which variables are so significantly related as to suggest the possibility of a causal relationship' (1974: 59). Singer too states

---

where the relevant laws are not known in detail we can still give an *explanation sketch* must therefore be distinguished from his claim that not only universal laws but statistical ones can yield an *explanation* (1965c: 381–412). For Hempel, explanation by *genuine statistical laws* is a full explanation; explanation by *mere statistical generalizations* is only an explanation sketch. For a succinct discussion of this and related issues, see Benton (1977: 57–60).

that 'few scientists would object to the proposition that the establishment of covariation—while not *sufficient*—is indeed *necessary* to the search for causation' (1979*b*: 181; emphasis original; see also Singer and Small 1968: 257, 283).

These remarks are essentially Hempelian. As is clear from his wording, Hempel is not saying that where there is a well-known regular conjunction between $C_1, C_2 \ldots C_n$ and E, that knowledge is *sufficient* to make us say that $c_1, c_2 \ldots c_n$ caused e in a given instance.[3] This is untrue anyhow. Still, he holds that such knowledge (or particular confirming instances of such general knowledge) will *supply evidence* that $c_1, c_2 \ldots c_n$ caused e in a given instance (1965*c*: 350-1). This position seems defensible in fact, and is supported, for example, by Rom Harré (1964) and J. L. Mackie (1980: ch. 3, esp. 78).

Contrary, however, to what Hempel appears in fact to want to say (1965*c*: 350)—and contrary to the suggestions of Rummel and others cited above—even in the *absence* of such evidence we can still come to make a singular causal assertion, for example, by eliminating all other likely candidates. And we may not necessarily be mistaken in advancing such an assertion (Mackie 1980: 78–80, 121–3).

On this Mackie writes:

> it is worth stressing that the generalization need not be known in advance: it may be discovered and (tentatively) established by the observation of the very sequence of events about which the causal statement is made. Not even the vaguest foreknowledge about what often happens is needed to smooth the way even for a physical causal discovery. The doctor (Sir Norman Gregg) who discovered that German measles in pregnancy had caused eye defects in a number of children had no previous reason for regarding this as anything but the mildest of ailments, with no lasting effects. It is true that previously known generalizations may contribute to a causal conclusion, but they do so by supporting the belief that the *other* features present on this occasion would be unlikely to have produced the observed result. (1980: 78–9; emphasis original)

In any case, even if we were to concede that the knowledge of relevant laws was required to supply *indispensable* evidence for making a singular causal statement, we would still want to know

---

[3] Here, following Hempel's use of '*a*', '*b*', '*A*' and '*B*', '$c_1, c_2 \ldots c_n$' are used to denote concrete instances of '$C_1, C_2 \ldots C_n$', and '*e*' a concrete instance of '*E*'.

what else we would have to show in order to be able to say that $c_1, c_2 \ldots c_n$ caused e in a given instance. This is not explained by Hempel.

An Interim Summary

It is only after considerable dilution, then, that Hempel's responses to questions (1) and (2) gain some plausibility. To summarize the points made so far, only the weaker version of the view that a singular causal statement entails corresponding laws is plausible: what it entails is *at best* not laws but their existence. But there seems little point in insisting that their existence is entailed while admitting not to know their substance.

Moreover, while the knowledge of an underlying regularity (or its supporting instances) may supply evidence for a singular causal remark, such evidence is certainly not sufficient, and may not even be indispensable, in order for us to arrive at a singular causal statement.

Thus the link between a singular causal statement and a law or laws supposedly involved in it is rather tenuous, and more so than is suggested by Hempel's initial assertions. Might it be the case, however, that stating the cause of an event *explains* its occurrence because and only to the extent that we can produce the law or laws linking the cause-type events and the effect-type event? Clearly, Hempel thinks so. But he is quite mistaken in this belief as explained below.

Do Causes Explain their Effects by Laws?

In assessing Hempel's response to question (3) 'how it is that stating the cause of an event also explains its occurrence', we should note that the following six moves are involved in his argument:

(i) stating the cause of an event supplies not only the assertion that the cause-type events occurred but, implicitly with it, also the assertion that the circumstances were such that the relevant laws operated;

(ii) these two assertions together yield a deductive argument conforming to his model of explanation;

(iii) therefore stating the cause of an event satisfies his model of explanation;

(iv) when a deductive argument satisfies his model of explanation, it is shown that an effect-type event was to be expected;

(v) when it is shown that an event of that type was to be expected, we can understand why the event occurred;

(vi) therefore, stating the cause of an event also makes us understand, or explains, its occurrence (1965c: 337).

Hempel's first move (i), upon which (ii) and (iii) are built, is due to his acceptance of the regularity theory of the meaning of singular causal statements, which we have criticized. Further, his move (iv) causes some anxiety. It states that when a deductive argument satisfies Hempel's model of explanation, it is shown that *an effect-type event was to be expected*. A moment of reflection reveals, however, that this is not actually so: when a deductive argument satisfies his model of explanation, what is shown is merely that *the statement* that an effect-type event occurred has to be true. But this move is quite unhelpful as explained below.

When in our search for an understanding of why a given event occurred we ask ourselves whether it was to be expected, we have surely already presupposed that such an event did occur. But if such an event did occur, then *the statement* that it occurred has to be true: it cannot be otherwise. Thus nothing is added by a further demonstration that *the statement* that an event of the type occurred has to be true. Indeed, it is on the assumption that *this* requires no further demonstration that we became interested in why such an event occurred, or whether it was to be expected.

The argument here may be reformulated as follows. To show that a given event was to be expected is to show that such an event had to happen. But there is a clear difference between saying (1) that such event had to happen and (2) that it has to be true that such an event happened. Whereas it is (1) that we need, logical deduction within the covering-law model of explanation only gives (2). But, of course, it has to be true that such an event happened because such an event did happen.

To this line of criticism, Hempel would reply as follows. Admittedly, we cannot necessarily show that a given type of event was to be expected merely by revealing that the statement that such an event occurred has to be true. But we *can* in fact show this where we produce a deductive argument conforming to his model of explanation. This is so, according to Hempel, because such a deductive argument contains as a premiss a general statement to the effect that such an event *always* occurs under the circumstances specified (Hempel 1965c: 337–8). Since an event of the kind concerned *always* occurs under the circumstances specified— so the argument goes—given that the circumstances of the kind obtained, the event of the type concerned was to be expected.

However, this in turn leads to a problem relating to the next move Hempel makes. When it is shown that an event of that type was to be expected, can we, as Hempel claims under (v) above, necessarily understand *why* the event occurred?

To examine this point, suppose, for example, that someone is suffering from a given symptom (S_2). Can we claim to understand why this is so when we are told that S_2 always accompanies, or follows, another symptom (S_1), that the sufferer also has, or already had, S_1, and that his now having S_2 was therefore to be expected? Can we claim this even though S_1 and S_2 are in fact causally unrelated collateral effects of the disease with which the sufferer was infected? Perhaps we *do* claim this, but only in ignorance of a better explanation.

An important point to note here is this: whether we can claim to understand why an event occurred, when we realize that an event of that kind was to be expected, will depend on *the nature of the grounds* on which we realize that it was to be expected. Thus Hempel's move (v) above cannot be accepted wholesale. As the above example of a sufferer of two symptoms shows, where the ground is simply that 'it always happens like that' we cannot claim to understand why the event occurred, even though we may claim to know that it was to be expected.

In short, Hempel's contrary assertion notwithstanding (Hempel 1965c: 366ff.; see also Popper 1961: 124), a retrodiction (or a backward prediction) is not the same as an explanation of a past event, any more than a prediction is an explanation of a future event. Hempel's account of explanation does not address this issue satisfactorily (Hempel 1965c: 374–5).

It appears then that, despite the influence they have had on the discussion of causation and explanation, Hempel's views on singular causal statements cannot be accepted without some serious qualifications, and that his covering-law theory of explanation must be rejected as misguided. Clearly, a fresh start is required on both these issues if we are to work out a more satisfactory position.

Causes versus Reasons/Natural versus Human Sciences

One of the implications of discarding the Hempelian views of causation and explanation relates to the distinction between a causal explanation of a natural event and an account of a human action in terms of the actor's reasons.

There are a number of grounds on which they are distinct. For example, the latter involves intersubjective understanding of the actor's reasons, whereas this dimension is conspicuously absent from the former. It is on this basis that some writers have stipulated a linguistic convention whereby a sharp distinction is drawn between 'understanding' and 'explanation': human actions are said to be 'understood' whereas other occurrences are 'explained'. Within the field of International Relations, Hollis and Smith (1991) are among the latest in adopting this dichotomy as a key principle.[4]

Another important difference is that reasons can be assessed in a way in which causes cannot: it is possible to evaluate whether or not the actor's reasons for his or her action were good, appropriate, or honourable, whereas such normative considerations find no place with respect to causes of occurrences other than human actions.

In short, reasons for actions and causes of events other than human actions appear to be different with respect to (i) how they can be identified, and (ii) how they can be assessed. But there is another ground on which the distinction has been drawn. This has to do with the claim that laws are implicit in a singular causal statement concerning events other than human actions, but not so in a statement of reasons for an action (Hart and Honoré 1985:

---

[4] This convention, however, is not followed here. Instead, an 'explanation' is taken to be 'essentially a linkage of what we do not understand to what we do understand' (Scriven 1959: 449). 'Explanation' necessarily involves 'understanding' inasmuch as there can be no such linkage, and hence no such thing as an explanation, if we understand nothing. As N. R. Hanson remarks: 'We have had an explanation of *x* only when we can set it into an interlocking pattern of concepts about other things, *y* and *z*. A *completely* novel explanation is a logical impossibility' (1958: 54). Even explanation in natural science involves intersubjective understanding of the assumptions and concepts shared by the community of scientists. As Thomas McCarthy, in his exposition of Jürgen Habermas, remarks, 'the objective knowledge produced by empirical-analytic [or natural scientific] inquiry is not possible without knowledge in the form of intersubjective understanding' (1984: 690). On the so-called hermeneutical dimension of science, see further Bernstein 1983.

55–7); and, further, that an account of an action in terms of the actor's reasons does not satisfy the covering-law model of explanation (D. M. Taylor 1970: esp. chs. 2 and 6; Lessnoff 1974: 83 ff.).

However, given the now clear tenuousness of the link between a singular causal remark and laws, and given also the defectiveness of the covering-law theory of explanation itself, this standard basis for the distinction becomes implausible. Specific laws are neither entailed by, nor perhaps required as evidence for, any singular causal statement at all. Further, it is not because of the laws involved that causal events explain their effect. Therefore, the apparent fact that a statement of reasons for an action does not involve any specifiable laws need not worry us. This fact does not by itself disqualify a statement of reasons for an action from being a variety of singular causal statement. We will return to this point briefly in Section 4.3.[5]

Now, some writers maintain that the covering-law model of explanation is, and should be, applicable to any empirical study whether it be of human actions or occurrences other than human actions (Hempel 1965c: 463 ff.; Davidson 1980b). Against them, there are also those who argue that the study of human actions is categorically different from the study of occurrences other than human actions because the covering-law model of explanation applies only to the latter (Winch 1958).

Between the two positions the latter might appear to be the more plausible. However, as the foregoing discussion shows, it cannot be on the basis of the applicability or otherwise of the covering-law model of explanation that the two kinds of study may be distinguished. This model fails as a model of explanation *per se*, that is, irrespective of the nature of the subject matter.

This, of course, does not mean that there are no differences between the study of human actions and that of occurrences other than human actions. As we noted, reasons for actions are different from causes of events other than actions with respect to how they can be identified and assessed. To the extent that the study of human actions is indispensable to the understanding of history and society, but not to that of nature, there are some important

---

[5] On 'reasons' and 'causes', see further Keat and Urry (1975: 151–9); Benton (1977: 128 ff.).

differences between History and Social Science, on the one hand, and Natural Science, on the other. The point here, however, is that, contrary to a commonly entertained view, the applicability or otherwise of the covering-law model of explanation is not among the differences. This is one of the implications of discarding the Hempelian views of causation and explanation.

4.2 A CAUSE AS A NECESSARY CONDITION

There exists a tension in David Hume's understanding of 'a cause'. He defined it to be '*an object, followed by another, and where all the objects similar to the first are followed by objects similar to the second*' (1777: 76; emphasis in original). But he defined 'a cause' also as '*[an object followed by another] where, if the first object had not been, the second never had existed*' (1777: 76; emphasis in original). Hempel's view of causation, discussed in Section 4.1, stems from Hume's first definition.[6] A view of causation which reflects Hume's second definition is found in Mackie's analysis of a singular causal remark, which we shall discuss below.[7] In the course of the discussion, it will be shown that, although promising, the second approach in turn requires a number of qualifications to cope with certain standard counter-examples, leading us to suspect that perhaps a less cumbersome alternative might be found by another route.

Mackie's analysis of a singular causal statement

According to Mackie, a singular causal statement (1) that an event *a* caused an event *b* entails:

(2) that *a* occurred;
(3) that *b* occurred;
(4) that *a* and *b* are distinct events; and

---

[6] See, however, Mackie (1980: 20, 77), where he points out that Hume himself did not subscribe to the regularity theory of the *meaning* of singular causal statements.

[7] As Mackie (1980: 30) and Lewis (1975: 181) point out, Hume's second definition is not a mere restatement of his first definition, although Hume himself carelessly treated his second definition as his first definition 'in other words' (1777: 76).

(5) that if in the circumstances *a* had not occurred *b* would not have occurred.[8]

Philosophical problems associated with (2), (3), and (4)—for example, what is meant by 'distinct events', or whether it is in principle possible for *b* to have occurred before *a*—need not detain us here. An issue relating to (5), however, requires brief treatment. The problem is that there are occasions where we would say (1) that *a* caused *b*, yet might not say (5) that if in the circumstances *a* had not occurred *b* would not have.

Causal overdetermination

Suppose, for example, that *X* (an assassin) lured *Z* (a Rasputin-like figure) to take a lethal amount of poison, but that soon afterwards, whether unaware of this or just to make sure, *Y* (another assassin) shot *Z* in the head, and that *Z* died instantly—before the poison would have killed him. In such a case, we would say that *Y*'s shooting *Z* caused him to die, but we would not say that, if, in the circumstances, *Y* had not shot *Z*, he would not have died: the circumstances were such that the poison administered by *X* would have killed *Z* anyway. This example seems to show that the statement (1) that *a* caused *b* does not necessarily entail the key statement (5) that if, in the circumstances, *a* had not occurred *b* would not have occurred.

This problem, however, can be overcome by the following move. Admittedly, in the above example, if *a* stands for '*Y*'s shooting *Z* in the head', and *b* stands for '*Z*'s dying', then even though we can say (1) that *a* caused *b*, we cannot say (5) that if, in the circumstances, *a* had not occurred *b* would not have occurred. However, '*Z*'s dying' and '*Z*'s dying of a head injury' are distinct descriptions (though of the same event). And, of course, if *a*, as before, stands for '*Y*'s shooting *Z* in the head', but *b* now stands for '*Z*'s dying of a head injury', then we can say (1) that *a* caused *b*, and (5) that if in the circumstances *a* had not occurred *b* would not.[9]

---

[8] See Mackie (1980: ch. 2). This is an analysis of a singular causal *statement*. It is an answer to the question 'what does it mean to *say* that *a* caused *b*?'. It is important to bear in mind that this is not the same as asking 'what went on in the objects when *a* caused *b*?' See Mackie 1980: pp. viii–ix, 77.

[9] 'To die of', however, is an implicitly causal notion. Therefore, it will be objected that this move has not enabled us to explain the nature of a singular causal remark in non-causal terms. Nonetheless, the argument that (1) entails (5) is kept

But what if, in the above case, W (yet another assassin) also shot Z in the head at the same time as did Y? In such a case, if *a* stands for 'Y's shooting Z in the head' and *b* stands for 'Z's dying of a head injury', it still does not follow that if, in the circumstances, *a* had not occurred *b* would not: the circumstances were such that 'W's shooting Z in the head' (call this *c*) would have killed Z. However, it turns out that this case need not trouble us. This is because in such a case as this we would hesitate to say in the first place that *a* caused *b*: we would not know whether to say *a* caused *b*, or *c* caused *b* (Mackie 1980: 43–7).

Hypothetical examples of the kind just considered are known as cases of 'causal overdetermination'. Using such unlikely examples as mentioned above to challenge what appears in the main a correct thesis is a habit of certain contemporary philosophers, and may alienate further those who are already sceptical of the relevance of philosophy to empirical disciplines. However, one of the main concerns of philosophy is to elucidate basic concepts which are often fuzzy at the edges. To do this, it is often necessary to test one's analysis of a given concept against 'hard cases', and these sometimes inevitably take on somewhat outlandish qualities.

Moreover, the idea of 'causal overdetermination' is not something philosophers have invented for their indulgence, but is relevant to 'real-world' causal enquiries. For example, a dispute may arise over whether an arms race was part of the cause of a given war. Those who deny that it was may contend that in their judgement the circumstances were such that a war would have occurred anyway even if the arms race had not taken place. Against this, however, it might be argued as follows: in the circumstances 'a war' might well have occurred without the arms race; but the circumstances were causally overdetermining; and 'the war', which actually occurred, took on certain specifiable features (e.g. its severity, or the speed with which it broke out once the situation began to deteriorate) because the arms race was part of its cause. The point of using hypothetical examples like the ones discussed above (constructed so as to enhance their power of illustration) is to help us grasp the concept of 'causal overdetermination' at a stroke, and thereby clarify the structure of a dispute like this one

---

intact by this move. Whether it is possible to analyse the concept of causality in non-causal terms will be touched on later.

with respect to 'real-world' issues. The idea of 'causal overdetermination' will be employed again in the next chapter.

A condition necessary but not causal

An analysis of a singular causal remark, according to which statement (1) entails statements (2), (3), (4), and (5), needs to be supplemented by consideration in the opposite direction. Are there cases where we would say (2) that a occurred, (3) that b occurred, (4) that a and b are distinct events, and (5) that if in the circumstances a had not occurred b would not, and yet *not* say (1) that a caused b?

There are indeed such cases. For example, in response to a question 'what caused Z's death?', we would not seriously reply 'his birth', or even 'his birth *among other things*'. We would not think of his birth as 'a cause' of his death, even though it is true to say that if he had not been born he would not have died. The reason why we would not count his birth as 'a cause' of his death (even though the former is a necessary condition of the latter) is that a causal remark is offered as an answer to some question, in this case, 'what caused Z's death?', and this question is asked on the presupposition that Z was alive beforehand. His birth therefore is taken for granted, requires no mention, and hence does not count even as '*a* cause' in the context of *this* question.

There is another type of case where we may not mention a as 'a cause' (and *a fortiori* as '*the* cause', meaning, in this case, 'the most significant causal condition of all') of b even though, if a had not occurred, b would not. As noted, a singular causal remark is offered in response to a question of the type 'what caused b?', but such a question is asked not only with certain presuppositions as just noted, but often also with a clear purpose, for example, in order to determine who or what is to blame for the occurrence of b, or how to prevent a repetition of b-like events.

Thus, for example, in accounting for a car accident involving Smith and Jones (in a country where cars are driven on the left), we may agree that in the circumstances the collision would not have occurred if Smith had not deviated to his right without warning, *or* if Jones had not driven straight ahead. Nevertheless we may conclude that it was Smith's deviating to his right without warning that *caused* this collision. In so concluding, we are guided by what we see as the point of the question: we understand 'what caused this collision?', in an ordinary conversational context, to be asking 'who or what is to blame for it?', and further 'how might an accident like this be prevented in future?' (Carr 1964: 104–105).

Thus we may tentatively conclude as follows. In order to say (1) that *a* caused *b*, we need to be able to say *not only*:

(2) that *a* occurred;

(3) that *b* occurred;

(4) that *a* and *b* are distinct events; and

(5) that if in the circumstances *a* had not occurred *b* would not; *but also*

(6) that *a*'s occurrence is not presupposed by the question 'what caused *b*?'; *and further*

(7) that the mention of *a*'s occurrence is not thought to be irrelevant from the pragmatic viewpoint of the questioner.

However, it is not unreasonable to enter a qualification here: it is not that those conditions which do not satisfy requirements (6) and (7) are definitely not causes; the point is rather that referring to such conditions as causes does not constitute a good answer, given the specific interest of the questioner (Mackie 1980: 34–6, 118–20; Hart and Honoré 1985: 32–44).

Collateral effects, manipulability, and explanation

The cases which led us to add (6) and (7), formulated above, are not the only kinds where we are inclined to disqualify a necessary condition from being treated as a cause. For example, we would not say that Mary's having suffered from morning sickness caused her to give birth to a child; nevertheless it would be true to say that if, in the circumstances, Mary had not suffered from morning sickness she would not have given birth to a child. More generally, where *a* and *b* are causally independent collateral effects of *c*, we would not say (1) that *a* caused *b* since it was *c* that caused both; nevertheless it would be true to say (5) that if, in the circumstances, *a* had not occurred *b* would not.

Thus we must now add a further qualification (8) that *a* and *b* are not independent collateral effects of a common cause. However, we are here trying to analyse what it means to say that *a* caused *b*, and in analysing this we cannot use words like 'collateral *effects*' and 'common *cause*' since these are precisely the terms we are trying to analyse (or render intelligible by substituting other terms). How might we overcome this problem?

One suggestion is to introduce the idea of manipulability. This idea has in fact been touched on when we discussed (7), where the idea of prevention (e.g. of a car accident) was mentioned. But we are now using it to distinguish not between *relevant* causes and *irrelevant* ones from the pragmatic viewpoint of the questioner, but between a *cause-and-effect* sequence and a *collateral-effects* relationship.

In the above example, Mary can, by contraception, prevent developing morning sickness *and* giving birth to a child; but she cannot prevent giving birth by taking anti-morning-sickness tablets (provided, of course, that such tablets exist and that they do not have the side-effect of causing her to abort the child). More generally, where a and b are collateral effects of c, a and b are controllable by manipulating c, but b is not controllable by manipulating a (Collingwood 1938; Gasking 1955; von Wright 1971: 69 ff.).

Thus in the place of (8), formulated above, we may say (8'): that b is controllable by manipulating a. However, the idea of manipulability cannot be taken *literally* since there are many instances where we are willing to say (1) that a caused b even though we know well that manipulating a is not within human power.

For example, whatever caused a star to explode many light-years ago must be said to have caused its explosion, even though we know well that human beings could not have suppressed the occurrence of the cause, in contrast to the case of Mary, who could have used contraception. Of course, if we had in mind the particular instance where God was the cause of Mary becoming pregnant, we would readily concede that *that* was beyond human control. But, again, this concession would not prevent us from saying that Mary's becoming pregnant caused her to give birth to Jesus.

Therefore, the idea of manipulability must be formulated in a somewhat extended sense: 'manipulability in principle', or 'hypothetical manipulability'. Since 'manipulability' is in turn a causal concept, however, we still have not succeeded in rendering the notion of cause intelligible in non-causal terms. Perhaps this only suggests that the concept of cause is not reducible to a sum of non-causal concepts (R. Taylor 1975: 42–3; Scriven 1966: 261; 1971: 66).

But perhaps there is another way out. In the place of resorting to the idea of 'manipulability in principle' in order to distinguish a cause-and-effect sequence from a collateral-effects relationship, why not seek help in the idea of 'explanation'? For where we are willing to say that *a* and *b* are collateral effects of *c*, we are also willing to say that *c* 'explains' *a* and *b*, but that *a* does 'not explain' *b*. If we fail to reject a remark (i) that *a* caused *b* in favour of a remark (ii) that *a* and *b* are caused by *c*, we may be said to do so in ignorance of a 'better explanation'. This suggests that the idea of explanation is in fact central to our notion of cause.

4.3 CAUSATION AS AN EXPLANATORY RELATION

Earlier we examined how it is that, according to Hempel, stating the cause of an event also explains its occurrence. His response, which we studied earlier, combined the regularity theory of the meaning of singular causal statements and the covering-law theory of explanation. But instead of wondering how it is that stating the cause of an event also explains its occurrence, we may perhaps begin by suggesting that it *is* so. Stating the cause of an event, we may say, is such that *in* so doing (not *by* so doing) we explain its occurrence, and unless in so doing we do explain its occurrence we cannot properly be said to be stating the cause of it.

Causation and explanation

Of course, our everyday activity of 'explaining' is wide-ranging. For example, we may 'explain' what in an exceptionally obscure passage Mackie is trying to say, or 'explain' how to use a computer (Passmore 1962: 106–7). Thus the category of 'explanatory statements' is broader than that of 'causal statements'. But as far as explaining the occurrence of an event is concerned, we may perhaps say that we do this by stating the cause of it because to state the cause of it *is* to explain its occurrence.

Such an idea of what it is to state the cause of an event has some support among philosophers. It was suggested already by Thomas Hobbes when he wrote (inevitably in somewhat archaic language):

a CAUSE simply, or *an entire cause, is the aggregate of all the accidents both of the agents how many soever they be, and of the patient, put together; which when they are all supposed to be present, it cannot be understood but that the effect is produced at the same instant; and if any of them be wanting, it cannot be understood but that the effect is not produced.* (1655: 121–2; emphasis in original)

Note that 'understanding' is an integral part of 'a cause' in Hobbes's definition, unlike in Hume's, cited earlier.

A more recent endorsement of the same view is found in an insightful passage by William Kneale: 'If, then, we are to give a definition which will cover all the various usages of the word, we must say that a cause is anything by the thought of which we can render a happening *intelligible* to ourselves' (1949: 60; emphasis added). By this criterion, it should be noted, an actor's reason for his or her action is also a cause of it, and intersubjective understanding (or, to be more precise, intersubjective 'intelligibilifying') is a variety of causal explanation.

A similar position to Kneale's is suggested by Michael Scriven, who, strikingly, claims that 'causation can only be understood as a special case of explanation (and not as a specific case of the totally unrelated notion of correlation . . .)' (1975: 4), that a 'cause is *an* explanatory factor (of a particular kind)' (1975: 11, emphasis in original), and that causation 'is the relation between explanatory factors (of this kind) and what they explain' (1975: 11).

In short, 'the cause' of an event is that which the event happened *because of*, which is the same as that which *explains* the occurrence of the event in question.[10]

Explanation as narration

Now to explain the occurrence of a given event is to render its occurrence more intelligible than before by solving specific puzzles we have about it: 'to explain' is 'to make plain'.[11] This point can be clarified in the light of a famous example by which Hempel intended to illustrate how his covering-law model of causal explanation worked. He wrote:

[10] How then does our explanation of the occurrence of an event relate to its causation which takes place independently of our knowledge or thoughts? A few plausible positions concerning this question are examined in Kim (1993).

[11] Explanations are not divided sharply into valid and invalid ones, but, as David Lewis (1993: 193) remarks, '[a]n act of explaining may be more or less satisfactory, in several different ways' (1993: 193–5). This being so, the question of whether an 'unsatisfactory' act of explaining deserves to be so-called is not pursued here.

Let the event to be explained consist in the cracking of an automobile radiator during a cold night. The sentences of group (1) [asserting the occurrence of certain events $C_1, \ldots C_n$ at certain times and places] may state the following initial and boundary conditions: The car was left in the street all night. Its radiator, which consists of iron, was completely filled with water, and the lid was screwed on tightly. The temperature during the night dropped from 39°F. in the evening to 25°F. in the morning; the air pressure was normal. The bursting pressure of the radiator material is so and so much. Group (2) [asserting a set of universal hypotheses reasonably well confirmed by empirical evidence] would contain empirical laws such as the following: Below 32°F., under normal atmospheric pressure, water freezes. Below 39.2°F., the pressure of a mass of water increases with decreasing temperature, if the volume remains constant or decreases; when the water freezes, the pressure again increases. Finally, this group would have to include a quantitative law concerning the change of pressure of water as a function of its temperature and volume. (1965b: 232)

Hempel is right to add that '[f]rom statements of these two kinds the conclusion that the radiator cracked during the night can be deduced by logical reasoning' (1965b: 232). But he is not right to think that 'an explanation of the considered event has been established' by this deduction specifically (1965b: 232).

This, of course, does not mean that no information provided in the above paragraph can render the cracking of the radiator intelligible *vis-à-vis* our specific initial puzzles. Suppose, for example, that we did not know that the car was left in the street all night, but that we knew the rest of the story told by Hempel at least in as much detail as is supplied by him, and perhaps even more, so that we were not puzzled by *that* part of the story. If so, the information that the car was left in the street all night (contrary to our assumption, for example, that it was kept in the garage, and was therefore protected against the inclement weather) renders the cracking of the radiator more intelligible than before in a relevant way and thus solves our initial puzzle.

We may say that *this* was the explanatory factor we were in search of, and that we have now obtained 'the cause'. However, we need not identify this particular factor alone with '*the* cause' as though other factors did not matter causally. We may suggest instead that by adding this initially missing explanatory factor the story is now complete to our satisfaction, and that the entire story, thus obtained, constitutes 'the cause'. The same point can be made with respect to any other condition noted by Hempel above, and to any combination of such conditions. Such conditions, either individually or in combination, complete the story to our satisfaction with respect to our specific initial puzzles, and supply the 'telling' part of 'the cause' or 'the story'.

Laws and explanation

The same point, however, cannot be made with respect to the empirical laws mentioned by Hempel as necessary components of a full explanation. Suppose we are puzzled as to why the radiator cracked given all the conditions enumerated by Hempel. This specific puzzle is not in fact solved, contrary to Hempel's belief, when he produces the relevant empirical laws as the missing information and simply points out that it always happens like that under similar circumstances. What is missing is not the knowledge of such laws, but an explanation linking the drop in the temperature of water with the rise in its pressure, leading to the cracking of the radiator.

Here is another example. It is well known that the appearance of sunspots is regularly followed by widespread radio disturbance. But the knowledge of this law, or regularity, does not itself explain how the two phenomena are linked. The link, as it stands, is no less mysterious than a link, if there were one, between the appearance of sunspots and widespread *economic* disturbance, said in fact to have been identified by William Stanley Jevons, the English economist (Blainey 1988: 101). We need something other than subsumption of the particular under the general to understand either the particular or the general.[12]

What we need therefore, it is sometimes said, is to explain the general, the law, and this is done by showing that the law is deducible from higher laws. This move, however, not only simply assumes that deduction necessarily equals explanation, but also creates the problem of how to deduce the higher laws in turn. It is also irrelevant to solving our initial puzzle since what we want to understand, or want explained, is what lies behind any one

[12] Incidentally, sunspots and radio disturbance are linked, not as cause and effect, but as collateral effects of a common cause, intense magnetic fields formed on the sun.

case of the link between the two phenomena concerned, or what really connects the two events. This is not shown by demonstrating the logical deducibility of the law in question from higher laws.

Of course, we may not always be interested in obtaining an explanation on such matters, just as, for example, a historian of the First World War, as a historian, would not be interested in finding out why the bullets, once fired by Princip, reached their victims, the Archduke and his wife, rather than, shall we say, dropping mid-flight to the ground. But if we are interested, scientists can supply an explanation with reference among other things—to return to the radiator case—to the molecular structure of water, the crystalline structure of ice, and the relevant physical properties of a radiator made of iron.

In so doing, scientists resort to a theory or theories. However, a theory explains the occurrence of a given event to the extent that it enables us to *see* (i.e. understand) the sequence of relevant events, or causal chains, resulting in the event concerned (Hanson 1958: ch. 3). It is interesting to note here that the word 'theory' originally meant 'a sight, a spectacle'.[13]

Finally, it is worthwhile to remark that the very common practice of representing the cause of an event by a set of symbols such as '$c_1, c_2, c_3 \ldots$' or 'c_1 & c_2 & c_3 & $\ldots$' is misleading, even pernicious because its misleading nature is not easily noticed. These symbolic representations are, of course, helpful in reminding us that the cause of an event consists of a number of conditions. But using notations such as 'c_1, c_2, c_3' tends to obscure the fact that such conditions may be of radically different kinds. But, more crucially, these representations use commas and ampersands quite thoughtlessly, failing thereby to draw attention to the most important aspect of 'the cause', namely that the conditions must be combined and arranged as part of a whole in such a way that the outcome is rendered intelligible (Keat and Urry 1975: 31-2).

[13] The view presented here is supported by a number of philosophers of history, social science, and natural science. See Dray (1957: ch. 3); Scriven (1959); Ryan (1970: chs. 3 and 4); Keat and Urry (1975: part 1); Benton (1977: chs. 3 and 4). Of course, each 'causal chain' requires an explanation, and again this cannot be done by merely pointing to the relevant law or laws. The chain must be broken into further chains. How this is done in natural science is lucidly illustrated in Harré (1972: 178-80). See also Lewis (1993: esp. 192).

4.4 STORY CONSTRUCTION IN HISTORY OF
WAR ORIGINS

The position we have reached so far through a maze of philosophical arguments can be summarized as follows. To state the cause of an event is to explain its occurrence. To explain the occurrence of an event is to render its occurrence more intelligible than before. To do this we show the sequence of relevant events, leading to the event in question, in such a way that a specific puzzle or puzzles we have about the occurrence of the event concerned can be solved.[14]

We may term such an exercise 'story-telling' or 'giving a narrative account'.[15] In the case of an event in the world of nature (or a natural scientific event), this exercise involves getting the help of a scientific theory. This leads to the question of how in natural science a theory is constructed or selected. But this question, important though it is, cannot be dealt with here (see e.g. Harré 1972; Suppe 1977: esp. afterword). What we must do now is to see how our argument so far regarding causation, explanation, and narration relates to the case of historical events in the social world, and outbreaks of war in particular.

One thing has already been made clear, however: stating the cause of a given war is inextricably intertwined with telling a story about how the war came to be fought, or giving a narrative account of its origins. Thus (c′) 'what caused this particular war?' can justifiably be equated with our question (c) 'how did this particular war come about?'. A narrative account given in response to (c) is not a weak substitute for a more scientifically rigorous answer supposed by some to be required by the question (c′). Indeed, if we are right in our argument, events in the world of nature, too, require a narrative account, and science explains these events to the extent that scientific theories help us construct an intelligibilifying narrative about them. Likewise, a narrative account made in response to question (c) renders the outbreak of the war more

---

[14] Here, as before, 'actions' and 'states' are included under the general category of 'events'.

[15] It is interesting to note that the words 'narrative', 'narration', 'to narrate', etc., derive via the Latin *gnarus* ('knowing', 'acquainted with', 'expert', 'skilful', etc.) and *narro* ('relate', 'tell') from the Sanskrit root *gna* ('know') (H. White 1987: 215 n. 2).

intelligible to us than before, *the sequence of events thus narrated* constituting the cause of the war.

Of course, if a particular event in this sequence stands out as especially noteworthy from some viewpoint, for example, from the standpoint of preventing future wars, then there may be a case for saying that this event was *the* cause of the war. A parallel point has already been made in the case of a car accident involving Messrs Smith and Jones. But this is a question of causal weighting, or of ordering causal factors in terms of their relative importance considered from some particular standpoint. Whether this can be done in an objective manner, or whether causal weighting is inevitably subjective, especially in historical explanation, is a complex question (D. M. Taylor 1970: 79–80; Hammond 1977; Dray 1980*b*; Martin 1982; Pork 1985). What is more fundamental to reflect upon now, however, is how a narrative account is constructed in response to question (*c*).

Three Kinds of History

Clearly, this is an instance of a larger question, 'how is a historical narrative constructed?' From around the mid-1960s or early 1970s in particular, this question has stimulated much discussion among philosophers of history. This can be seen, for example, from the large number of relevant articles in a leading journal, *History and Theory*.[16] It seems, however, that there is no straightforward answer to this general question for it is the case that there are at least three kinds of historical works.

First, there is what may be labelled the 'portrait of an age' variety. Huizinga's *The Waning of the Middle Ages* is a standard example of this type. This kind of history, which is 'cross-sectional' with respect to the passage of time, characteristically eschews a narrative form (Gruner 1969: 284; Dray 1971: 154–5). Secondly, there is a type which may be labelled 'the career of a subject'. Historical works under a title such as *A History of the United States* are examples. This type of history is written characteristically in a narrative form, but the content of the narrative is determined crucially by the historian's decisions as to which events are worth

---

[16] There are some excellent articles containing a very informative critical survey of the literature on the question of narrative in contemporary theory of history. Among them are Dray (1971), H. White (1984), and Ankersmit (1986).

accounting for in the career of the subject (M. White 1965: ch. 6). Thirdly, there is a kind of history which may be labelled 'genetic'. The term 'genetic' is borrowed from Hempel (1965c: 447). 'Culminatory' is another possible label. This is about how the end state came to be. Historical works on the origins of wars belong to this type, as do, for example, works on the origins of an institution, such as the United Nations.

Unlike the first type of history, the third kind takes a narrative form. And unlike the second type, where the aim of the narrative is to explain what happened to the subject during a given period, the central concern of the narrative in the third type is to explain the event at the end of the period by going back in time.

In practice, however, what is classifiable mainly as the third type of history inevitably contains elements of the first two. Thus, in accounting for the origins of a given war, some background information needs to be supplied from time to time, and particularly at the beginning of the narrative, regarding the circumstances of the age. W. H. Dray (1971: 155) aptly calls this 'a cross-sectional "breather"' without which the narrative becomes harder and harder to follow. Furthermore, what is classifiable as a history of the origins of a war may not concentrate strictly on the outbreak of the war as such, but aim to depict the transition from peace to war in the relations of the states concerned in a given period. This necessitates narrating what happened to the relations of the states during the period (regardless of whether the events narrated form part of the explanation of the outbreak of the war as such), and thus the second type of history is brought in (Danto 1965: 652–3).

Nevertheless, we may say that the closer a historical work approximates to the third type, the narrower the freedom of choice becomes on the part of the historian in deciding which events are worth accounting for. Thus, in contrast to the second ('career of a subject') type of history, the third ('genetic') type may be said to have a more tightly integrated form: in principle, only those factors relevant to the understanding of what comes at the end of the narrative should be included in it.[17]

[17] A. J. P. Taylor once observed: 'Continuous narrative works when you are confined to a single theme, such as the origins of a war. It is harder, indeed almost impossible, when you have to handle every aspect of national life' (1977c: 14). He is here comparing the third type of history and a hybrid between the first two types.

History of War Origins: A Preliminary Structural Analysis

Moving on without any further delay to the history of war origins, the question we must now ask is how in this type of history a narrative account is structured. A number of philosophical works exist which are of relevance to this question.

Chain of events versus actions

Carl Hempel, Morton White, and Arthur Danto among others see a narrative explanation essentially as a chain of events, each segment of the chain instantiating a regular causal pattern (Hempel 1965c: 447–53; M. White 1965: ch. 6; Danto 1965: ch. 11; the latter two works are reviewed extensively in Mink 1967–8, and Olafson 1970). These writers see a narrative explanation essentially as a series of covering-law explanations.

By contrast, according to G. H. von Wright and Frederick Olafson, what is essential to a historical narrative is a chain of actions, each action being described as an intelligible, purposive move performed by the actor in response to the situation created by the previous action of another actor (von Wright 1971: ch. 4; Olafson 1979: ch. 4). For them, a historical narrative is essentially a series of explanations of the relevant actors' actions in terms of their reasons.

However, the covering-law theory of explanation has been found to be defective, and with it goes the position advanced by the first three authors. The position of the latter two authors is promising in that making sense of the relevant actors' actions is indispensable, even central, to a historical narrative (Walsh 1951: 30). However, a historical narrative cannot be reduced to a series of purposive interactions among the relevant actors: other ingredients are also present.

Chance, freedom, and necessity

A very perceptive remark in this connection is found in the work of a French historian, Paul Veyne (1984: ch. 6). In writing history, he suggests, we must, and cannot but, pay attention to three kinds of causes or explanatory factors: the nature of things, human freedom, and chance. A historical narrative invariably contain these elements. According to Veyne (1984: 307 n. 18), this tripartite division is an ancient one, going back to the Greeks, and was revived by Wilhelm von Humboldt (see also Heller 1982: 173).

A corresponding classification of explanatory factors is found, for example, in Johan Huizinga, who refers to 'blind necessity', 'human will', and 'God's providence and continual act of creation' (1973: 293). Very interestingly, an identical point has been made by J. David Singer: 'All social events may be thought of as the outcome of a concatenation of some deterministic, stochastic, and voluntaristic elements' (1979*b*: 184). Singer's 'deterministic' element corresponds to Veyne's 'nature of things', and to Huizinga's 'blind necessity'; Singer's 'voluntaristic' element corresponds to Veyne's 'human freedom', and to Huizinga's 'human will'; and Singer's 'stochastic' element corresponds to Veyne's 'chance', and to Huizinga's 'God's providence and continual act of creation'.

This tripartite division is also implicit in E. H. Carr's discussion of historical causation (Carr 1964: ch. 4). It is also highly significant that, no doubt unnoticed by himself, Hempel's explanation of the cracking of a radiator, discussed earlier, has precisely these three components: the owner's voluntary (and perhaps thoughtless) act of leaving his car in the street all night; the (perhaps unexpected) chance coincidence that the temperature dropped *that* night; and the mechanistic processes which supply the rest of the story, which, if required, can be explained in more detail by recourse to scientific theories.[18]

In the light of this tripartite classification—of determinism, freedom, and chance—and also in the light of some of the observations made earlier about the three kinds of history, we may tentatively suggest that a historical narrative of the origins of a war comprises four essential elements:

(1) background information regarding the relevant characteristics or circumstances of the historical period, particularly at the beginning of the narrative, and whenever necessary to supply a 'cross-sectional breather';

(2) reference to significant chance coincidences;

(3) mention of relevant mechanistic processes at work in nature, in society, and in human beings (which students of history

---

[18] Like Arthur Danto earlier (1965: 237), George Reisch (1991: 19) notices the narrative nature of Hempel's explanation of the exploded radiator: 'Once upon a time, there was a radiator. Then, it got really cold and the radiator burst because it couldn't withstand the pressure exerted by the freezing water it contained.' This interpretation does not bring out the human element (the owner's voluntary act and expectation) no doubt unintentionally contained in Hempel's story.

may take for granted to such an extent that they, as historians, may not feel it necessary to mention them explicitly,
but which can in principle be explained by other empirical
disciplines); and

(4) descriptions of significant actions and inactions on the part
of key individuals or governments in response to the historical circumstances, chance coincidences, mechanistic processes, and to the actions and inactions of the other key
individuals or governments, resulting in the outbreak of the
war.

In addition, we may recall that where the narrative deviates from
the purely 'genetic' type towards the 'career of the subject' variety,
element (5) reference to events of some interest in the history of
transition from peace to war will become incorporated to a greater
extent even though such events may not form part of the explanation of the outbreak of the war as such.

Briefly, (1) provides the setting; (2) alerts us to unexpected turning-
points in the development of the story; (3) reminds us that the
story being told is about a segment of the same real world as the
one about whose segments (including the one in question) countless
other stories are told; (4) makes us understand the moves made by
the actors on the stage; and (5) gives us an appreciation of the
meandering through which we none the less recognize a pattern
that emerges, resulting in the war's outbreak.

Naturally, such a structural description is a simplification. A
less simplified analysis will be developed in the next chapter where
we will investigate what sorts of things, in the context of war
origins, fall under the categories of 'the background', 'chance coincidences', 'mechanisms', and 'government actions and inactions'.
But even as it stands, the description given here is more in line with
what is actually contained in narrative explanations of war origins
than are the over-simplified pictures found in the works cited
earlier by Hempel, M. White, Danto, von Wright, and Olafson.[19]

Intelligibility

But all this is still essentially to enumerate, in very general terms,
what a historical narrative about the origins of a war typically

---

[19] See in this regard von Wright's skeletal explanation of the origins of the First
World War in von Wright (1971: 139 ff.).

consists of. Before we move on to a more detailed analysis in the next chapter, we may briefly consider what it is about such a narrative that makes us say that it is an *intelligible* account of the origins of a given war.

Stories, plots, and arguments

Now, an essential test of whether we can be said to have understood a historical narrative of this sort is to see whether we can summarize the overall argument of the historian. Conversely, an essential test of whether a historian can be said to have advanced an intelligible account of the origins of a war is to see whether the narrative offered has a clear argument showing that the outcome, in the end, was inevitable.

The word 'argument' is here used advisedly. It is an appropriate term partly because historians, when explaining the origins of a war, 'argue' a case. It is also because, in literary use, 'argument' means 'an abstract or summary of a plot prefacing a work' as is found, for example, in Milton's *Paradise Lost*. As Roland Barthes notes, 'narrative lends itself to *summary* (what used to be called the *argument*)' (1966: 291; emphasis in original).

What is summarized by 'the argument' is 'a plot', and the word 'plot' has in turn been favoured by a number of writers who advance an analysis of historical explanation very similar to the one offered here.

Thus, according to Michael Scriven:

An illuminating comparison can be found between many historical explanations and straightforward procedures such as explaining the way to a certain place ... But the most interesting analogy of all, perhaps, is to be found between explanatory narrative in history and the development of the dramatic plot in a play or novel ... What must be given by the playwright to make the plot's unfolding seem inevitable in retrospect is not unlike what must be found and given by the historian to make his narrative explanatory. (1959: 470–1)

Similarly Paul Veyne writes:

Everyone knows that when he opens a history book, he understands it, as he understands a novel or what his neighbors are doing; put in other words, explaining, for a historian, means 'to show the unfolding of the plot, to make it understood.' Such is the historical explanation ... we will keep the name 'comprehension' for it. (1984: 88)

And according to W. H. Walsh:

What every historian seeks for is not a bare recital of unconnected facts, but a smooth narrative in which every event falls as it were into its natural place and belongs to an intelligible whole. In this respect the ideal of the historian is in principle identical with that of the novelist or the dramatist. Just as a good novel or a good play appears to consist not in a series of isolated episodes, but in the orderly development of the complex situation from which it starts, so a good history possesses a certain unity of plot or theme. And where we fail to find such a unity we experience a feeling of dissatisfaction: we believe we have not understood the facts we set out to investigate so well as we should. (1951: 33)

Such remarks point to an essential aspect of understanding involved in the reading and the writing of history. In Louis Mink's insightful words, which effectively summarize the passages just cited from Scriven, Veyne, and Walsh, the historian 'must in an act of judgment hold together in thought events which no one could experience together' (1964: 44); and the essence of historical understanding is '*synoptic* judgment' (1964: 42; emphasis added), the grasping of what we are calling here 'the argument'.

'Understanding' is often associated with 'grasping what went on in the minds of other human subjects' (e.g. Hollis and Smith 1991). The latter, of course, is an indispensable element of 'historical understanding', but is not identical with it. 'Historical understanding' is rather a subspecies of 'grasping the plot' (see, for similar views, Collingwood 1961: 245–56; Gallie 1963; White 1978; Ankersmit 1986). In short, being able to follow the argument is a key to reading history; realizing what the argument should be is a key to writing it. It is interesting to note in this connection that A. J. P. Taylor, critical of some of the volumes in the *Oxford History of England*, asked of them: 'Where was *the story line*?' (1977c: 14; emphasis added).

Science, fiction, and history

Interestingly, one authoritative account of 'understanding' in science, one which Werner Heisenberg attributes to Wolfgang Pauli, suggests that it 'probably means nothing more than having whatever ideas and concepts are needed to recognize that a great many different phenomena are part of a coherent whole' (Heisenberg 1971: 33). Now, as is often remarked, science and history differ in their characteristic orientations: science is said to be 'nomothetic', concerned with phenomena subsumed under the laws of nature, and history 'idiographic', in search of the specific, seeking to establish what happened at a particular place in a given period.[20] Yet, as R. G. Collingwood observes, historians, too, are in search of a 'coherent whole' (1961: 245). Paraphrasing Wolfgang Pauli, we may say that historical understanding probably means grasping the plot which is needed to recognize that a great many specific events are part of a coherent story.

This does not mean that history is only a form of fiction. The former must necessarily be about actual time, place, and people, and must be written on the basis of evidence available. The latter need not. Two genuinely incompatible historical claims, therefore, cannot both be right, although they may both be wrong or lack sufficient evidence. But, in fiction, there are no disputes, only differences (Collingwood 1961: 246–7).

There is a vital disanalogy also between history and science. Unlike in the latter, intersubjective understanding of human actions forms a central and indispensable part of the former (Collingwood 1961: 205–31). With respect to any human action, we noted, it is possible to ask whether its reasons were appropriate, and this is to ask whether a different course of action could and should have been taken. If, as we suggested, being able to follow the argument is a key to reading history, and realizing what the argument should be is a key to writing it, it is also an important part of 'doing history', then, to explore how a different outcome might have been reached as a result of a historical process (Joll 1979; Hawthorn 1991). This question is particularly pertinent to historical investigations into the origins of wars.

If, however, as Collingwood believes, the historian's job, like that of the novelist, is to present 'a coherent and continuous picture' (1961: 245), in which, 'nothing is admissible . . . except what is necessary' (1961: 245–56), and in which 'every character and every situation is so bound up with the rest that this character in this situation cannot but act in this way' (1961: 245), how then will it make sense even to ask how a different outcome might have been reached as a result of a historical process?

On this issue, Michael Scriven is right when he remarks that we

[20] The 'nomothetic'/'idiographic' distinction is Windelband's. See Collingwood (1961: 165–8).

can begin by eliminating certain exaggerations (1959: 470). As he maintains, it is too much to claim even with respect to a well-written play that '*no* changes in the plot or character development are possible, since even large changes if made earlier (with appropriate later changes) must be possible' (1959: 470; emphasis in original). Scriven's subsequent remarks are worth quoting in full:

After all, the early part of the play constitutes the only foundations on which one can *base* judgments of inevitability thereafter, the plot not being inevitable before the first line is written. So in history, given the data we have up to a certain point, there are a number of possible subsequent turns of fortune, none of which would seem to us inexplicable. Is it not an inadequate sense of explanation which makes it possible to explain each of several alternatives (though not 'anything that happens')? No; for to say that we can and would explain several different alternatives does not mean we could give the *same* explanation for each. In so far as the act itself is required for the explanation of the act, so far inevitability is only retrospective. (1959: 470; emphasis in original)

The inevitability of a given historical outcome, such as an outbreak of war, is not incompatible with the thought that it could have been avoided.

Conventions of intelligibility?

Charles Reynolds holds a view of historical explanation which is similar in some respects to the one advanced so far. According to him, 'ideally, a historical narrative or interpretation is a process of reasoning based upon a selection from surviving evidence of past events or "facts" which is organised into a logically consistent argument, rendering its subject both intelligible and communicable' (1973: 120). One important question which remains to be asked is how an argument, and hence a plot, which structures a historical narrative, and can thus be extracted from it, is in turn intelligible. An answer to this can be suggested here only tentatively.

    It seems that, both generally and perhaps more specifically with respect to a given kind of outcome such as the outbreak of war, we have certain conventional ways of making sense of our interactions and reactions to events. It also appears that, with respect to a given type of subject-matter such as the outbreak of war, and no doubt more generally, there are conventionally accepted types of argument (or plot). If so, we may suggest that an argument (or plot) of a historian is intelligible to the extent that, in addition to being internally consistent, its constituents and the argument (or plot) as a whole conform to such conventional ways.

The suggestion made here is in accord with W. H. Dray's remark cited below, and is a simplified version of Hayden White's line of thought (1973, 1978, 1987) on the nature of historical narratives:

> It should be noted that . . . notions of what historical causes can or must be like are not the inventions of historians (or philosophers). They belong to very familiar ways of thinking about the world: ways in which those to whom historians wish to communicate their results will naturally think, and in which, indeed, it is difficult not to think. Historians who succeeded in renouncing them altogether would produce accounts that would scarcely be recognizable as history. (Dray 1980*b*: 95)

This amounts to suggesting that our explanation is ultimately sanctioned by our, perhaps unspoken, conventional assumptions regarding how things are to be explained, how things are to be made sense of, or what it is to understand. As Geoffrey Hawthorn remarks: '[An explanation] succeeds, where it does, by giving descriptions which in the conventions of telling that story to that kind of audience, are relevant *as* explanations' (1991: 25; emphasis in original). To the extent that a cause is an explanatory factor, what counts as a cause is also conventionally sanctioned, and is thus perhaps historically contingent.

This is not a surprising conclusion to reach when we learn about the historical evolution of natural science as presented, for example, by Rom Harré (1972). But, it must also be said, our (or our scientists') conventional assumptions regarding how things are to be explained—their epistemological principles—are bound to be affected, in turn, by the evolution of scientific practice itself. It may well be that, as Dudley Shapere is reported as saying, '[w]e learn how to learn as we learn' (cited in Suppe 1977: 704). It is not suggested here, therefore, that science is a convention-bound, non-rational activity.[21]

The issue of intelligibility and conventionality of our explanation is too large a topic to be dealt with fully in the present volume. However, as we proceed to the next chapter, the ideas suggested

---

[21] See Suppe (1977: afterword). On the cultural relativity of how the past is represented, however, see Hastrup (1992).

above tentatively will gain some plausibility in the specific context of understanding war origins.

CONCLUSION

Starting with a very commonly held view about 'causation' and 'explanation', we have reached a rather unexpected conclusion. The regularity theory of the meaning of singular causal statements has been criticized, and the covering-law theory of explanation has been rejected.

Instead, causation, explanation, and narration are seen to be inextricably intertwined both in relation to events in nature and with reference to historical events in the social world. The view that historical understanding reduces to intersubjective understanding of the individual actions performed by key figures has also been found inadequate, and the idea of 'synoptic judgment'—the grasping of the argument/plot—has been given prominence.

To answer the question 'what caused this war?' either requires or is equivalent to answering the question 'how did this war come about?' In answering this, an intelligibly structured, or argued, narrative must be presented. Constituent units of such a narrative have been indicated, although only very broadly.

The main conclusion we have reached is this: we can see what, according to a historian, caused a given war when we grasp the argument of a story he or she tells; as historians, we can say what caused a given war when we come to realize what the argument should be which structures the story we are to tell about the origins of the war.

This is very different from a view which is derived from a crude application of Hempel's analysis, that is, that we can say what caused a given war when we come to realize what conditions are associated regularly with the occurrence of wars, or wars of that type.[22]

Against this, our view suggests that the sequence of events narrated, or 'related', in such a way that the occurrence of the war can be made (more) intelligible (than before) constitutes the cause

---

[22] This is a *crude* application because Hempel himself will probably offer what he calls a 'genetic explanation' stringing together a series of causal explanations, each given in accordance with the covering-law model. See Hempel (1965c: 447 ff.).

of the war. This is a qualified endorsement of the statement by Paul Veyne cited at the beginning of this chapter: 'the "causes" of the war between Octavius and Antony are the events preceding that war, exactly as the causes of what happens in Act IV of *Antony and Cleopatra* are what happened in the first three acts' (1984: 91).

In this connection, it is highly interesting to note J. David Singer's remark that 'an adequate explanation is one that tells the story, step by step, of how a given event or condition sets in motion a sequence that regularly culminates in a given outcome' (1989: 13). This reveals that, perhaps unexpectedly, Singer's position is much closer to that of this chapter than to Hempel's. Singer even stresses the 'need to distinguish explanation from both prediction and covariation' (1989: 13), and sees the essence of explanation in story-telling 'step by step'.

There is, of course, one significant difference between Singer's remark and the position suggested here: whereas he is interested in explaining the *regular* sequence of events which culminates in war, this chapter has been concerned with the question of how to explain the occurrence of *particular* wars.

Nothing should stop anyone from seeking an answer to any question he or she finds interesting to ask. Despite considerable efforts on the part of many investigators, however, no regular sequence has been identified concerning *war as a whole*. Still, it may be that there are certain *statistically dominant paths* to war, each path leading to a particular *type* of war. It is sensible to attempt to identify such paths (Vasquez 1993). Contrary to some writers' insistence (e.g. Seabury and Codevilla 1989: 50), therefore, it is not suggested here that those interested in the causes of war should only be concerned with particular wars, and not wars in general.

There is, however, one point that this chapter finds worthwhile to insist on: that it is unnecessary to know about wars in general to be able to give an account of specific wars. A causal explanation of a particular event, as we saw, does *not* involve statement of the law(s) covering it. The idiographic does not presuppose the nomothetic. On the contrary, it is one of the contentions of this chapter that we will be in no position to grasp why a statistically frequent path to war, if and when one has been identified, produces war at all, if we are incapable of seeing how a particular sequence of events, instantiating this pattern, led to war. The argument we need to grasp in order to understand the latter also makes the former intelligible (Lewis 1993: 192–3).

A telling illustration of this point is to be found in John Vasquez's recent contribution (1993) to the causes of war debates. By synthesizing a number of key statistical works on the onset and expansion of war, he claims that he has identified one typical causal path to one type of war, one which takes place between rivals of roughly equal power. What explains the occurrence of this type of war, however, is not the statistical regularity with which war has followed the path identified, but the followability of the path Vasquez constructs as a narrative.

In order to answer (c′) 'what caused this particular war?', then, we need not return to our question (b) 'under what sorts of circumstances have wars occurred more frequently?', but should proceed to (c) 'how did this particular war come about?'

5

ORIGINS

> True, the events [subsumed under a single term 'war'] have
> a common observable factor—organized violence perpetrated
> by groups of people upon each other. But this is near the
> extent of the commonality.
>
> (Rapoport 1975: 44)

It is significant that the above remarks come from Anatol Rapoport,
one of the most committed social scientists specializing in peace
research. Scientifically oriented though he undoubtedly is, he has
conceded what, historians tend to insist, would have to be conceded: our question (c)—'How did this particular war come about?'
—would be given different answers depending on which 'this particular war' was.

However, as we saw in our detailed discussion earlier in this
volume, Kenneth Waltz, one of the most influential theorists of
international relations, and of war in particular, has paid very
little attention to the variety of ways in which war comes about.
His main concern, we noted, is the constant possibility and recurrence of war, not the occurrence of any particular war. He therefore
has little to say about actual wars, and, accordingly, what he says
about differences and similarities among particular wars is re-
markably underdeveloped. Wars may be different in terms of their
immediate causes, Waltz appears to concede. But, in his judgement, they are all the same with respect to their underlying cause.
This is said to be 'international anarchy'.

This, however, is prima facie implausible: conditions other than
international anarchy must have been among the underlying causes
of *some* wars. This point seems to have escaped Waltz. Further,
there may be some similarities, as well as differences, among some
wars with respect to their *immediate* causes. But this is not explored by Waltz, who thinks that immediate causes of war are
often trivial.

In this final chapter, we attempt to replace Waltz's third-image
theory, and his tripartite analysis itself, with a more comprehensive

overview, or understanding, of war origins. What is offered here
is a theory of war origins which takes more seriously than Waltz
has done the fact that wars come about in different ways. It pays
attention to various paths to war, and, unlike Waltz, takes note of
a variety of underlying causes. It also considers afresh the question
of whether, given the apparent diversity of war origins, there are
any noteworthy similarities at all in the ways in which wars come
about, other than the fact, stressed by Waltz, that international
anarchy is an enabling condition of them all.

To pursue these aims, we shall investigate in the main sections
of this chapter what sorts of thing fall under the categories of the
background, chance coincidences, mechanisms, and government
actions. These, we argued in Chapter 4, are the four building
blocks commonly used in constructing narrative explanations, or
stories, of war origins. To paraphrase an important passage from
W. H. Dray (1980b: 95), cited in the previous chapter, historians
who succeeded in doing away with these elements altogether would
produce works which would scarcely be recognizable as stories of
war origins, and which would hardly make war origins intelligible
to us.

In the course of the discussion below, the nature and the sources
of similarities and differences among the origins of wars will come
to be clarified. In particular, it will be revealed that the very way
in which we conventionally make sense of war origins constitutes
one important source of similarities amongst them. It is therefore
integral to our understanding of origins of wars that we understand what is involved in understanding our subject-matter. Philosophical reflection, then, is not just a methodological preliminary,
but a key to development in the study of war and peace. Such is
the conclusion towards which the discussion of this long chapter
is directed. But first we shall take a look at a number of historical
works on the origins of wars.

5.1 THE BACKGROUND

The background is indispensable to any story of war origins. It
shows the nature of the circumstances where a story begins by
revealing the setting and latent forces within it.

Historians decide on what should be included in the background, and what should not, in the light of their story lines; but their story lines are, in turn, influenced by what they regard as important features of the background. As we saw, to explain is to link what we do not understand with what we do understand. Therefore, the level of knowledge writers assume in their audiences also influences what is to be contained in the background. Accordingly, the background is constrained, but not determinate, and the substantive content of the background varies from one story to another, whether of the same war, or of different wars. A comparison of several works in the Origins of Modern Wars series, edited by Harry Hearder, illustrates well the extent of this diversity.

Typically, the background is depicted cross-sectionally in the form of 'a portrait of the age'. The portrayal may be very brief, as we find, for example, in Ian Nish's *The Origins of the Russo-Japanese War* (1985). The theme of this book is the 'deteriorating Russo-Japanese relationship' (Nish 1985: 18), leading to the war's outbreak in 1904, and the 'story starts in 1894 with the Sino-Japanese war' (Nish 1985: 3). In the introduction of this work, however, the author succinctly explains the nature of foreign policy making in Russia and in Japan, and takes a brief look at Russia's expansion of railways in North China, and the Russo-Japanese rivalry over the building of railways in Korea. These supply minimum background information, enough to get the story going.

Sometimes the background section, though perhaps quite brief, is made to play a key role in support of a particular argument advanced by a historian. T. C. W. Blanning's *The Origins of the French Revolutionary Wars* (1986) illustrates this well. His basic thesis is that these wars, which began in 1792, were not the genuine ideological wars they are often supposed to be.

According to Blanning, they were rooted in a deeply ingrained assumption of the old-regime European international politics which saw war as an efficient and relatively painless method of settling disputes; and they stemmed from mutual grievances, phobias, and hostilities among the European powers which predated the Revolution.

Blanning therefore finds it imperative to supply a background chapter (1986: ch. 2), outlining conflicts and antagonisms in Europe before the Revolution. It is only in the context of these old-regime conflicts and rivalries, he claims, that we can properly understand the nature of the 'revolutionary wars', which he places in inverted commas to suggest continuity from the pre-revolutionary ones (1986: 36).

A much more substantial portrayal of the background than is given by Nish or Blanning is found with respect to the Second World War in P. M. H. Bell's *The Origins of the Second World War in Europe* (1986). His narrative proper begins with the Geneva Disarmament Conference of 1932–34, and ends with the German invasion of the Soviet Union in 1941 (Bell 1986: 201–95). As a preliminary to this, however, Bell analyses in considerable detail the ideological, economic, and military strategic features of the major European powers in the inter-war period, aptly calling this part of the volume 'The Underlying Forces' (1986: 49–200).

The background, however, may itself be written as part of a continuous historical narrative. For example, Peter Lowe devotes the first three-quarters of his *The Origins of the Korean War* (1986), in varying degrees of detail, to a narrative account of Japan's colonial occupation of Korea, Japan's defeat in the Pacific War, the establishment of two Koreas, confrontation between them, the reforms and recovery of Japan, the defeat of the Kuomintang regime in China, and the emergence of the Cold War in Europe. All this clarifies the regional and global setting, and the Cold War frame of mind, in the light of which the sequence of events leading to the outbreak of the Korean War, treated in Chapter 7 of his eight-chapter volume, is made more fully intelligible.

Similarly, Ritchie Ovendale gives a detailed narrative account of the creation of Israel in the first half of his *The Origins of the Arab–Israeli Wars* (1984), and this provides the relevant background information regarding the wars. Since, in a non-trivial sense, the Arab–Israeli Wars could not have occurred without the creation of Israel, it is understandable that considerable weight should be given to this topic.

Clearly, 'the background' forms an indispensable part of the whole explanation, whether it is presented in an analytical mode, stylistically separated from the narrative proper, as in the case, for example, of Bell (1986); or whether it is given in a narrative form, and merges into the rest of the story, as in the case, for example, of Lowe (1986), or Ovendale (1984).

It appears that many kinds of things can fall under the category of 'the background' in stories of war origins. Some of the following features, however, appear relatively frequently to be treated as part of 'the background': (1) geographical and demographical aspects of the countries involved; (2) characteristics of the existing international system, for example, the distribution of power, alliance configurations, the nature of the key international regime, the relevant countries' attitudes towards it, and changes taking place with respect to any of these items; (3) the governmental structures of the relevant states, and characteristics of their foreign policy-making; (4) the political, social, economic, and military strategic features of the powers concerned; (5) ideological motivations of the leaders and the peoples, and prevalent assumptions about the nature of international politics, diplomacy, and war; (6) past history, particularly with respect to the sources of grievance and rivalry; and so on.[1]

Clearly, some of these are 'personal', 'domestic', and 'international' features, which could therefore be accommodated within the tripartite scheme popularly associated with Kenneth Waltz. However, the items noted above are sufficiently wide-ranging to make it somewhat artificial to try to force all of them into the three categories.

It should be stressed that a two-way relationship exists between the background and the story: while the background information contributes to making the story more fully intelligible, the argument of the story in turn shapes what must be included in the background. The sorts of items which are treated as part of war's background, therefore, vary from one story to another, whether with respect to the same war, or regarding different wars.

Now, the sorts of items which constitute the background are also part of what we often treat as underlying causes of war. It appears, then, that underlying causes of war, or at least some of them, are not things which exist independently of our attempt to make sense of particular wars. In this sense, there is some truth in Blanning's statement that 'war *per se* is only the aggregate of all wars' (1986: 4). In any case, Waltz's claim to the effect that the underlying cause of war is found exclusively in the nature of the international system cannot be accepted. Underlying causes of wars are found also in other places within, and beyond, his tripartite scheme.

---

[1] The explanatory power of several of the features listed here is discussed extensively by James Joll (1984) with respect to the origins of the First World War. Joll is well known for his stress on the role of what he called the 'unspoken assumptions' (Joll 1972; 1979; see also Farrar 1972).

5.2 CHANCE COINCIDENCES

In some cases, the background depicted appears already so war-prone that, in retrospect, we think that only a final spark was needed to set fire to the heap. The First World War is a classic example of a war which has been described in this fashion. An early instance of this is found in Sidney Fay's *The Origins of the World War* (1930: 1). A more recent and much shorter piece, which judiciously synthesizes many existing works, and points in the end to the importance of the exceptionally war-conducive circumstances of the time, is Jack Levy's 'Preferences, Constraints, and Choices in July 1914' (1991: see esp. 259–61).

A highly war-prone background, however, at best only shows that *a* war would most probably have occurred sooner or later involving roughly the same set of states as those which came to fight the actual war. This is not the same as explaining how *the* war, the one that in fact occurred, came to be fought. To explain this, it is necessary to fill the gap between a highly inflammable background and an actual outbreak of war. In this, 'chance coincidences' may play a significant part. First, we need to be clear about what 'chance coincidences' are.

Chance coincidences: Mundane, extraordinary, and historically significant

By 'a chance coincidence' is meant an intersection of independent causal chains, or a simultaneous occurrence of two or more events which are causally unrelated to one another (Kneale 1949: 114–17; Carr 1964: 98–100). Though largely unnoticed, our world of events is infested with chance coincidences: a leaf falls off a lime tree across the street as I turn on the radio in my study; my cat yawns as a next-door neighbour seals an envelope. We could find any number of such 'mundane' and apparently insignificant chance coincidences if we bothered to look for them. The fact that we do not is a sign of the world's infestation.

Of course, there are also some quite 'extraordinary' chance coincidences, leading us at times to suspect a mysterious causal mechanism, or agent, in operation. If an old friend, with whom I have lost contact for many years, suddenly phones me just as I begin to think of him, 'telepathy' may be invoked, jocularly. If, every time the police come close to catching a suspected drugdealer in the act, incriminating evidence is somehow never found, they will seriously begin to think that the dealer may have 'a hidden hand', an accomplice in the forces. When, in 1274, a typhoon struck Japan, and caused many of the Mongol ships to sink, forcing the Mongolians to abandon their invasion which they had just launched, and when, unbelievably, the same thing happened again in 1281, forcing them to abandon their plan of conquest altogether, it was not unnatural for the Japanese to begin to believe in 'Kamikaze', the divine wind.

Whether extraordinary or mundane, however, only a few such coincidences, it seems, survive to play an important part in the production of any given outcome which we want to explain. These are 'historically significant' chance coincidences—chance coincidences which play a vital role in completing a given story.

A historically significant chance coincidence

As we noted, chance coincidences seem particularly pertinent to explaining how *the* war that did occur came about. A. J. P. Taylor's BBC television lecture on the origins of the First World War supplies a particularly good illustration. The relevant passage (Taylor 1977*a*: 138) is worth quoting in full.

The only way one can answer this [question of the origins of the First World War], I think, is to describe what happened—or some of it.

On 28 June 1914, Archduke Franz Ferdinand visited the town of Sarajevo, in Bosnia. Bosnia is a Slav, a Serbo-Croat province which was acquired by Austria/Hungary in 1908, and there was a good deal of discontent there . . .

The Serbian government certainly did not want to provoke a crisis, of that we can be quite sure. There were, as there have been in later times, of course, plenty of national conspirators. Half-a-dozen of these were schoolboys working for what we now call their A levels. They said: 'We oughtn't to let the archduke's visit go without some sort of demonstration.' Although they did not, in fact, belong to the secret society, the Black Hand, which was supposed to organise conspiracies, they got a couple of revolvers and a couple of bombs, and they turned up on the day. As the archduke drove along, the first conspirator could not get his revolver out of his pocket because the crowd was too tight; the second of them thought a policeman was looking at him; and the third felt sorry for the archduke's wife. The fourth of them simply went home. The fifth of them threw his bomb, which missed, though it injured one equerry. The sixth of them, having heard the bomb go off, thought, 'Oh, well, it has succeeded,' so he stepped over. At that moment, the procession drove by and he realised that it had failed, so he sat down in a café, feeling very gloomy.

The archduke drove on to the town hall, where he arrived in a great rage and said: 'I come here and you greet me with bombs. I am not stopping; I am driving straight out. I am not going back through the old town.' However, the chauffeur had not been told that they were driving straight on, not turning, so when they came to the turn where the original route had been, he turned; and there was the schoolboy, sitting at the edge of the pavement in a café. Princip, he was called. To his astonishment, he saw an open car with the archduke and his wife stationary in front of him. He walked out of the café, stepped on to the running-board, took out his revolver, shot the archduke, and then aimed at the governor of Bosnia, who was sitting in the front of the car, and hit the archduke's wife, who was sitting at the back. That was the assassination at Sarajevo.

Not quite. Taylor gave lectures without notes (Taylor 1977c: 6), and his television lectures were meant primarily to entertain. 'History is fun to write and, I hope, fun to read. That to my mind is its justification,' Taylor wrote (1977c: 17). His account is certainly 'fun to read', but may in fact contain some inaccuracies.

Although there are many uncertainties which surround the Sarajevo affair, a rather different story is found, for example, in the second volume of Luigi Albertini's *The Origins of the War of 1914*. It is noteworthy that, reviewing this volume, Taylor had himself remarked: 'The strength of the book lies in its intense examination of these well-known details, just as Sherlock Holmes made discoveries by looking again at what everyone else had looked at already' (1953).[2]

According to this and another detailed study, it appears that Colonel Dragutin Dimitriević, who was the Chief of Intelligence in the Serbian General Staff, and, under the pseudonym 'Apis', also the leader of the Black Hand, not only helped the conspirators, but actually instigated the plot (Albertini 1952–7: ii, chs. 1–2; Remak 1959). Furthermore, two or three of the assassins, Princip amongst them, are believed to have been members of Black Hand (Albertini, 1952–7: ii. 42; Remak 1959: 60–2, 95), and the weapons used on the day were supplied by a Black Hand agent (Albertini 1952–7: ii. 72; Remak 1959: 67). Taylor in fact concedes the last point in his book, *War by Time-Table* (1969: 54–5), but is adamant

[2] I am grateful to Alex Danchev for alerting me to the existence of this review.

that Dimitriević was not the instigator, any contrary speculation being, in his words, 'so much poppycock' (1969: 54).

Despite such disagreements, one central point in Taylor's reconstruction appears to be in accord with some other historians' views. Had the chauffeur driving the Archduke's car not turned, but driven straight on at a high speed as was now arranged, he would not have been told to stop and reverse the car at that corner; and had Princip not been there in the vicinity just at that moment, a second attempt at assassination would probably not have been made; and had it been made, it would probably have failed. Albertini himself, after a very detailed study of the sequence of events, reaches the same conclusion (1952–7: ii. 38).

According to Taylor's interpretation, what followed the assassination at Sarajevo was inevitable, or readily intelligible, in the circumstances. But the Archduke would most probably not have been assassinated had it not been for the chance coincidence that his car stopped just in front of where Princip happened to be. And, since it is impossible to know for certain what would have happened if the assassination had not taken place then, we can at least amuse ourselves with the thought that war might never have broken out after all.

Indeed, in the original television broadcast, Taylor had added the following remark to the passage cited above, although this does not appear in the version printed in the *Listener*, from which the above passage was quoted: 'If the, you know how tempting it is to say ifs, if the chauffeur had not made his turn—no assassination—[Taylor visibly shrugs his shoulders here]—no war' (Taylor 1977*b*). Taylor appears quite persuaded by the view that 'human blunders . . . usually do more to shape history than human wickedness' (Taylor 1964: 265–6; see also Taylor 1977*c*, in which he describes his own life as a series of accidents).

The shrugging of his shoulders, noticeable to the television viewers, indicates that Taylor was not entirely serious in his suggestion here. However, it is noted by a number of historians (e.g. Fischer 1967: 50; Jarausch 1969; Mommsen 1973: 32 ff.; Kaiser 1983: 468–9; Trachtenberg 1991*b*: 91–2) that in Germany's governing circles at this time the idea of a preventive war against Russia was in the air: some, particularly certain military leaders, viewed the prospect with equanimity, others in the end tried to persuade themselves that this might not be a bad thing for Germany after all. However, Germany would not have been keen to make a move towards a preventive war unless it could rely on Austria to join in the fight. The assassination gave Germany an opportunity: now Germany would fight for Austria, not Austria for Germany, and this Austrian dependence on Germany made it virtually certain that, in making a move to fight Russia, Germany could count on Austria's full participation (Van Evera 1984: 79–83). This line of reasoning strengthens the argument that, without the assassination, war might not have come after all.

But this interpretation requires an obvious qualification. If Germany was bent on preventive war, it might perhaps have resorted to war sooner or later. What we could reasonably say, therefore, is that, if the assassination had not taken place, 'there would have been neither an Austro-Serbian War, nor a World War, *in the summer of 1914*' (Fay 1930: ii. 53; emphasis added). This is also Taylor's view. According to him (1977c: 10), 'the actual war that broke out in August 1914 would not have occurred *as it did* if Archduke Franz Ferdinand had not gone to Sarajevo on June 28 or even if his chauffeur had not taken a wrong turning' (emphasis added). A chance coincidence, leading to the assassination, was, therefore, a key component of the explanation of the origins of the war *as it came about*, although, given the highly unstable circumstances of the period, another war, similar in some important respects to the one that actually occurred, might perhaps have come about sooner or later through a different causal path.

There is in fact an interesting twist to the story of coincidences in the Sarajevo affair, which deserves a brief mention. The assassination of the Archduke and his wife, Sophie, took place on 28 June. It was on the same day, in 1900, that the Archduke had married Sophie. By curious coincidence, 28 June was Serbia's sacred national day: on that day in 1389 the last army of old Serbia had been destroyed by the Ottoman Turks at the legendary battle of Kosovo Field (Taylor 1969: 49–50).

Taylor at one point toys with the idea that the Archduke might have gone to Sarajevo on that day partly to please his wife on their wedding anniversary by a ceremonial visit, and partly to demonstrate Austria–Hungary's defiance of Serb nationalism. As Taylor acknowledges, however, there is no evidence to sustain the view that without the coincidence of dates the Archduke would not have visited Sarajevo, and hence would not have been killed there, on that day (Taylor 1969: 49–50; cf. Taylor 1977*a*: 138). Charac-teristically, Taylor remarks: 'The Habsburgs knew nothing of the national traditions of the peoples over whom they ruled. Probably the Archduke and his advisers had never heard of Kosovo. At most, they were vaguely aware that 28th June was some sort of holiday in Bosnia and therefore suitable for a ceremonial visit' (1969: 50).

In any case, even if we were to subscribe to the view that, with-out the coincidence of dates, the assassination would not have taken place, we would still argue perhaps that a war, like the First World War, would have come about sooner or later, given the existing conditions. This is to see the First World War as having been 'causally overdetermined'.

The Sarajevo case, then, aptly illustrates one sense in which Geoffrey Blainey is right in his remark that 'an "accidental" war is more likely if the non-accidental factors are strong' (1988: 142): a chance coincidence is more likely to ignite a major catastrophe where war-conducive factors have already accumulated in the background.[3]

One observation may be added here concerning the question of causal weighting. It is often said that the war-prone background was *a more important cause* of the First World War than was the assassination of the Archduke, the former constituting the 'pre-conditions', 'the underlying cause' of the war, the latter its 'pre-cipitant'. Sometimes, it is also held that this causal weighting, attributing more importance to the preconditions than the precip-itant, is an *objective* judgement based on a plausible view that a major war, like the First World War, was more probable in the absence of the assassination *than* in the absence of the background conditions (Hammond 1977: 114).

As was noted, however, the Sarajevo assassination was an es-sential component of the origins of the First World War *as it came about*. The judgement, therefore, that the background was a more important cause than the assassination involves a prior judgement to the effect that the knowledge of the conditions from which a major war, such as the First World War, is likely to result is in some sense more important than the knowledge of the specific sequence of events which led to the First World War itself.

[3] This, however, may not rule out the possibility that a war-conducive back-ground in turn arises to some extent out of a series of chance coincidences.

This prior judgement is in turn likely to be based on the belief that generalizable knowledge of war-conducive conditions is more useful, from the viewpoint of prescribing for future peace, than historically specific knowledge. Clearly, a major war is more likely to be averted by modifying some of those conditions than by guaranteeing the lives of archdukes, and it is this that leads to the view that those conditions were causally more important than the assassination. Such a view, then, is not an objective judgement (in the sense in which, for example, it is an objective judgement to say that a kilo of potatoes is heavier than a pound of tomatoes), but one which reflects the particular interest of those who subscribe to it. This does not mean that causal weighting is arbitrary, but that it involves value judgement.

5.3 MECHANISMS

To show what sorts of thing fall under the category of mechanisms in the stories of war origins, it is necessary first to clarify what a 'mechanism' is. This is important, because the term 'mechanism' is much used in the social science literature, but the concept is rarely analysed, and, in particular, the difference between a 'mechanism' (a causal process) and a 'mechanical device' (a physical object) appears at times to be forgotten.

Mechanisms as narratives

We know by experience that mechanical devices have their conditions of workability: sometimes they work; at other times, unfortunately, they fail. We are in fact unable to state exhaustively what such conditions are, but well-trained mechanics are familiar with standard sources of mechanical failure. They become familiar with these because they know how a given mechanical device works when it works.

Explaining how a mechanical device works involves revealing its 'mechanism', showing step by step how a particular input leads to a particular output when the device is isolated from unwanted disturbances. To show 'what is the mechanism of it all' is to complete a narrative with respect to a given device's workings from the beginning, through the middle, to the end.

Now, the world we live in contains not only, as we saw, a vast number of chance coincidences, but also a variety of standardized processes or routines, relatively uncomplicated, and isolated from intervening forces (Kneale 1949: 64–5). Such standardized processes are found not only in the workings of nature, but also in the operations of our minds, and in the functioning of our society. To explain such processes found in nature, mind, or society, we show their 'mechanisms'. And to ask 'what is the mechanism which operates here' is to demand an intelligible narrative with respect to the phenomenon in question.

Mechanistic processes are relatively easily repeatable, and produce noticeable regularities when repeated. But they are neither ineluctable nor uncontrollable processes. A mechanism, whether of a man-made mechanical device, or of nature, mind, or society, operates only under appropriate conditions, free of disturbances. Admittedly, the mechanisms of nature, mind, and society are perhaps less easy to control than those of man-made mechanical devices, since these may be 'turned off' at will; but the former are not inevitable processes sealed off from our attempts to manage them.

Still, a 'mechanistic process' is seen as having 'its own momentum', and is thus distinguished from what may be called 'completion of a purposive process' where we perform a certain act with a given intention, and achieve our intended aims; where, in short, 'we are in control'.

Thus, 'mechanisms' are said to be in operation, for example, where we are induced to behave in a certain way because of the workings of our mind or body, or because the social environment induces us to think and act in a particular manner; or where, through the workings of the system in which our actions take place, they lead to unintended consequences. In the last case, an *invisible* hand' is said to be in operation, which, incidentally, may be contrasted to those cases where we invoke a *'hidden* hand' to explain extraordinary chance coincidences.

There are then a variety of standardized processes in the world, physical, physiological, psychological, or social, some of which are simply taken for granted, and some of which are thought to demand an explanation because they are puzzling, though perhaps noticeably often encountered. When called upon to explain, we, like a competent mechanic explaining the workings of a mechanical device, try to give a narrative account of how a given input, not ineluctably, but when appropriate conditions are met, leads through the middle part to a given output.

In short, a mechanism, being a causal process, is story-shaped. It is no coincidence that Robert Axelrod, in outlining the mechanism whereby cooperation emerges among egoists under anarchy, refers to the three stages of the mechanism he has identified as the 'beginning of the story', the 'middle of the story', and the 'end of the story' (1990: 21).

A mechanism, then, is a mini-story of a repeatable, or often encountered, non-purposive process, sometimes with the middle part omitted because the story is too familiar to tell. On hearing that a tense relationship is developing between certain siblings, we will treat it as 'the same old story'. In such cases, it is generally felt to be unnecessary to fill in the middle: the input, as if through a smooth operation of a very simple and familiar mechanical device, leads to the output. In somewhat more complex cases, however —where, for example, a boy brought up by a dominant mother grows up into a misogynist—the less than immediately obvious linkages need to be clarified, and specialists in abnormal psychology may be called in.

Two observations must be added to the discussion so far. First, certain outputs, as we just saw, are sometimes treated as though it were in 'the nature of things' that, given the inputs, they were brought about. The linkages are so familiar that there is little need felt to explain them. But this does not mean that it is always easy to fill in the middle, to explain the linkages. Familiar processes, when de-familiarized, often strike us as being quite hard to explain. None the less, implicit in the assertion that a given consequence followed mechanistically from an antecedent condition is the view that there is some more detailed story to tell.

Secondly, a mechanism of human mind or society 'causes' its effect in exactly the same way as, for example, boiling a kettle 'causes' its lid to lift. It may perhaps be objected, firstly, that the lid is physically or literally pushed by the air pressure in the kettle, but that psychological or social pressures do not literally push people to do anything; or, secondly, that the process, or causal mechanism, whereby the kettle lid is lifted is directly observable, but that psychological or social mechanisms are not.

The first objection ignores the obvious, but often neglected, point that 'causing' is not the same as literal 'pressing' or 'pushing'. As W. V. O. Quine suspects, the notion of cause may have begun 'with the feeling of effort, of pushing' (Magee 1978: 146;

see also Hanson 1958: 65). But if 'pushing' were a necessary ingredient of 'causing', then even 'a fire' could not properly be said to have been 'caused', let alone 'a war', for neither is literally 'pushed' into existence. The second objection is equally faulty. A mechanism, unlike a mechanical device, is never in fact 'observable'—although it is 'followable' by, and in that sense 'visible' to, the comprehending mind. Thus, Alexander Wendt's view of scientific explanation as involving 'the identification of the underlying causal *mechanisms* which physically generated the phenomenon' (1987: 353; emphasis in orginal) is curious, for what is meant here by 'physically' is uncertain. A mechanism *necessitates* an outcome, but does not *physically* generate it. His reference to 'the (*often* unobservable) causal mechanisms' (1987: 354; emphasis added) is also curious.

One of the implications of the points made in the previous two paragraphs is that, in attributing any degree of causal power or efficacy, as is often done, to the structure of the international system, such as anarchy or multipolarity, there is no need to feel anxious at all that such a structure is not literally like that of a building. Perhaps it is worthwhile developing this point further, because some confusion is detectable in certain recent theoretical works on the systemic causes of international phenomena.

For example, we may note Steve Smith's remark that, even though the structure of the international system, like patriarchy, is not the sort of thing of which we can say that it is either 'hard' or 'solid', it is none the less 'real' because its effects are noticeable. In any case, he suggests, we are committed to thinking of it as 'real' to the extent that we attribute any causal power to it (Hollis and Smith 1991: 105, 115, 207). This is similar to Wendt's argument (1987: esp. 350–61) for the scientific legitimacy of the belief in the reality of social structures despite their unobservability.

Smith is, of course, entirely right to think that what counts as a cause need not be 'real' in the sense in which it would be 'unreal' if it were found, for example, not to be 'hard' or 'solid'. Otherwise, neither 'events' nor 'facts', but only 'bodies' and 'things'—those which could literally 'shape and shove' (Waltz 1986: 343)—could have 'effects', which, of course, would be quite absurd. But if we are claiming that a cause-event occurred, or a causal fact (such as anarchy or multipolarity) obtains, nothing is added by remarking further that it 'really' happened, or it 'really' obtains. The adverb is redundant, and so also is the question of the 'reality' or otherwise of the structure of the international system. This is one question we need not investigate.

War-conducive mechanisms

Returning now to the issue of war, there clearly are a wide variety of mechanisms relevant to the occurrence of war, some contributing to the preparation of a war-prone background, others more directly linked to war's outbreaks. The American political-science literature on the origins of the First World War, which has grown in depth markedly in recent years, supplies a rich source of illustration. Several examples are given below to show how psychological, bureaucratic/organizational, and international mechanisms might cumulatively bring states closer and closer to the brink of war. The story begins with some common observations about the military profession.

Notoriously, the military tend to adopt a worst-case analysis of international relations because their profession nurtures, or reinforces, such an attitude of mind. Since the military are thus inclined to take for granted the hostility of other states, they tend to find it prudent to be prepared to launch preventive wars and pre-emptive strikes in case they become necessary. As a result, there may be a marked tendency for the military to prepare offensive military plans (Snyder 1984: 118–19). Here we already have an example of mechanism, a particular social environment inducing those within to think and act in a characteristic manner. Of course, it is not true that the military will always prefer offensive plans, or that they will never be interested in defensive ones: mechanistic processes, as we noted, do not always complete themselves, any more than do purposive processes.

As with many large and complex organizations, however, the military need to prepare detailed plans with which to enable the subordinate units to follow standard operating procedures. It happens that, whereas offence tends to be seen as simply carrying out a plan of attack by seizing the initiative at the right moment, defence tends to be seen as reacting to circumstances created by the enemy which are difficult to predict or control. This tends to produce an illusion that offence is easier to plan, and an offensive plan is easier to put into practice, even where the military in principle acknowledge that deviations from standard operating procedures are necessary both in defence and offence. This compound of organizational and psychological mechanisms may reinforce the military's tendency to prefer offensive war planning (Snyder 1984: 119–21).

Furthermore, as with most organizations, the military compete for their institutional autonomy and prestige. However, the military are more likely to enjoy autonomy from the civilian politicians when the operational goal is to disarm the adversary quickly and decisively by offensive means than when it is to negotiate a diplomatic solution by limited or defensive means. To seek their own autonomy, therefore, the military tend to force their doctrine and planning into the offensive mould. Moreover, the image of the military as specialists in victory by a decisive offensive move is more likely to heighten their prestige than their image as specialists in attrition. Here is another mechanism in operation. The military, as one organization among many, are induced by the circumstances to seek their institutional autonomy and prestige, and to choose those means which they believe are likely to help them achieve these ends (Snyder 1984: 121–2).

Where a military organization matures without firm civilian control, as in Germany before 1914, its offence-dominated thinking may become its institutional ideology, thus making it harder to challenge or revise it. Here a psychological mechanism may work in such a way that any perceived inadequacies of the offensive military plans, either in fighting a war or as a means of coercive diplomacy, come to be rationalized away (Snyder 1984: 122–9).

Also in the absence of firm, unified civilian control, a factional rivalry may develop within the military, as in Russia before the First World War. In such circumstances, the absence of strong civilian control may help intensify factional competition—another organizational mechanism at work—and exacerbate the offensive preferences exhibited by each in pursuit of its own autonomy and prestige, leading to the adoption of a disunited offensive strategy despite its obvious disutility for the state (Snyder 1984: 133–7, 140).

The mechanism whereby the military, like most other organizations, compete for their institutional autonomy and prestige operates even where there exists civilian control. This occurred in France, especially after the infamous Dreyfus affair of 1898, which intensified civilian attempts to control the military. Against the civilian

pressure to reduce the terms of conscription and introduce a more
defence-oriented, reservist-based strategy, the military tried to pro-
tect their tradition, size, and prestige by insisting on the virtues of
their offence-dominated plans, which they argued could not be
implemented without maintaining a large and well-trained stand-
ing army at a high level of readiness. In such cases, where strategic
doctrines are used more as a means of defending institutional
interests in the context of intragovernmental politics, offensive
military plans may be advanced irrespective of their operational
values (Snyder 1984: 129–33).

When one country adopts an offence-dominated strategy, the
neighbouring countries are forced to respond to it. It does not
necessarily follow that they are in turn forced to adopt offence-
dominated strategies. Jack Snyder (1984: 138) refers to the Russian
response to the German Schlieffen Plan as an illustration of how
one offensive war plan begets another in a neighbouring country.
Indeed, the knowledge of the Schlieffen Plan led the Russian military to believe that the window of opportunity provided by the
Plan's initial westward move must be exploited, leading them
eventually to adopt an offensive strategy against Germany's rear.
However, this Russian response reflected the peculiarities of the
Schlieffen Plan itself, and does not demonstrate how an offence-
dominated strategy *as such* tends to produce a similarly offensive
strategy in response.[4]

None the less, a militant policy adopted in one country may
tend to increase the influence of the military in the neighbouring
countries. Added to this mechanism is the military's quickness,
already noted, to view war as inevitable and their penchant for
offence. Furthermore, strategic writings in one country tend to be
read in other countries. These mechanisms combine to produce a
tendency for offence-dominated strategies to spread internation-
ally (Snyder 1984: 137–40).

The international spread of the offensive doctrines and offence-
dominated strategies is highly destabilizing (Jervis 1978: 186 ff.).
Such doctrines and strategies encourage states to think that expansion is relatively easy and tempts them to take advantage of any
opportunity to expand. Even status-quo powers are tempted to

---

[4] A very succinct account of the Schlieffen Plan is found, for example, in (Levy
1986: 197). See also Turner (1979).

behave in a similar fashion to deny the opportunity to their adversaries. A security competition intensifies, fuelling the arms race. The likelihood of preventive wars and pre-emptive strikes increases, making states feel even more insecure, more in need of allies and of tighter control of military secrecy. Offensive doctrines, by making improvisation seem costly, also tend to produce tight alliances based on detailed plans, and contribute to their rigid implementation. Most of these mechanisms appear to have operated in the period prior to the First World War (Jervis 1978: 190–2; Van Evera 1984; Levy 1986: 215).

Competition for security is one notable feature of the international system. However, the absence of a central authority from the international system means that states are highly sensitive not only about their security, but also about their stature, and these two objectives depend to a great extent on the states' reputations for strength, readiness to fight, and for fulfilling their alliance commitments.[5] Where a country's alliance with another involves specific military plans, the former's concern for reputations may lead it to implement the plans rigidly: what has been planned must be carried out when the occasion demands it, because failing to do so may be seen as a sign of weakness, indecision, or duplicity. In this scenario, there is a mechanism in operation, leading from the decentralized nature of the international system, through the perceived importance of reputations, to a rigid implementation of existing military plans. This contributes to the outbreak of war by reducing the governmental freedom of action. Levy (1986: 206–7) suggests that such a mechanism may have been at work in making Russia fight Germany strictly in accordance with its commitments to France.

Military contingency plans result from the tendency inherent in the military to minimize uncertainty. But in order to maintain their autonomy, the military often tend not to supply civilian policy-makers with full information regarding operational tactics. As a result, civilian policy-makers are in danger of devising policies not consonant with existing military plans. In critical circumstances resulting from the pursuit of such policies, the civilian policy-makers may be forced to become subservient to the military to

---

[5] On the role of 'honour' in international disputes, see Northedge and Donelan (1971).

whose contingency plans no viable alternative may readily be found. Thus having gained influence, the military often tend to 'elevate narrow operational requirements above the needs of state policy' (Levy 1986: 208). Years of work in developing, revising, and perfecting a plan generate a psychological commitment to it, and make improvisation difficult even where desirable (Levy 1986: 212). Such a process, leading from the natural and relatively innocuous need for the military to devise contingency plans, and resulting in the plans themselves dictating the solution, is another war-conducive mechanism. According to Levy (1986: 207–12), the German implementation of the Schlieffen Plan in the summer of 1914 illustrates this and certain other related mechanisms (1986: 207–12; see also Taylor 1969).

Furthermore, when under considerable stress, the decision-makers may become so exhausted that they may lose the normal flexibility of their minds (O. R. Holsti 1990). To cope with extreme anxiety, they may seek refuge in the certainty of known routines, and hence in existing plans. They may also begin, for example, to feel that their own options are limited, forced by the circumstances, and narrowing, while those of the adversary are larger in number, freely chosen, and even expanding. Such a trend may be reinforced by what Irving Janis (1982) has called 'the groupthink syndrome', which Levy (1986: 214) sums up as 'a concurrence-seeking tendency which can increase resistance to policy change through illusions of unanimity and invulnerability, moral certainty, self-censorship, and collective rationalization'. Such psychological mechanisms may operate to reduce decision-makers' mental flexibility at critical junctures when innovative moves are desperately required to avert the approach of war.

Given that there are so many war-conducive mechanisms, it is fortunate that they, like any other mechanisms, only work under requisite conditions free of disturbances. Otherwise, there would be many more wars than we already have for, undoubtedly, the above list is only a very small sample of a much wider set. None the less, when requisite conditions are met, such mechanisms contribute to increasing the likelihood of war, and, in specific instances, come to constitute part of what is usually treated as the underlying causes of war. Further, since mechanistic processes are relatively easily repeatable, they contribute to standardizing, to an extent, the processes of deterioration from peace to war.

'Mechanistic processes', we noted earlier, are contrasted to 'completion of purposive processes' where 'we are in control'. This does not mean, of course, that mechanistic processes cannot be controlled. However, war-conducive mechanistic processes, when uncontrolled, contribute to curtailing governments' freedom of action, and can, in extreme cases, effectively trap them in a collision course. The extent to which the outbreak of the First World War exemplifies this 'loss-of-control' scenario is a much debated issue (Trachtenberg 1991*b*).

War resulting from a 'loss of control' is one plausible definition of 'accidental war'. However, even in those circumstances where governments have lost much of their freedom of action through their failure to control various war-conducive mechanisms, it is still the actions of the governments which bring about a war's outbreak. In any case, governments' actions are at times more significant in bringing about a war than the uncontrolled operation of some war-conducive mechanisms. We turn to this topic next.

5.4 GOVERNMENT ACTIONS

To a narrative account of war origins the element of government actions (which include 'inactions') is not only indispensable, but central. It shapes the plot by revealing the key moves relevant governments make in the development of events leading to an outbreak of war. However, the main kinds of act governments are said to have undertaken are limited in variety. They are:

(1) resistance,
(2) acts with belligerent intent,
(3) acts of contributory negligence,
(4) insensitive acts,
(5) thoughtless acts, and
(6) reckless acts.

This sixfold categorization is a revised version of the scheme adopted originally in Suganami 1990*a*, and derives from the discussion of legal responsibility found in Aquarius (1945), and Smith and Hogan (1992: 53 ff.).

Resistance

The first of these is the easiest to explain. When a state is given by its adversary a clear choice between immediate surrender and war, say, in the form of an ultimatum, or a surprise attack, the target state may choose to surrender, as Denmark did to Germany on 8 April 1940. But when, as is more usually the case, the target state refuses to surrender immediately, and resorts to arms in response to the challenge, it may be said to act 'in resistance'.

'Resistance', as defined here, is the refusal by a state immediately to surrender, and therefore does not include activities of 'resistance' movements after the state's formal capitulation. Despite this slight terminological awkwardness, the label 'resistance' is still to be preferred to 'defence', another possible term, because the former is more neutral in connotation: whereas a state which is said to be acting 'in defence' may be thought not to have acted 'offensively' to provoke the challenge, this is not necessarily so with a state 'resisting' other states. The more neutral term is preferable here since a state 'refusing to surrender immediately' may or may not be an entirely innocent victim of aggression, as Norway was in 1940 when Germany attacked, and Iraq was not in the Gulf War in the winter of 1991.

Acts with Belligerent Intent

Clearly, war cannot begin where there is no resistance, but this in turn, by definition, presupposes a state confronting its target explicitly with a choice between immediate surrender and war. Such an act is said to be undertaken 'with belligerent intent'.

A variety of wars

However, 'an act with belligerent intent' need not be directly linked to an outbreak of war. As defined here, the term refers to any act motivated by clear intent, immediately *or at some later stage*, to force upon the opponent a choice between surrender and war. Such acts can therefore take place at various points leading up to an outbreak of war, and may take various forms, ranging from a variety of preparatory measures to an actual use of force at the start of a war. It is the presence of clear belligerent intent that is central to the concept of 'acts with belligerent intent', not their outward features, nor their temporal location.

Some wars are described as 'premeditated'. For example, according to a popular interpretation, Hitler is thought to have premeditated the Second World War in Europe. It is well known that A. J. P. Taylor (1964) challenged this interpretation. Taylor's argument, however, was partly that the state of war between Germany on the one hand, and France and Britain on the other, which came into existence on 3 September 1939, was not premeditated by Hitler (Taylor 1964). In a brief essay written in response to one of his critics, Taylor therefore remarked:

> On 1 September 1939 the German armies invaded Poland. On 3 September Great Britain and France declared war on Germany. These two events began a war, which subsequently—though not until 1941—became the Second World War. Perhaps I should have called my book: The Origins of the Outbreak of war in 1939. (Taylor 1971, 140–1)[6]

Given that premeditation is a long-term process, it is not difficult to show that a particular war, especially when characterized as one which broke out between specific belligerents at a particular time, even on a particular day, was not premeditated. A perfectly premeditated war would be a rare thing. What is more likely is war whose origins cannot be understood fully without reference to some acts undertaken by a state with more or less clear intent to bring about a war at some later stage with some more or less clearly identified adversaries.

The fact that acts based on belligerent intent, as defined here, are motivated by clear intent, immediately or otherwise, to force upon the opponent a choice between surrender and war does not necessarily mean that such acts are undertaken gratuitously, without any sense of being compelled by the circumstances to do so. Indeed, such acts are often undertaken in a genuinely desperate mood: Japan's decision to call off diplomatic negotiations with the USA, and resort to a surprise attack on Pearl Harbor, is an example (Iriye 1987: ch. 6; Sagan 1989; Dockrill 1992; Asada 1993: ch. 5).

Further, an act with belligerent intent is not necessarily an aggressive act. Whereas such acts may, of course, be aimed aggressively at an entirely innocent victim, it is also possible for such acts to be undertaken in response to varying degrees of hostile

---

[6] See also Taylor (1977c: 13).

provocation. Where war results from one country's acts with belligerent intent against an entirely innocent victim, which merely resists, the war is an 'aggressive war' by the former against the latter. Germany's war against Belgium resulting from implementing the Schlieffen Plan at the beginning of the First World War is an example. Where, by contrast, a country becomes exasperated by another country's aggressive foreign policy, and resorts to acts with belligerent intent which lead to war, the former may be said to be engaging in a 'punitive war' against the latter. The war of 1991 conducted by the US-led coalition against Iraq is a recent example of this, as was the war declared by Britain and France in 1939 against Germany.

Somewhere between the two extremes is a 'preventive war', where one party, fearing that its power is soon to decline relative to its hostile rival, resorts to acts with belligerent intent against the latter, leading to a war then rather than later. Pakistan's war against India in 1965 over Kashmir is an example (Brines 1968: 293; Barnds 1972: ch. 9; Blinkenberg 1972: 238–43; Paul 1994: ch. 6).

It is also possible for the target of acts with belligerent intent to respond in parallel at various stages, or resist in anticipation by resorting to a pre-emptive strike, thereby making it at times difficult to say clearly who the aggressor was. The deterioration of the German–Russian relationship leading to the outbreak of the First World War illustrates this (Turner 1968).

It is clear from the foregoing remarks that, where State A's acts with belligerent intent against State B form part of an explanation of war between them, A's war against B is not necessarily 'aggressive', 'gratuitous', or 'premeditated'. However, where A is seen to have resorted to a premeditated, aggressive, and/or gratuitous war against B, a good deal of stress will be placed, in explaining the war, on the string of acts undertaken by A with belligerent intent. In such a case, the story of war origins becomes effectively reduced to that of the origins of A's bellicosity. Fritz Fischer's *The War of Illusions* (1975), attributing to Germany a major share of responsibility for the outbreak of the First World War, to some extent illustrates this point.

'Unintended' wars

War is impossible without resistance, and seems virtually impossible without acts with belligerent intent. Imagine, however, that

A's nuclear missiles are launched, without any belligerent intent, through a series of technical errors, hitting their targets in *B*; and that *B*, assuming *A*'s intent to be belligerent, resorts to retaliatory strikes. In such circumstances, according to our definitions, *B*'s retaliation is not an 'act with belligerent intent', but 'resistance', though misconceived. Here then perhaps is a picture of what a war without belligerent intent might look like.

However, what is happening here is not yet really a 'war', but an 'incident'. Such an incident might come to an abrupt end if, immediately after the initial exchange of missiles, *A* were to apologize to *B*, explaining the circumstances. The initial exchange of missiles is more likely to develop into a war where *A* and *B* are long-standing adversaries, having a good reason to go to war in the first place. Here then is another illustration of Geoffrey Blainey's remark, cited earlier, that 'an "accidental" war is more likely if the non-accidental factors are strong' (1988: 142).

By an 'accidental war' here is understood a war the decision to resort to which was triggered by an accident, such as an unintended launching of missiles. What is accidental about such a war, it is important to note, is not the war itself, but what triggered the key decision: the war itself remains an outcome of belligerent intent.

If, therefore, stories of war origins invariably contain reference to acts with belligerent intent, they are also likely to contain reference to acts of other sorts apart from 'resistance' which was already noted. In most cases, acts with belligerent intent do not occur out of the blue, but in the context of deteriorating international circumstances in which a variety of war-conducive acts have already been undertaken. These are here classified into the following four types: 'acts of contributory negligence', 'insensitive acts', 'thoughtless acts', and 'reckless acts'.

Contributory Negligence

The first of these differs from the rest of the set in that 'acts of contributory negligence' are not themselves offensive acts. On the contrary, a 'contributorily negligent' act, in the context of war origins, is a failure to resort to standard countermeasures against an adversary's offensive policy, thereby unduly encouraging the adversary to take even more offensive steps, receiving harm as a result. In retrospect, the appeasement of Hitler is a classic example of this.[7]

A more recent and much-debated case is Britain's failure, in early March 1982, to take a precautionary naval action against Argentina's possible attack on the Falkland/Malvinas Islands, which may have contributed to the invasion the following month. The Franks Committee, reviewing the British Government's conduct, therefore, examined the view held by Lord Carrington, the then Foreign Secretary, that a naval deployment in early March, if covert, would not have worked as a deterrent, but, if overt, would have jeopardized the prospect of keeping negotiations going (Franks *et al.* 1992: paras. 324–9, introduction by Alex Danchev, pp. xiii–xiv). The Committee noted:

We do not think that this [Lord Carrington's view] was an unreasonable view to take at the time, but we believe that there would have been advantage in the Government's giving wider consideration at this stage to the question whether the potentially more threatening attitude by Argentina required some form of deterrent action in addition to the diplomatic initiatives and the contingency planning already in hand. (Franks *et al.* 1992: para. 330)

None the less, to the dismay of some of the critics, the Committee concluded:

if the British Government had acted differently in the ways we have indicated [and resorted to some form of deterrent action earlier], it is impossible to judge what the impact on the Argentine Government or the implications for the course of events might have been. There is no reasonable basis for any suggestion—which would be purely hypothetical—that the invasion would have been prevented if the Government had acted in the ways indicated in our report. Taking account of these considerations, and of all the evidence we have received, we conclude that we would not be justified in attaching any criticism or blame to the present Government for the Argentine Junta's decision to commit its act of unprovoked aggression in the invasion of the Falkland Islands on 2 April 1982. (Franks *et al.* 1992: para. 339)[8]

[7] See e.g. Bullock (1971: 221); Aster (1989). A more recent and extensive 'counter-revisionist' thesis, criticizing Chamberlain's appeasement policy, is found in Parker (1993).
[8] The Franks Committee's assessment of Carrington's decision in March 1982 not to resort to precautionary naval measures is discussed by Alex Danchev in Franks (1992: introd. by Alex Danchev, pp. v–xxiv, esp. p. xiii ff.); see also Danchev (1991: 309–12).

The Franks Committee's assertion, just cited, that there is '*no reasonable basis for any suggestion*—which would be purely hypothetical—that the invasion would have been prevented if the Government had acted in the ways indicated in our report' (emphasis added) is an overstatement. One reasonable basis would be statements from the members of the Argentinian junta to the effect that they would have hesitated to launch an invasion at that time had it been the case, and had they been informed of the fact, that a British submarine was there, ready to torpedo any Argentinian ships approaching the Islands (see Franks *et al.* 1992: introd. by Alex Danchev, p. xiv). Such statements would add some credibility to the necessarily counterfactual claim that the invasion could have been prevented, and thereby supply a firmer ground for the assertion that the British Government was to some extent negligent contributorily. But, of course, the extent of negligence must be judged in the light of what can reasonably be expected of a government in similar circumstances.

Insensitive, Thoughtless and Reckless Acts

Of the four kinds of acts listed earlier, the remaining three types ('insensitive', 'thoughtless', and 'reckless' acts) can be explained as follows.

Suppose that State *A* is about to undertake what amounts to an offensive act against its adversary *B*, and that a reasonably attentive mind would notice the act's offensiveness. If, in such circumstances, *A* performs the offending act, unaware even that *B* will, with good reason, consider the act as offensive, then *A* can be said to act 'insensitively'.

If, however, *A* performs the offending act, having noticed its offensiveness, but failed to give any serious thought to the resultant risk of war, obvious to a reasonably attentive mind, then *A* can be said to act 'thoughtlessly'.

Finally, in the course of deliberating whether or not to perform the offensive act, *A* may come to calculate as follows: the probability of war resulting from the act, and/or the cost of such a war, might be considerable; but still the probability and/or the cost would be tolerably low when judged in the overall context of what *A* could probably gain by resorting to the act in contrast to not doing so at that time. If, on the basis of such a calculation, *A* carries out the offensive act, even though a reasonably prudent person would not take the risk, then *A* can be said to act 'recklessly'. This category covers cases of controlled risk-taking—where *A* resorts to the offending act, along with some softening measures to reduce the risk of escalation into war, and/or the probable cost of such a war, speculating that the risk and/or the cost has thereby become tolerable in the overall calculation.

It should be added here that each of the three types of act identified above, as in the case of acts of 'contributory negligence', can vary in magnitude. Some 'insensitive' acts are more so than others, and the same point can be made with respect to 'thoughtless' and 'reckless' acts, as well as those of 'contributory negligence'.

Insensitive acts

'Insensitivity' is illustrated well by Tsarist Russia's actions towards Japan. From the time of the so-called Three Power Intervention (1895), at the end of the Sino-Japanese War, by Russia, Britain, and Germany to undo some of Japan's gains, and then in return to obtain concessions from China, until the very eve of the Russo-Japanese War (1904–5), when Russia utterly failed to appreciate the degree of Japan's exasperation, the Tsar's government exhibited unyielding and condescending attitudes towards Japan, then full of juvenile pride.

As Nish (1985: 6) observes, Tsar Nicholas was noted for his peace-loving personality, but wanted peace on Russia's terms and 'failed to understand how objectionable her actions appeared to others or when a conciliatory approach was desirable'. As depicted in Nish's work in considerable detail, this was reflected in Russia's insensitive attitude towards Japan in dealing with matters of mutual concern, especially issues relating to hegemony and influence in Korea and Manchuria, gradually pressurizing even the more conciliatory faction inside Japan to consider war with Russia as inevitable and justified (Nish 1985: esp. 48, 189, 210–11, conclusion).

Thoughtless acts

In addition to 'insensitivity', there were also elements of 'thoughtlessness' in the Russian leaders' attitudes towards Japan: they never gave any serious thought to the idea that Japan might dare to resort to war against the mighty imperial forces (Nish 1985: 168,

209, 218, 240–1, 244, 249; Paul 1994: ch. 3). According to Nish (1985: 168):

Colonel Vannovskii, who had occupied the position of military attaché at the Tokyo legation since 1900 and was the man capable of reporting most authoritatively, seems to have taken the view that the Japanese would need about a century to develop a modern army comparable to that of the weakest army in Europe and that their army was one of infants.

Baron Rosen, the head of the Russian legation in Tokyo, was adamant only ten days before the war broke out that 'we had only to mobilize one Division and the Japanese will climb down' (Nish 1985: 209; see also Nish 1985: 249).

However, 'thoughtlessness' of this magnitude may be relatively uncommon. Argentina's decision to invade the Falkland/Malvinas Islands, apparently with the intention of forcing the British government into serious negotiations on a transfer of sovereignty, may perhaps be noted as a possible exception from the recent past (Charlton 1989: 99–124; Freedman and Gamba-Stonehouse 1990: 68, 79, 81; Levy and Vakili 1992; Paul 1994: ch. 8, 169).

By contrast, 'recklessness', of various shades, is encountered quite frequently in the war-origins literature. An early, but still much-debated, case is Bethmann Hollweg's thinking regarding the probability of British intervention in the event of Germany implementing the Schlieffen Plan (Albertini 1952–7: ii. 466–527; Fischer 1967: 50–92; Jarausch 1969; Berghahn 1973: 208–9; Mommsen 1973: 38; Fischer 1975: 400; Steiner 1977*a*: 126; Fischer 1988; Levy 1991: 238–42; Lynn-Jones 1991: 181–9; Sagan 1991: 124–9).

Bethmann Hollweg's recklessness

In the summer of 1914, German Chancellor Theobald von Bethmann Hollweg was aware that Britain might not remain neutral in case the conflict could not be localized to the Austrian–Serbian level but expanded to a continental war in which Germany would fight France and Russia in accordance with the Schlieffen Plan. He hoped, and appears to have believed, at a minimum, that Britain, in such circumstances, would not intervene until the defeat of France was imminent. But he also had considerable doubts, and wished, as far as possible, to avoid expanding the war beyond the European Continent.

Bethmann therefore tried to reduce the likelihood of British intervention, or at least encourage indecision in Britain, and so delay British entry into the war. It was partly with this end in view that he went to great lengths to ensure that Germany did not mobilize before Russia. To increase the likelihood of British neutrality, Germany must at least be seen to be fighting in response to Russian aggression. He also appears to have thought that British intervention could perhaps be avoided if Germany guaranteed to Britain that no territorial concessions were to be demanded from France.

Contrary to his hopes but in line with his fears, Bethmann was to receive an unequivocal warning from Sir Edward Grey, the British Foreign Secretary, that Great Britain could not remain neutral in a war involving France. When, at the very final stage of the July crisis, this message was brought to him, Bethmann immediately reacted by a complete reversal of the German policy towards Austria. He now warned that Germany might not support Austria unless it accepted mediation of its dispute with Serbia, and Kaiser Wilhelm's compromise 'Halt-in-Belgrade' proposal, pressing Austria to stop its advance into Serbia once Belgrade had been taken.

Bethmann Hollweg's reversal of policy, apparently prompted by an unequivocal warning from Britain at the very last phase of the crisis, indicates that throughout most part of the crisis Bethmann was acting on the assumption that Britain was unlikely to intervene immediately. If so, his policy may be said to have been 'reckless'.[9] However, this thesis needs to be qualified by an observation that Britain itself was uncertain until the final stage of the July crisis as to whether it would remain neutral in a continental war.[10] Therefore, Bethmann Hollweg was not entirely to blame for his, in retrospect, highly wishful thinking.

Still, it can be argued that he was 'reckless' in underestimating, or perhaps even 'thoughtless' in not giving any serious thought to, the readiness with which Britain, a guarantor of Belgian neutrality, would intervene to defend it (Jarausch 1969: 71; Fischer 1988: 387). However, although Bethmann apparently knew that the

[9] Trachtenberg (1991b: 83 ff.), however, challenges the view that it was an unequivocal warning from Britain that prompted Bethmann Hollweg's sudden reversal of policy. See also Levy, Christensen, and Trachtenberg (1991).
[10] Sources of British hesitancy are explained in Steiner (1977b: 401); Levy (1991: 243–5); Lynn-Jones (1991: 182 ff.).

Schlieffen Plan envisaged the seizure of Liège, he did not know until 31 July 1914, the day before the German mobilization took place, that, according to the Plan, the invasion of Belgium had to begin on the third day of mobilization. This may have encouraged him to assume that Britain would not join in the war at an early stage (Turner 1979: 213; Joll 1984: 84; Levy 1991: 258 n. 115).[11] If so, the lack of coordination between the civilian and military leaders in Germany, and the latter's 'recklessness' or even 'belligerent intent' with regard to Britain would need to be noted as vital elements in the origins of the First World War.[12]

Hitler's recklessness

Another much-disputed case also concerns Germany: Hitler's decision to invade Poland in September 1939. The dispute centres on two contending interpretations: (1) that Hitler's primary aim was to take Poland with—or perhaps without—a war, but that he acted in deliberate disregard of the danger that this might escalate into a war with France and Britain; and (2) that Hitler's aim was confined to taking Poland without a war if possible, but that, to his dismay, he found himself confronted with France and Britain, neither of which at that time he intended to fight or assumed he would have to fight.

The first interpretation is advanced by a number of historians, among them H. R. Trevor-Roper (1971: esp. 96–8), T. W. Mason (1971: esp. 111), Alan Bullock (1971: esp. 207 ff.), and, more lately, P. M. H. Bell (1986: ch. 15, esp. 257, 262, 263), and D. C. Watt (1989: esp. 252, 623–4). The second interpretation is famously associated with A. J. P. Taylor (1964: 17–18, 136–7, chs. 9–11), finds support in H. W. Koch (1971), and is followed more recently by Jeffrey L. Hughes (1989: 307). A third possible view that Hitler in 1939 set out on a premeditated course towards war with Poland, *and with France and Britain at the same time* seems to find little support among historians, although this thesis is attributed by H. W. Koch (1971: 158) to the German Historian, Walter Hofer.

---

[11] Albertini (1952–7: iii. 249) and Moses (1975: 87) also depict Bethmann as being ignorant of the details of the Schlieffen Plan, but this view is challenged by Trachtenberg (1991b: 61–2); see also Fischer (1975: 168).

[12] It is noteworthy that, unlike Bethmann Hollweg, General von Moltke, the Chief of the German General Staff, considered English neutrality as an illusion (Fischer 1988: 377).

A careful reading of these works, however, shows that some degree of reconciliation is possible between the first two positions. This might seem somewhat implausible given the much-publicized bitterness of the dispute on this issue between, in particular, Taylor and his critics (see e.g. Robertson 1971; Dray 1980*b*). Taylor's intention, however, was to develop an argument, as far as it can plausibly go, against the then too-readily accepted dogma that Hitler, Attila-like, loved destruction for its own sake and was bent on war without thought of policy. Against this, he presented an image of Hitler as an opportunist, wicked undoubtedly, but not necessarily so in foreign policy, who in the end blundered. 'At any rate,' Taylor wrote, 'this is a rival dogma which is worth developing, if only as an academic exercise' (1964: 266). When deliberate overstretching, resulting from Taylor's explicitly stated purpose, is removed, there is much in his work that can be reconciled with the main argument of some of his major critics.

It appears that, in the summer of 1939, Hitler intended to take Poland with or without a war, but wanted as much as possible to avoid getting involved in war with Britain and France *at that time*. He had already signed the so-called Pact of Steel with Mussolini's Italy as a partial deterrent against British support of Poland (Morewood 1989: 190). Hitler's other precautionary measures included, most importantly, the Nazi–Soviet non-aggression pact of 23 August 1939, with which he hoped, among other things, to discourage Britain from implementing its guarantee of Polish independence.

When this had the opposite effect of hardening the British attitude, resulting, on 25 August, in a formal treaty of alliance between Britain and Poland, Hitler attempted to circumvent the danger of escalation by pressing for a compromise. His apparent policy now was to demand minimum concessions from Poland along the lines of German national self-determination, on the assumption that Britain, preferring another Munich-type settlement to war, would pressure Poland to negotiate with Germany (Robertson 1989: 349–50).

But Poland, unlike Czechoslovakia a year before, would not budge. Hitler, for his part, could not afford not to move. Having ordered the armed forces to be prepared to attack Poland at any time from 1 September 1939 (Taylor 1964: 303; Bell 1986: 257; Watt 1989: 190), having, in a moment of optimism, put back the planned date of invasion to 26 August (Taylor 1964: 320; Watt

1989: 479), having once confirmed that order (Taylor 1964: 326; Bell 1986: 262; Watt 1989: 489), and then, in a sudden moment of pessimism, having abruptly countermanded it (Taylor 1964: 326; Bell 1986: 262; Watt 1989: 495), in the end he decided to implement the initial plan: Poland was invaded at dawn on 1 September 1939. Throughout the Polish crisis, Hitler's moods vacillated as the probability of intervention fluctuated. But ultimately he carried out the invasion, perhaps underestimating British and French resolve, but in any event preparing for the worst case by taking precautionary defensive measures in Germany's western borders (Bell 1986: 262, 263).

Now, clearly, not even Taylor is suggesting that Hitler acted 'thoughtlessly', that Hitler never gave any serious thought to the idea that his offensive policy towards Poland might lead to a war with Britain and France in 1939. Hitler did take this possibility very seriously indeed. Hence the Pact of Steel with Italy, and more importantly, the Nazi–Soviet Pact. Hence also Hitler's last-minute diplomatic manœuvre and hesitation; 'his haggard appearance and temperamental outbursts' (Bullock 1971: 215); and a defensive posture in the west (Bell 1986: 263). But he calculated, it would seem plausible to say, that what he could probably gain by invading Poland, *in contrast to not doing so then*, was quite substantial.

There were a number of reasons why Hitler wanted to take Poland *at that time*. He was much exercised by fear of an early death, and the need to accomplish his aims before he was struck down (Bell 1986: 263; Watt 1989: 619; Parker 1993: 330). Economic pressures for annexation of Poland at that time were strong (Bell 1986: 263), and any delay would have meant, because of the autumn rains, that the defeat of Poland could not be accomplished in 1939 (Bell 1986: 262; Robertson 1989: 345; Watt 1989: 319, 509). In Hitler's estimation, Germany's relative superiority in air power at that time gave him an opportunity which might not recur (Bell 1986: 263), and since he was concerned to impress his generals, he could not afford to abandon the plan once prepared (Taylor 1964: 304, 333; Koch 1971: 178–89).

Hitler was, as we noted, aware that he would lose much if British/French intervention were to take place; but this, while more likely than in 1938 (Koch 1971: 160, 177), was by no means assured. On 29 August, two days before the invasion order was finally released, Hitler still indicated his belief that Britain would not fight (Taylor 1964: 332–3; Bell 1986: 264; Robertson 1989: 350). In any case, Poland would have been conquered before the intervention could take place (Taylor 1964: 336; Koch 1971: 182).

Therefore, in Hitler's overall calculation, the invasion of Poland was worth a gamble at that time. If, as Taylor says, 'wars are much like road accidents' (1964: 135), Hitler's decision to invade Poland resembles a heavily drunken man's choice to drive home late at night from a dinner party: his hosts insist he should stay the night; but he would rather drive now and wake up in his own bed the next day than face his hosts the morning after and then drive; in this context, the negative factor—for example, the probability (if not necessarily the cost) of having an accident—begins to appear tolerably low; and he decides to drive home.[13]

This interpretation of Hitler's thinking is in fact closely in line with the view advanced by Bullock in opposition to Taylor. Bullock, however, sums up his position as follows (1971: 215): 'This [Hitler's invasion of Poland, leading to war with Britain and France] was no stumbling into war. It was neither misunderstanding nor miscalculation which sent the German army over the frontier into Poland, but a calculated risk, the gambler's bid . . .'. These remarks are misleading. It must not be thought that because Hitler was making 'the gambler's bid', his decision could not have involved any miscalculation. Clearly, Hitler gambled, but on this occasion he badly miscalculated because, among other things, he misunderstood British intentions.

Taylor's view that Hitler miscalculated the British/French factor is not, therefore, incompatible with the interpretation advanced here: Hitler did underestimate the probability of British/French intervention, though not perhaps the cost of such an eventuality, relative to his estimation of the probable gains accruing from invading Poland then. At the same time, the view held by some of Taylor's critics that Hitler invaded Poland in deliberate disregard of the danger of a British/French intervention, too, is compatible with the interpretation: Hitler was, of course, aware of the danger, but he chose not to let it override his decision because

---

[13] Hitler, incidentally, was a teetotaller (Watt 1989: 462). His power of self-intoxication was sufficient, no doubt. He was also vegetarian, adamant, characteristically, that 'the world of the future will be vegetarian' (Bullock 1962: 388).

when everything was taken into account it appeared to him to make sense to invade Poland at that time.[14]

The main disagreement between Taylor and his critics is a *normative* one, as has been skilfully exposed by W. H. Dray (1980b).[15] According to Taylor's critics, the probability of escalation was so obviously high that Hitler, like a dangerous driver, must be said to have acted irresponsibly. It is, according to them, preposterous to say that Hitler *just* miscalculated.

'Clearly Hitler would have preferred Britain and France to remain inactive, but the risk was obvious enough for him to be presumed to have been ready to accept the consequences if they did not,' says T. W. Mason (1971: 111). 'That Hitler would have been happy to accept a Polish surrender without a fight does not mean that he was not deliberately playing with fire,' notes P. S. Wandycz (1986: 203). And P. A. Reynolds reproachfully remarks:

In law, and in common sense, the consequence of an action is presumed to have been intended if a reasonable man would suppose that the particular consequence would follow from the action in question. Whether Hitler was a reasonable man or not, the actions that he said he would perform, and that he did perform, were such as any sane man would expect eventually to lead to war, protest as Taylor may (and as Hitler sometimes did) that this was not his intention. (1961: 217)

These would appear to be reasonable claims.[16] Hitler was behaving dangerously; he ought not to have behaved like that. Taylor would dispute this, however, suggesting in effect that, even though Hitler was taking a risk, he was not—judged by the standard expected of European leaders at that time—grossly negligent in so doing (Taylor 1964: 14–15, 97, 100; Dray 1980b: 79 ff.).

In any case, whether Hitler's recklessness can be *the whole point*

---

[14] There is some parallelism between the case of Bethmann Hollweg considered earlier and that of Hitler. Characteristically, Waltz (1979: 171) explains this in the light of the multipolar structure of the international system in 1914 and 1939. Compare Snyder (1990: 18–19), where the reckless foreign policies of Germany (and Japan) are explained in terms of the absence of mature democracy.

[15] See also Dray (1960: 578–92), and Dray (1964: ch. 4), where he exposes the normative element in the debates about the causes of the American Civil War.

[16] However, P. A. Reynolds's statement is imprecise if he has English criminal law in mind when he remarks that '[i]n law ... the consequence of an action is presumed to have been *intended* if a reasonable man would suppose that the particular consequence would follow from the action in question' (1961: 217; emphasis added). See Smith and Hogan (1992: 53 ff.).

of the narrative may be debated because there are also certain
other ought-not-to-have-dones which, in retrospect, we cannot
ignore. As Bullock (1971: 189) writes:

the British and French governments of the 1930s have been blamed for
their policy of appeasement and for failing to secure an agreement with
Russia; Mussolini for his alliance with Hitler; Stalin for the Nazi-Soviet
Pact; the Poles for the illusions which encouraged them to believe that they
could hold Russia as well as Germany at arm's length. Taking a wider
sweep, historians have turned for an explanation of the origins of the
Second World War to the mistakes made in the peace settlement that
followed the First; to the inadequacies of British and French policy between
the wars; the retreat of the United States into isolation; the exclusion of
the Soviet Union; the social effects of the Great Depression, and so on.

The culpability of Hitler and Germany as a whole must be
judged relative to such commissions and omissions on the part of
other governments and peoples in the period before 1939. Even
D. C. Watt, who goes so far as to claim that 'Hitler willed, wanted,
craved war and the destruction wrought by war', concedes that
'he did not want the war he got', and that 'its origins lay through
his own miscalculations and misperceptions, *as much as* through
those of his eventual opponents, not least in their belief that he
was bluffing, that he would recoil' (1989: 623; emphasis added).
None the less, as Watt stresses, 'when it became clear that settling
with Poland would, despite all his hopes, involve war with Britain,
[Hitler] did not postpone that settlement for more than a week'
(1989: 624). Given such an extraordinary degree of bellicose recklessness as was exhibited by Hitler, other parties' contributory
negligence would not supply him with a very strong defence even
though it forms an indispensable part of the story of the origins
of the Second World War in Europe. Bullock concludes:

If the Western Powers had recognised the threat earlier and shown greater
resolution in resisting Hitler's (and Mussolini's) demands, it is possible
that the clash might not have led to war, or at any rate not to a war on
the scale on which it had finally to be fought . . . This is their share of
responsibility for the war . . . None of the Great Powers comes well out
of the history of the 1930s, but this sort of responsibility, even when it
runs to appeasement, as in the case of Britain and France, or complicity
as in the case of Russia, is still *recognisably different* from that of a
government which deliberately creates the threat of war and sets out to
exploit it. (1971: 221; emphasis added)

Danchev (1994: 103–4) accepts Bullock's view that the primary, if not the sole, responsibility for the war of 1939 lies with Hitler and the nation which followed him. It is interesting to note Danchev's view that the same point can be made about Saddam Hussein in the Gulf War (see also Stein 1992). Whether a party to a war can be said to have been contributorily negligent, and how far, in view of the aggressiveness of its opponent, that party can be held responsible for the war's outbreak is clearly a recurrent question in the war-origins literature.

Those who argue along the Bullock–Danchev line may be said to follow the kind of reasoning enshrined in criminal, as opposed to civil, law. As Hart and Honoré state (1985: 352):

When the concurrent cause [of a harm] is the contributory negligence of the victim, civil law allows this to be pleaded as a complete or partial defence, while *in criminal law contributory negligence is no defence* though the victim's reckless or grossly negligent behaviour or his voluntary decision to court death or injury may negative causal connection, on ordinary principles, between accused's act and the harm. (emphasis added)

The view that an act of aggression committed by a state against another should be seen analogously to a crime within domestic society became an influential doctrine from about the time of the First World War (Suganami 1989a: esp. 89). Interestingly, it is about this time that causes of war became a major intellectual concern among historians, and works on war origins came to proliferate (Howard 1983b: 8–9). Before then, as a historical theme, origins of wars were more naturally an integral part of works on the wars themselves (see e.g. Kinglake 1877). Writing a *self-contained book* on a war's origins as such, that is, on deteriorating international conditions resulting in the outbreak of a war, is a practice familiar only since 1914.

This shift of camera angle, among notable historians, from war to war origins, and the extension of criminal-law thinking from the domestic realm to war in international society, are both manifestations of the attitudinal change brought about by the experience of the First World War. War came to be seen more in a negative light than ever before—as a disaster to be avoided, a crime to be prevented, an evil to be eliminated. It is the rise of such a pacificistic view of war that partly explains the growth of the war-origins literature, and the moralistic and quasi-juridical tone with which historical controversies concerning the origins of the major wars of this century tend to be conducted.

5.5 PATTERNS OF WAR ORIGINS

War comes about in different ways. Its background conditions are quite diverse. In some cases, chance coincidences may play a part in preparing a war-conducive background. Perhaps more often, they contribute to setting the timing of a war's outbreak. Yet in others, they may not play any very significant part at all. A wide variety of mechanisms also play a part in the process of deterioration from peace to war, some in preparing war-conducive backgrounds, others in escalating crises into wars. Origins of wars are so diverse that, contrary to Waltz's view, examined in Chapter 1, there is no one item which can be considered as *the* underlying cause of all wars. Yet, it is also possible to see *family resemblances* in war origins.

The notion of 'family resemblances' is associated with Ludwig Wittgenstein. In his well-known analysis, he notes that no one feature may be found to be common to all 'games'. But, he suggests, as we go through many examples of games, we see 'similarities crop up and disappear', 'we see a complicated network of similarities overlapping and criss-crossing'. He adds:

I can think of no better expression to characterize these similarities than 'family resemblances'; for the various resemblances between members of a family: build, features, colour of eyes, gait, temperament, etc. etc. overlap and criss-cross in the same way. (1968: sects. 66 and 67)

The argument to the effect that there are family resemblances among war origins is most persuasive with respect to the element of government actions. In the actual processes of deterioration from peace to war, governments of course perform a myriad of acts: sending cables, envoys, and bombers—sometimes all at once; bluffing, guessing, or miscalculating; intimidating, restraining, or cajoling; making a pledge to assist an ally, or backing down at the last minute; and so on, *ad infinitum*. But the key moves governments make, which broadly shape the course of events leading to a war's outbreak, appear in fact to be limited in variety. As we noted, they are broadly of six types: (1) resistance; (2)

acts with belligerent intent; (3) acts of contributory negligence; (4) insensitive acts; (5) thoughtless acts; and (6) reckless acts. These general categories of government actions constitute *a common pool* such that interactions among relevant governments leading to outbreaks of war can be outlined by combinations of some or all of them. This produces clear family resemblances in war origins, as can readily be noted from several examples mentioned below.

In the relatively simple case of the Falkland/Malvinas War of 1982, Argentina, in invading the Islands, acted thoughtlessly, or perhaps recklessly, regarding potential British reactions to the Argentine resort to arms (Freedman and Gamba-Stonehouse 1990: 142, 323). Britain, perhaps having been contributorily negligent to a small degree, now responded by sending a naval task force to the South Atlantic. In so doing, Britain appears to have calculated that the cost of failing immediately to take military actions far outweighed the probable cost of war, which, of course, would be unnecessary if Argentina, under the threat of war with Britain, were to back down (Freedman and Gamba-Stonehouse 1990: 124). Not unnaturally, Argentina could not face the humiliation of defeat without a fight (Freedman and Gamba-Stonehouse 1990: 143), but was in the end forced to withdraw.

In a comparably simple case, in the Gulf War, Iraq resorted to an act with belligerent intent when it invaded Kuwait in the summer of 1990. Kuwait, perhaps having been to some extent insensitive or thoughtless in its handling of Iraq, barely had time to register its resistance. By the following winter, however, the USA had acted with belligerent intent, and carried out a punitive war against Iraq, sanctioned by the UN and supported by other countries. Iraq resisted, but was compelled to withdraw (Freedman and Karsh 1993).

The Russo-Japanese War of 1904–5, though with much interesting meandering, is again reasonably straightforward in its outline. Russia acted insensitively and thoughtlessly towards Japan. Exasperated, Japan became firmer in its resolve to dictate a military solution, resorting in the end to a war to challenge Russian hegemony in Manchuria and influence in Korea.

The origins of the Second World War in Asia and the Pacific also involve some meandering, but the modality of the three major participants' entry into the war is relatively simple: Japan's aggressive war against China; China's resistance; Japan's intent, in desperation, to launch a war against the USA, which, assuming that Japan would yield to the pressure, had resorted, with other powers, to punitive measures short of war against Japan; and the USA's resistance.

The immediate origins of the Second World War in Europe, too, are relatively straightforward in outline: Germany's invasion of Poland, which was an act with belligerent intent as regards Poland, but an act of recklessness regarding the prospect of war with Britain and France; Polish resistance; the belligerent intent on the part of Britain and France, having been contributorily negligent and by now exasperated by Germany's excessively reckless provocations, to resort to a punitive war; Germany's resistance; Germany's belligerent intent to cause an aggressive war against the Soviet Union; and the Soviet resistance.

The origins of the First World War are notoriously complex, but the following is one plausible outline: Austria–Hungary's ultimatum to Serbia, which was an act with belligerent intent against Serbia, and a reckless act with respect to the prospect of war with Russia (Williamson 1991: 190 ff.); Germany's support of Austria–Hungary, reflecting Germany's reckless thinking to the effect, initially, that the war could perhaps be limited to the Austrian–Serbian level, but, later, that if Germany were to have to face Russia and France, Britain would at least not enter the war immediately (Levy 1991); Russia's stage-by-stage mobilization, which, by the time general mobilization was ordered, became an act with belligerent intent to resort to a punitive war against Austria, and a pre-emptive war against Germany (Turner 1968; Trachtenberg 1991*b*: 72 ff.; Levy, Christensen, and Trachtenberg 1991: 194–7, 201–3); Germany's implementation of the Schlieffen Plan, which was an act with belligerent intent against Belgium, France, and Russia; resistance by Belgium and France; and, finally, Britain's resort to a punitive war against Germany.

These illustrations indicate that, although every war, when looked at in detail, has its unique origins, there are nevertheless certain family resemblances amongst the origins of different wars. Similarities crop up and disappear as we compare different cases at a certain level of generality in terms of key government actions which contributed to the outbreaks of war. Can the same point be made about war origins with respect to their other elements, 'background conditions', 'war-conducive mechanisms', and 'chance coincidences'?

As far as war's 'background conditions' are concerned, a particular combination of factors, with all the relevant details, is of course unique to the war which resulted from it. Yet some features, under certain general descriptions, may find their equivalents with respect to some other wars: for example, the absence of a balancer in the international system of the region; multipolarity, or the presence of a relatively large number of decision-making centres, in a crisis situation; the rising power of the 'have-not' states; the lack of civilian control of the military; and so on.

As in the case of government actions, there might even be a common pool of general features such that the background conditions of particular wars are its subsets in concrete forms. Such a common pool, however, might not be a closed set comprising a finite number of items. Unlike in the case of government actions, the variety of background conditions relevant to war's outbreaks may be unlimited. A parallel remark could no doubt be made with respect to 'war-conducive mechanisms'. They, too, are likely to contribute towards family resemblances among war origins, but may also be unlimited in variety.

By contrast, it would be difficult to see how family resemblances might ever emerge among war origins if we compared them with respect to the element of chance coincidences. When given relevantly detailed descriptions, chance coincidences do play interesting parts in some stories of war origins. Yet, it is difficult to visualize a common pool, closed or otherwise, comprising *types* of chance coincidences such that—as in the case of background conditions or war-conducive mechanisms—those contributing to particular wars are the subsets, in concrete forms, of the entire pool.

We can with some confidence, then, advance a hypothesis regarding patterns of war origins. It is that despite a wide diversity in the origins of wars, there are family resemblances among them; and that this is to a great extent the result of the limited number of things governments can be said to have done when their key moves are described at the level of generality embodied in the six broad categories noted above; however, family resemblances may also be found with respect to certain general features of background conditions, and also to the war-conducive mechanisms, which may recur in various combinations.

We may note here that, in the field of literary theory, a similar, though much stronger, claim has been made by Vladimir Propp with respect to Russian fairy tales. According to his investigation, the moves made by the characters in fairy tales (or what he calls the 'functions' of the characters) are limited in variety, thirty-one at a maximum, *and always appear in the same sequence* (Propp 1968; Scholes 1974: 59 ff.). War-origins stories are much more diverse by comparison, but the argument advanced here is similar in spirit to Propp's.

In Chapter 4, in discussing Carl Hempel's covering-law theory of explanation, we observed that laws connecting particular events hold only under relevant descriptions of them. It is unsurprising therefore to find that resemblances in war origins are also a function of the level of generality at which their key elements are depicted. We may note in this connection a parallel observation made by Evan Luard regarding similarities and differences among *issues* that states fight about in war. He writes (1986: 83):

> If the word were defined in sufficiently general terms, it would not be difficult to show that the 'issues' about which wars have been fought have been the same throughout history: conflicts of national interest; mutually incompatible objectives; rivalry for power, status or influence. Conversely, the more specific the definition used, the more unique are the issues over which particular wars have been fought: for example, only one war has been fought about Jenkin's [*sic*] Ear (if that). There is probably little that can usefully be said about issues if interpreted in either of these extreme ways. Issues of the first type are so general and so interchangeable that almost all wars could be shown to be alike; issues of the second type so particular that almost no useful general conclusions can be drawn about them.
>
> We shall be concerned therefore with issues at a middle level: specific enough to distinguish one war from another, but not so specific as to relate only to one or two conflicts each.

Correspondingly, all war origins are alike in that every war results from a conscious decision, however reluctant, on the part of the key decision-makers to go to war. There is no such thing as an 'unintended outbreak of war' (and, at least in this sense, there is no such thing as an 'accidental war'), although what happens in war may well be largely unintended at the time of its outbreak (Howard 1983*b*: 12; Blainey 1988: 292). However, when recounted in detail, as is done in historical works, origins of wars are naturally all very different. Family resemblances in war origins will begin to weaken and disappear if, for example, key government actions are depicted at a more specific level than is adopted in the sixfold categorization discussed above. Still, wars do not come about in any way they like any more than can brothers, sisters, or cousins differ entirely in their appearances.

CONCLUSION

In some cases, the background conditions appear already so war-prone that the particular path through which the actual war broke out seems only to have been one of a number of alternative routes through which a war like that could have been brought about. Of course, even in such cases, actions of the relevant governments cannot be ignored. In any case, the war-prone background itself will be found to have resulted partly from commissions and omissions by these governments and certain others. None the less, in such cases, where the conditions are ripe for war, the governments concerned will appear to have had very little freedom of action left to them. The circumstances, we suspect, were such that the outcome was causally overdetermined, almost. Only fine skills, combined perhaps with extraordinary luck, could have saved the day.

Even in such cases, the actual outbreak of war, and in particular the timing of it, may have been determined to a great extent by some chance coincidences. Further, the circumstances surrounding the decision-makers are likely to have been so full of war-conducive mechanisms that the outbreak of war can easily be depicted as a result of their loss of control over the development of events. Moreover, since governments are not very likely to act in accordance with a detailed plan, prepared a long time in advance, to start a war precisely at a given time with a given country, it is not difficult to show that the war that actually broke out at a particular time was not premeditated by any government. Further, given what often happens in war, it may be easy to show that most governments involved would like to have avoided most or some of the consequences of the war's outbreak. From here, it is only a short step to suggest that no one really wanted the war, that the war was quite unintended, and that the war was inadvertently entered into.

Too much stress on chance coincidences, loss of control, and inadvertence, however, may tend to obscure the significance of the war-prone setting. It may be because of the dangerous setting in which the actors found themselves that particular chance coincidences could become historically significant; that the governments lost control over the development of events relatively easily; and that they found themselves having to enter a war which they neither planned long in advance, nor particularly wanted to fight.

Of course, not all wars are produced in this way, exemplified well by the First World War, where *the setting* dominates. There are some wars which are more deliberately brought about. The Suez War of 1956, for example (Stephens 1971: chs. 6–7; Nutting 1967). There are also some wars which could easily have been avoided, but were brought about because of some extraordinary ineptness on the part of some key decision-makers—the Falkland/Malvinas War, for example, in which the Argentinian government appears to have acted excessively thoughtlessly or recklessly. There are, therefore, also cases where *the actions* dominate. Whether, *in general*, the setting dominates more than the actions, or vice versa, is an idle question: the ratio varies.

The background, chance coincidences, mechanisms, and government actions thus combine in various ways to yield diverse origins of wars. But there are some family resemblances among them. Some background conditions may recur in various wars, as may some war-conducive mechanisms. Most importantly, there are only a limited number of things governments do to bring about a war. These are: (1) resistance; (2) acts with belligerent intent; (3) contributory negligence; (4) insensitive acts; (5) thoughtless acts; and (6) reckless acts. It is when these labels are used to characterize key government actions that family resemblances emerge most vividly among diverse origins of wars.

It is worth emphasizing here that these categories of government actions have not been invented artificially for the sake of forcing similarities to emerge from what are after all very diverse origins of wars. These are in fact the categories which are conventionally used by anyone who tries to give an account of government interactions leading to war. To do this, one must answer a number of key questions about government actions, and such questions are formulated in the light of those categories.

For example: 'What motivated a country to resist the invader when other countries in similar circumstances did not?'; 'Was the invasion premeditated?'; 'Was the decision to invade made in genuine desperation, or were clear alternatives available to the invader to attain its aims?'; 'To what extent did the invaded country fail to deter the invasion through its lack of preparedness?'; 'Had the invaded country acted offensively by committing any insensitive or thoughtless acts towards the invader?'; 'What were the invader's calculations concerning intervention by a third party, and, in particular, did it act entirely thoughtlessly on this issue, or did it gamble on the third party's inaction?'; 'If it did gamble, was it a reasonable thing to do in the circumstances, or was it excessively irresponsible?'; and so on.

Plainly, these questions are formulated in the light of the six types of government actions noted above, and these are the sorts of questions one quite naturally asks in trying to understand the origins of any war. Of course, in dealing with these questions, many others will have to be answered, and some of them will concern background conditions, mechanistic processes, and chance coincidences. It does seem, however, that understanding war origins *requires* us to answer questions of the type enumerated, and thus to think in terms of the categories listed, whether we like it or not. In any case, it is difficult to imagine how stories of war origins could be told, and war origins understood, without them.

Interestingly, a parallel case cannot be made with respect to background conditions, war-conducive mechanisms, or chance coincidences. This point deserves a brief discussion.

As far as background conditions and war-conducive mechanisms are concerned, it is of course possible to subdivide them, and their subdivisions are often accorded some standard labels. For example, P. M. H. Bell (1986) divides 'the underlying forces' of the Second World War in Europe into 'ideological', 'economic', and 'strategic' factors. Waltz's tripartite scheme may also be used in sorting out background and mechanistic factors. We noted in Chapter 1 that Waltz's scheme reflects a conventional view of modern world political order.

However, such classificatory schemes, well accepted though they may be, are not *integral* to our understanding of background conditions or war-conducive mechanisms in the way in which the sixfold scheme of classifying government actions appears to be to our effort to make sense of them in the course of explaining war origins. In short, background and mechanistic factors can be subdivided, labelled, and schematically presented, as they often are, but no particular scheme of classification concerning such factors is indispensable to our understanding of them.

As far as chance coincidences are concerned, no classificatory scheme is easily identifiable which is conventional, standard, or appropriate. This is probably because chance coincidences, so long as they are accepted as such, do not even require us to make sense of them. The fact that two events occurred simultaneously by chance becomes incorporated into our story without requiring us to understand *what sort of fact* that was. Indeed, the question does not appear to make much sense.

The situation is manifestly different with respect to government actions. Here we need to understand *what sort of act* was committed by a relevant government in order to be able to incorporate it, as a key element, into our story. And, in answering this question, it appears, we make use of the six categories, indispensably.

CONCLUSION

The question of what happened leads as fluently in historical investigation as in law, to the question of who did it. And in both arenas questions of causation are embedded in questions of responsibility, of what is responsible for the event. Such responsibility is not restricted in any way to human beings as such. Nations, churches, classes, ideologies can all partake in the problem of assigning responsibility for an event. But by handling the issue of causation in this way, as an issue of responsibility, what is entailed is that causality is conceived as the action of agents, as if events are precipitated by agents.

(Cousins 1987: 133–4)

WE began our enquiry by examining in Chapter 1 two major contributions to the study of how to reason about the causes of war: *Man, the State and War* by Waltz, and *Why War?* by Nelson and Olin. The two works, it was noted, share one serious shortcoming: neither of them pays sufficient attention to the important fact that, under the rubric of the causes of war, a number of distinct questions arise. In particular, it was argued, the following three types must be clearly distinguished as a preliminary move in any discussion of the causes of war: (*a*) 'What are the conditions which must be present for wars to occur?'; (*b*) 'Under what sorts of circumstances have wars occurred more frequently?'; and (*c*) 'How did this particular war come about?'

It was argued that separating these questions is a more fundamental move to make in clarifying how to reason about the causes of war than is identifying the three levels of analysis as was done, famously, by Waltz. It was also shown that, in analysing different ideas about the causes of war, a classification of suggested answers in terms of the types of question they aim at is more fundamental than the classification of the same in the light of their ideological underpinnings, as was undertaken by Nelson and Olin. A detailed analysis in Chapter 1 revealed furthermore that the failure on the part of Waltz, as well as Nelson and Olin, to separate questions (*a*), (*b*), and (*c*) clearly and consistently in their reasoning is partly responsible for leading them into advancing their respective causal theories of war, which are in turn defective.

Waltz's theory of war holds that 'international anarchy' is the permissive and underlying cause of war, accounting for the possibility and recurrence of war; that the immediate causes of particular wars are found in the levels of 'man' and 'the state'; but that in some cases these immediate causes are in turn derived from 'international anarchy'. Nelson and Olin, by contrast, subscribe to a version of the diversionary theory of war: a society suffers economic depression, or a noticeable disparity of wealth develops among its citizens; frustration deepens on the part of the relatively deprived class, which seeks reform; but this is resisted by the conservative force within; this upsets domestic stability, and the conservative force, anxious to maintain its position, attempts to unite the nation by resorting to an aggressive foreign policy, which results in war.

Of the two theories—one a third-image theory in Waltz's own terminology, and the other a second-image one—the weakness of the latter is more readily noticeable. One only needs to ask: which particular instance(s) of war does this scenario explain? And further: given that not all wars come about in the way suggested, how frequently do they do so? The major weakness of Nelson and Olin, in other words, is that they do not give sufficient weight to the fact that wars come about in different ways, and fail thereby to specify the range of wars which they expect their favoured theory to encompass. They would have avoided this error if they had taken seriously the distinction among questions (*a*), (*b*), and (*c*). They would have realized that their model of war origins did not provide an answer to question (*a*) or even question (*b*), although it might explain some particular instances of war; and this would in turn have led them to take seriously the idea that other models would be needed to account for other kinds of war.

Waltz, too, fails to pay sufficient attention to the fact that wars come about in different ways. This is one major inadequacy of Waltz's work, which we tried to remedy in Chapter 5. But, more fundamentally, we revealed in Chapters 1 and 2 that Waltz's main thesis itself—in particular, his central contention that 'international anarchy' is the permissive and underlying cause of war, accounting for the possibility and recurrence of war—cannot be accepted without certain serious amendments and qualifications.

To begin with, 'international anarchy' can only be *a*—rather than *the*—permissive cause (or necessary condition) of war, and it is so only if the term is understood to mean 'the absence from the international system of a *perfectly* effective anti-war device'. However, 'international anarchy' in this sense accounts for the possibility of war in a trivial manner: war would be impossible in the presence of a perfectly effective anti-war device anywhere. That is what 'a perfectly effective anti-war device' *means*. Furthermore, since such a device cannot possibly exist in the international system, it is difficult to think what point there is in making a reference to its absence as one of the necessary conditions of war: what cannot in principle be present cannot very meaningfully be said to be absent. Indeed, 'the absence from the international system of a perfectly effective anti-war device' can hardly be an appropriate definition of 'international anarchy', nor even a meaningful *structural* characterization of the international environment: such a device cannot be part of any *social* structure.

To be sure, Waltz himself equates 'anarchy' with 'decentralization' (1979: 88; 1989: 42). This is sensible. But then, this definition is insufficient to render 'international anarchy' a *necessary* condition of war. Waltz's thesis that international anarchy is a permissive cause of war therefore collapses in the face of a dilemma: either it is trivial, or it is untrue.

Admittedly, 'international anarchy' in the sense of 'the relatively decentralized institutional structure of the international system' *may partly* account for *some* aspects of disorder which are present to *some* degree in the international environment. Similarly, 'international anarchy' in the sense of 'a continuously tense and unstable international situation where war is effectively part of states' everyday expectations' *may be an* underlying cause of *some* wars. But it does not follow from either of these correct propositions that 'international anarchy' in either sense—let alone, any other— is *the* underlying cause of *all* wars. Another important reminder is that 'international anarchy' is at best a *necessary* condition of war. In whatever sense, it is not a *sufficient* condition of it. It does not make war *inevitable*.

In Chapter 2, which focused on question (*a*), those conditions whose necessity for the possibility of war is knowable through the analysis of the meanings of relevant words were provisionally separated from 'scientifically necessary conditions' of war, and

were termed 'logically necessary conditions' or 'logical prerequisites' of war. At the level of human beings, their 'discriminatory
sociability' and their ability to kill their own kind were counted as
among such conditions. At the level of societies, another logical
prerequisite was identified: sufficient prevalence of the belief among
a number of societies, in particular the states, that there are circumstances under which it is their function to resort to arms
against one another, and in so doing to demand the cooperation
of society members. It was also shown that 'international anarchy', in whatever sense, does not have causal priority over these
logical prerequisites of war at the human and societal levels of
analysis. Thus the view that 'international anarchy' constitutes the
most fundamental cause of war was shown, on this ground also,
to be unsatisfactory.

None of the theses identified in Chapter 2 pointing to logical
prerequisites of war, we found, could be, or could usefully be,
superseded by scientific reformulations. Moreover, occasional claims
to have identified scientifically necessary conditions of war, such
as those of Rummel and Bueno de Mesquita, turned out, upon
closer examination, not to be sufficiently well founded. There is,
it was noted, a reasonably clear agreement as to what the term
'war' means, and therefore it is relatively easy to formulate some
of war's logical prerequisites. However, actual instances of war
appear varied, and a single scientific theory pointing to a necessary
condition of all instances of war is unlikely to be found. War is
a multi-causal phenomenon not only in the oft-noted sense that a
variety of factors contribute to the making of a war, but also in
the less obvious sense that there are multifarious causal paths to
the outbreak of war.

But this has not deterred statistically minded researchers from
asking questions of type (*b*) regarding the correlates of war. Curiously, even though Waltz is explicitly concerned with the phenomenon of the *recurrence* of war, he has paid little attention to
statistical works on war. Of course, in the 1950s, when *Man, the
State and War* appeared, such works were relatively scarce. But
the latter part of the twentieth century saw a phenomenal increase
in the number of correlational studies concerning war. Chapter 3
was written partly in acknowledgement of this fact.

There we identified three key situations which have arisen in
statistical investigations into the correlates of war: (1) where the

researchers suspect a causal link between a given type of condition and the occurrence of war, but where no concomitant variation is clearly seen between the variables examined; (2) where, on the basis of a very strong association found over a long period between a given type of condition and the occurrence of war, the former is said to be at least a valuable early warning indicator of war, if not necessarily a cause of it; and (3) where a number of researchers have uncovered an exceptionally regular pattern on a war/peace issue, and where in addition they offer a plausible causal theory to explain it. These three situations were discussed, respectively, with reference to Rummel's classic work on national attributes and foreign conflict behaviour, Wallace's claim that a runaway arms race provides at least a valuable early warning indicator of the escalation of serious disputes into war, and a consensus among the leading scholars that constitutionally secure liberal states have hardly ever gone to war with one another.

The upshot of that chapter, however, was to stress the importance of familiarity with causal processes in various historical situations ending in war, or no war, as the case may be. This, it was argued, will assist researchers in hypothesis formulation by alerting them to potentially relevant contextual variables. Rummel's consistently negative statistical findings were likely to be due to the operation of those variables which were not included in his hypotheses. Notwithstanding the absence of a strong statistical correlation between national attributes and foreign conflict behaviour, there clearly are circumstances in which certain national attributes of a country or countries play an important causal role in bringing about a war. Such circumstances, however, are likely to be complex and varied.

One of the main functions of a correlational study of war is thought to lie in uncovering early warning indicators of war which may be used in predicting and controlling the development of events. However, the usefulness of any identified correlate of war as an early warning indicator must be judged case by case. In this context also, familiarity with causal processes in various historical cases will be helpful. In the particular case of Wallace's study, the value of a runaway arms race as war's early warning indicator was called into question on a number of grounds. It was also pointed out that the *scientific* concept of 'an early warning indicator' is not a purely correlational idea, but operates within the realm of causal notions.

Finally, even such a highly regular conjunction as has been found between dyadic liberalism and peace is very unlikely to be a uniform reflection of a single causal process. A historical enquiry is needed to reveal which, and how many significant, confirming instances of this regularity are plausibly explained by any particular causal scenario.

Realizing the importance of acquainting ourselves with causal processes in actual historical situations, our next move was to deal with the causes of particular wars. But first we needed to know what was required of us if we wished to answer a question of the type 'what caused this particular war?' Does this question perhaps force us to return to a correlational question? Is the popular view correct that correlation is not causation, but nevertheless a necessary condition of it? In Chapter 4, therefore, we analysed the concept of causation itself. This was a necessary philosophical interlude, for among the researchers on the causes of war there is much empiricism, but very little respect for conceptual disputation; much interest in wars, but very little concern for causation as such.

In the course of the discussion, the regularity theory of the meaning of singular causal statements, to which Hempel subscribes, was shown to be implausible, and his covering-law model of explanation was rejected. To explain a particular outbreak of war, therefore, we need not search for a regular sequence of events ending in war or any of its subtypes. As was stated, the idiographic does not presuppose the nomothetic. The analysis of a singular causal statement in terms of the idea that, without 'the cause', 'the effect' would not have occurred appeared more promising than did the regularity theory, but was in turn rejected in favour of the idea that a cause is an *explanatory* factor.

To explain the occurrence of an event, it was suggested, is to render its occurrence more intelligible than before by showing the sequence of relevant events, leading to the event in question, in such a way that a specific puzzle or puzzles we have about the occurrence of the event can be solved. In short, to explain the occurrence of an event is to narrate its origins, and the sequence of events narrated so as to explain its origins constitutes the cause of the event—although, of course, *'the* cause of the event' may also be taken to mean the most important feature, from some particular viewpoint, of the narrated sequence of events.

To answer the question 'what caused this war?', according to our reasoning, either requires, or is equivalent to, answering the question 'how did this particular war come about?' This is our question (*c*). In answering this form of question, an intelligibly structured narrative must be presented. Constituent units of such narratives were identified, which we found to fall into the following four categories: backgrounds, chance coincidences, mechanisms, and human actions.

These building blocks, however, do not by themselves explain the occurrence of any war; they function as ingredients of an explanation when they are put together to form an organic whole. In this connection it was observed in Chapter 4 that it is possible to see what, according to a historian, caused a given war when we grasp the argument of a story he or she tells. If so, it seemed to follow that as historians we can say what caused a given war when we come to realize what the argument must be which structures the story we are to tell about the origins of the war. The historian of war origins 'must in an act of judgement hold together in thought events which no one could experience together' (Mink 1964: 44).

Chapter 5 amplified and gave some substance to the key claims made in Chapter 4. Background conditions of various sorts identified in a number of historical works were contrasted, and the role of chance coincidences was discussed with reference to A. J. P. Taylor's account of the origins of the First World War. Using the Sarajevo incident as an example of 'precipitant', as opposed to 'preconditions', the view that the background conditions were more important than the Archduke's assassination as a cause of the First World War was shown to reflect the holder's interest in prescribing for future peace.

In Chapter 5, the essence of 'mechanism' was said to lie in its narrative character, and a large variety of war-conducive mechanisms were noted, operating in the organizational, psychological, and other spheres of human activity. Finally, government actions were said to be the key constituent of the story of war origins, and were analysed in the light of the six categories: (1) resistance; (2) acts with belligerent intent; (3) contributory negligence; (4) insensitive acts; (5) thoughtless acts; and (6) reckless acts. Each of these was illustrated with examples found in leading historical works on war origins.

The more ambitious goal of that final chapter was to advance a theory of war origins. This theory does not explain why war occurs by any simple formula. In fact it rejects such an approach because it recognizes war to be a multi-causal phenomenon in both senses of the term noted earlier: the theory acknowledges not only that many factors contribute to the making of a war, but also that there are many causal paths to war. The theory presented is therefore consonant with historians' usual claim that every war has its own unique cause. But, instead of issuing an injunction to the effect that 'the only investigation of the causes of war that is intellectually respectable is that of the unique origins . . . of the *particular* past wars' (Seabury and Codevilla 1989: 50; emphasis in original), the theory points to family resemblances amongst war origins, and locates the main source of such similarities in the way in which war origins are constructed by historians and others.

It will be recalled that, according to Waltz, the origins of wars may be quite diverse in terms of their immediate causes, which, in his view, comprise acts of relevant individuals and states, but that they are similar in terms of their underlying cause, which, he insists, is 'international anarchy'. The theory of war origins, advanced here, holds a markedly different view: that war origins are quite diverse especially with respect to their backgrounds, the operation of war-conducive mechanisms, and the influence of chance coincidences; and that the first two of these three items are often considered as the underlying causes of war; that there are, however, some family resemblances amongst war origins; and that these are due chiefly to the limited number of ways in which relevant governments can be said to have acted in making their key moves in the partially overlapping processes resulting in the outbreaks of war.

Several steps were taken in this volume to reach this conclusion, and many problems remain still to be considered. Of the various assertions made in the foregoing discussion, the following two are particularly important, and require further attention:

(1) that we can say what caused a given war when we come to realize what the argument must be which structures the story we are to tell about the origins of the war; and

(2) that in showing the origins of any particular war we cannot but pay attention to what relevant governments did or failed to do; but that in order to incorporate any key government

action into our story, we need to understand what sort of act it was; and that in answering this question, we unavoidably make use of the six categories of government actions, listed earlier.

Many questions may be raised with respect to these two assertions. Here we may very briefly deal with the following two. Concerning (1), we may wonder: how are we to know whether what we have come to 'realize' as a good argument is in fact a good one? In response to (2), we may ask: what is the function of story-telling concerning war origins which apparently takes place within a certain delimited boundary, especially with respect to the ways in which government actions are depicted? These are in fact part of larger questions concerning the nature and function of historical representation, and these in turn are central issues in the theory of history, to which a separate volume must be dedicated. What follows is a very tentative treatment of the two specific questions.

Concerning the first, the following observation by Kenneth Stampp on the causes of the American Civil War is noteworthy:

As one reflects upon the problem of causation it becomes perfectly evident that historians will never know, objectively and with mathematical precision, what caused the Civil War. Working with fragmentary evidence, possessing less than a perfect understanding of human behavior, and finding it impossible to isolate one historical factor to test its significance apart from all others, historians must necessarily be somewhat tentative and diffident in drawing their conclusions'. (1965: 3-4)

Indeed, working with evidence, which is not only fragmentary but also often susceptible of different interpretations, possessing far less than a perfect understanding of the workings of war-conducive mechanisms, and finding it impossible to assess objectively the relative significance of different causal factors, those who investigate the origins of wars cannot but be tentative when they come to realize what the argument must be. The most they can endeavour to arrive at is an intersubjective consensus, among professional historians and their readers, that their story is more persuasive—or at least no less so—than the pre-existing ones concerning the same war. Its persuasiveness may in turn be judged in the light, among other things, of breadth and judiciousness in its use of available evidence, and, more broadly, its coherence with

other well-accepted facts and stories about the world. As Walsh
has observed:

The problem of arriving at truth about the past thus becomes the problem
of whether, on the basis of such evidence as we can now command,
historical thought can arrive at a convincing account of what occurred.
But if that is so, historical facts are not so much discovered as arrived at
by processes of argument, and the question of whether we can accept
something as fact is the question of whether we can fit it in with the other
conclusions to which we have already committed ourselves, or without
disturbing those conclusions to an undue extent. (1977: 54)

The best we can do by way of identifying the origins of any
given war, then, is to construct a coherent and convincing narrative on the basis of available evidence and knowledge we have of
the world. Does this mean that we can never know what *really*
caused a given war? Surely, it may be said, it is the historian's task
to reconstruct the past 'as it actually was'—as the German historian Leopold von Ranke put it long ago (cited from Stern 1973:
16; see further Hexter 1967: 4–5; Ranke 1973: 137; Stanford
1986: 78).

Clearly, however, any claim to know what *really* caused a given
war is simply a claim to *know* what caused that war: nothing is
added by the adjective 'really'. And any claim to know what caused
the war (either in the sense of the sequence of events leading to the
war or in the sense of the most important feature of that sequence)
is liable to challenge by an equally good claim pointing to a different cause, and supersession by a better claim when one has
been found. There is no way of validating once and for all any
given answer to the question, 'What caused this war?'

Given this, what is the function of story-telling concerning war
origins which apparently takes place within a certain delimited
boundary especially with respect to the ways in which key government actions are depicted? This is the second question. In this
connection, we may recall A. J. P. Taylor's remark, cited earlier,
that '[h]istory is fun to write and . . . fun to read' (1977c: 17). But
there appears to be more to history than this, and historians of
war origins, in particular, fulfil an important social function,
whether they intend it or not.

Most obviously, they remind us of the magnitude of our potential folly and wickedness. We act recklessly, thoughtlessly, insensitively, and even aggressively—sometimes out of desperation, but

at other times quite gratuitously. Contributory negligence is another mistake we are liable to make in the process culminating in war. Historians of war origins also remind us that war is at least partly a human-made thing—for even though it might be true that almost anything could eventually lead to war, nothing would do so until 'acts with belligerent intent' have been committed, and responded to with 'resistance'.

Reminded of these things, we are encouraged to consider what could have been done, and ought to have been done, or not done, at various key junctures in the unfolding of events leading to outbreaks of war (Joll 1979). Historians are, therefore, capable of encouraging us to keep 'war' within the domain of normative discourse. Of course, a nationalistic historian might inevitably write a one-sided defence of his or her own country. Such a history, however, can be challenged and superseded by other historical interpretations. Historical works as a whole, therefore, are capable of making us realize the possibility that *our* country may have done wrong.

According to Hans Kelsen, 'the Greek word for cause, *aitia*, originally meant guilt: the cause is "guilty" of the effect, is responsible for the effect' (1967: 84; see also Collingwood 1940: esp. 291). An important part of enquiring into the causes of wars, then, is to keep alive the sense of responsibility towards what we can become guilty of—not because it is right to dwell on past mistakes and misdeeds, but because it is in our capacity to do better.

All this, it may be objected, is to overestimate the degree of freedom national leaders enjoy in performing their function. Often, it may be said, their freedom of action is so circumscribed that they cannot reasonably be expected to have acted in any significantly different way. They do not choose to go to war, but rather the choice is imposed upon them by the nature of the system they work in.

But this line of thinking in turn exaggerates the strength *and* uniformity with which the system, international and domestic, curtails national leaders' freedom of action. International anarchy makes no war inevitable. And between some states war is ruled out as an instrument of foreign policy in much the same way as genocide is ruled out as a means of governance in most countries. This shows that a war-conducive system cannot itself be a permanent fixture of the human social environment.

In explaining some wars much emphasis, of course, may be placed on the nature of the particular system within which the leaders had to work, but such an explanation in turn points to the need to transform the system itself. This is to keep 'social institutions' within the domain of normative discourse. Enquiry into the causes of war, then, is inseparable from our ethical concern.

REFERENCES

ALBERTINI, L. (1952–7), *The Origins of the War of 1914*, 3 vols. trans. and ed. I. M. Massey (London. Oxford University Press).

ALTFELD, M. F. (1983), 'Arms Races?—and Escalation? A Comment on Wallace', *International Studies Quarterly*, 7: 225–31.

ANKERSMIT, F. R. (1986), 'The Dilemmas of Contemporary Anglo-Saxon Philosophy of History', *History and Theory*, 25: 1–27.

AQUARIUS (pseudonym) (1945), 'Causation and Legal Responsibility', *South African Law Journal*, 62: 126–45.

ASADA, S. (1993), *Ryotaisenkan no nichibei kankei: kaigun to seisaku-ketteikatei (Japanese–American Relations between the Wars: Naval Policy and the Decision-making Process)* (Tokyo: University of Tokyo Press).

ASTER, S. (1989), '"Guilty Men": The Case of Neville Chamberlain', in Boyce and Robertson (1989), 233–68.

ATKINSON, R. L., ATKINSON, R. C., SMITH, E. E., and HILGARD, E. R. (1987), *Introduction to Psychology*, 9th edn. (New York: Harcourt Brace Jovanovich).

ATTRIDGE, D., BENNINGTON, G., and YOUNG, R. (1987), *Post-Structuralism and the Question of History* (Cambridge: Cambridge University Press).

AXELROD, R. (1990), *The Evolution of Co-operation*, with foreword by Richard Dawkins (Harmondsworth: Penguin Books).

BABST, D. V. (1972), 'A Force for Peace', *Industrial Research*, Apr.: 55–8.

BARNDS, W. J. (1972), *India, Pakistan, and the Great Powers* (New York: Praeger).

BARTHES, R. (1966), 'Introduction to the Structural Analysis of Narratives', in Sontag (1983), 251–95.

BATESON, P. (1989), 'Is Aggression Instinctive?' in Groebel and Hinde (1989), 35–47.

BEINER, R., and BOOTH, W. J. (1993) (eds.), *Kant and Political Philosophy: The Contemporary Legacy* (London: Yale University Press).

BELL, P. M. H. (1986), *The Origins of the Second World War in Europe* (London: Longman).

BENTON, T. (1977), *Philosophical Foundations of the Three Sociologies* (London: Routledge).

BERGHAHN, V. R. (1973), *Germany and the Approach of War in 1914* (London: Macmillan).

BERTRAND, C. L. (1977) (ed.), *Revolutionary Situations in Europe 1917–1922: Germany, Italy, Austria–Hungary* (Montreal: Interuniversity Centre for European Studies).

BERNSTEIN, R. J. (1983), *Beyond Objectivism and Relativism: Science, Hermeneutics, and Praxis* (Oxford: Blackwell).

BLAINEY, G. (1988), *The Causes of War*, 3rd edn. (London: Macmillan).

BLANNING, T. C. W. (1986), *The Origins of the French Revolutionary Wars* (London: Longman).

BLINKENBERG, L. (1972), *India–Pakistan: The History of Unresolved Conflicts* (Copenhagen: Munksgaard/Danish Institute of International Studies).

BLUNTSCHLI, C. J. (1879–81), *Gesammelte kleine Schriften*, 2 vols. (Nordingen: Beck).

BOOTH, K., and SMITH, S. (1995) (eds.), *International Relations Theory Today* (Cambridge: Polity).

BOYCE, R., and ROBERTSON, E. M. (1989) (eds.), *Paths to War: New Essays on the Origins of the Second World War* (London: Macmillan).

BRAND, M. (1976) (ed.), *The Nature of Causation* (Urbana: University of Illinois Press).

BRINES, R. (1968), *The Indo-Pakistani Conflict* (London: Pall Mall).

BUENO DE MESQUITA, B. (1978), 'Systemic Polarization and the Occurrence and Duration of war', *Journal of Conflict Resolution*, 22: 241–67.

—— (1981), *The War Trap* (New Haven: Yale University Press).

—— (1984a), 'Theory and the Advancement of Knowledge about War: a Reply' *Review of International Studies*, 10: 65–75.

—— (1984b), 'A Critique of "a Critique of The War Trap"'. *Journal of Conflict Resolution*, 28: 341–360.

—— (1985), 'The War Trap Revisited: A Revised Expected Utility Model', *American Political Science Review*, 79: 156–77.

—— (1987), 'Conceptualizing War: A Reply', *Journal of Conflict Resolution*, 31: 370–82.

—— (1989), 'The Contribution of Expected Utility Theory to the Study of International Conflict', in Rotberg and Rabb (1989), 53–76.

—— and LALMAN, D. (1992), *War and Reason: Domestic and International Imperatives* (New Haven: Yale University Press).

BULL, H. (1966), 'Society and Anarchy in International Relations', in Butterfield and Wight (1966), 34–50.

—— (1977), *The Anarchical Society: A Study of Order in World Politics* (London: Macmillan).

BULLOCK, A. (1962), *Hitler: A Study in Tyranny* (Harmondsworth: Penguin Books).

—— (1971), 'Hitler and the Origins of the Second World War', in Robertson (1971), 189–224.

BUTTERFIELD, H., and WIGHT, M. (1966) (eds.), *Diplomatic Investigations: Essays in the Theory of International Politics* (London: George Allen & Unwin).

BUZAN, B. (1991), *People, States and Fear: An Agenda for International Security Studies in the Post-Cold War Era.* 2nd edn. (Hemel Hempstead: Harvester Wheatsheaf).

—— (1993), 'From International System to International Society: Structural Realism and Regime Theory Meet the English School', *International Organization*, 47: 327–52.

—— (1995), 'The Levels of Analysis Problem in International Relations Reconsidered', in Booth and Smith (1995), 198–216.

—— JONES, C., and LITTLE, R. (1993), *The Logic of Anarchy: Neorealism to Structural Realism* (New York: Columbia University Press).

CARR, E. H. (1964), *What is History?* (Harmondsworth: Penguin Books).

CARROLL, B. A., and FINK, C. F. (1975), 'Theories of War Causation: A Matrix for Analysis', in Nettleship, Dalegivens, and Nettleship (1975), 55–71.

CEADEL, M. (1987), *Thinking about Peace and War* (Oxford: Oxford University Press).

CHALMERS, A. F. (1982), *What Is This Thing Called Science? An Assessment of the Nature and Status of Science and its Methods*, 2nd edn. (Milton Keynes: The Open University Press).

CHAN, S. (1984), 'Mirror, Mirror on the Wall . . . Are the Freer Countries More Pacific?', *Journal of Conflict Resolution*, 28: 617–48.

CHARLTON, M. (1989), *The Little Platoon: Diplomacy and the Falklands Dispute* (Oxford: Blackwell).

COHEN, R. (1994), 'Pacific Unions: A Reappraisal of the Theory that "Democracies Do Not Go to War with Each Other"', *Review of International Studies*, 20–3: 207–23.

COLLINGWOOD, R. G. (1938), 'On the So-Called Idea of Causation', *Proceedings of the Aristotelian Society*, new series, 38: 85–112.

—— (1940), *An Essay on Metaphysics* (Oxford: Clarendon Press).

—— (1961), *The Idea of History* (Oxford: Oxford University Press).

COSGROVE, C. A., and TWITCHETT, K. J. (1970) (eds.), *The New International Actors: The UN and the EEC* (London: Macmillan).

COUSINS, M. (1987), 'The Practice of Historical Investigation', in Attridge, Bennington, and Young (1987), 126–36.

DANCHEV, A. (1991), 'Life and Death in the South Atlantic', *Review of International Studies*, 17: 305–12.

—— (1994), 'The Anschluss', *Review of International Studies*, 20: 97–106.

DANTO, A. C. (1965), *Analytical Philosophy of History* (Cambridge: Cambridge University Press).

DAVIDSON, D. (1980a), *Essays on Actions and Events* (Oxford: Clarendon Press).

—— (1980b), 'Actions, Reasons, and Causes', in Davidson (1980a), 3–19.

—— (1980c), 'Causal Relations', in Davidson (1980a), 149–62.

DENNEN, J. M. G. VAN DER (1987), 'Ethnocentrism and In-group/Out-group Differentiation: A Review and Interpretation of the Literature', in Reynolds, Falger, and Vine (1987), 1–47.

DESSLER, D. (1989), 'What's at Stake in the Agent–Structure Debate?' *International Organization*, 43: 441–73.

—— (1991), 'Beyond Correlations: Toward a Causal Theory of War', *International Studies Quarterly*, 35: 337–55.

DEUTSCH, K. W. *et al.* (1957), *Political Community and the North Atlantic Area* (Princeton: Princeton University Press).

DIEHL, P. F. (1983), 'Arms Races and Escalation: A Closer Look', *Journal of Peace Research*, 20: 205–12.

—— (1992), 'What Are They Fighting For? The Importance of Issues in International Conflict Research', *Journal of Peace Research* 29: 333–44.

—— and KINGSTON, J. (1987), 'Messenger or Message? Military Buildups and the Initiation of Conflict', *Journal of Politics*, 49: 801–13.

DOCKRILL, S. (1992), 'Hirohito, the Emperor's Army and Pearl Harbor', *Review of International Studies*, 18: 319–33.

DONAGAN, A. (1964), 'Historical Explanation: The Popper–Hempel Theory Reconsidered', *History and Theory*, 4: 3–26.

DOYLE, M. W. (1983), 'Kant, Liberal Legacies, and Foreign Affairs', *Philosophy and Public Affairs*, 12: 205–34, 323–52.

—— (1986), 'Liberalism and World Politics', *American Political Science Review*, 80: 1151–69.

—— (1993), 'Liberalism and International Relations', in Beiner and Booth (1993), 173–203.

DRAY, W. H. (1957), *Laws and Explanation in History* (Oxford: Clarendon Press).

—— (1960), 'Some Causal Accounts of the American Civil War', *Daedalus*, 91: 578–92.

—— (1964), *Philosophy of History* (Englewood Cliffs, NJ: Prentice-Hall).

—— (1966) (ed.), *Philosophical Analysis and History* (New York: Harper and Row).

—— (1971), 'On the Nature and Role of Narrative in Historiography', *History and Theory*, 10: 153–71.

—— (1978), 'Concepts of Causation in A. J. P. Taylor's Account of the Origins of the Second World War', *History and Theory*, 17: 149–74.

—— (1980a), *Perspectives on History* (London: Routledge & Kegan Paul).

—— (1980b), 'A Controversy over Causes: A. J. P. Taylor and the Origins of the Second World War', in Dray (1980a), 69–96.

DUCASSE, C. J. (1975), 'On the Nature and the Observability of the Causal Relation', in Sosa (1975), 114–25.

ENLOE, C. (1983), *Does Khaki Become You? The Militarisation of Women's Lives* (London: Pluto).

——(1985), 'Bananas, Bases, and Patriarchy: Some Feminist Questions about the Militarization of Central America', *Radical America*, 19/4: 7–23.

EWER, R. F. (1968), *Ethology of Mammals* (London: Logos Press).

FARRAR, Jr., L. L. (1972), 'The Limits of Choice: July 1914 Reconsidered', *Journal of Conflict Resolution*, 16: 1–23.

FAY, S. B. (1930), *The Origins of the World War*, 2nd edn. (New York: Macmillan).

FISCHER, F. (1967), *Germany's Aims in the First World War*, with introd. by James Joll (London: Chatto & Windus).

——(1975), *War of Illusions: German Policies from 1911 to 1914*, with foreword by Sir Alan Bullock, trans. Marian Jackson (London: Chatto & Windus).

——(1988), 'The Miscalculation of English Neutrality: An Aspect of German Foreign Policy on the Eve of World War I', in Wank *et al.* (1988), 369–93.

FRANKS, LORD, *et al.* (1992), *The Franks Report: Falkland Islands Review*, with a new introd. by Alex Danchev (London: Pimlico).

FREEDMAN, L., and GAMBA-STONEHOUSE, V. (1990), *Signals of War: the Falklands Conflict of 1982* (London: Faber & Faber).

——and KARSH, E. (1993), *The Gulf Conflict 1990–1991: Diplomacy and War in the New World Order* (Princeton: Princeton University Press).

GALLIE, W. B. (1963), 'The Historical Understanding', *History and Theory*, 3: 149–202.

GALTUNG, J. (1967), *Theory and Methods of Social Research* (London: Allen & Unwin).

GARDINER, P. (1959) (ed.), *Theories of History* (London: Collier Macmillan).

GARNHAM, D. (1986), 'War-Proneness, War-Weariness, and Regime Type: 1816–1980', *Journal of Peace Research*, 23: 279–89.

GASKING, D. (1955), 'Causation and Recipes', *Mind*, 64: 479–87.

GEORGE, A. L. (1991) (ed.), *Avoiding War: Problems of Crisis Management* (Boulder, Colo.: Westview).

GLAD, B. (1990) (ed.), *Psychological Dimensions of War* (London: Sage).

GOCHMAN, C. S., and SABROSKY, A. N. (1990) (eds.), *Prisoners of War? Nation-States in the Modern Era* (Lexington, Mass.: D. C. Heath).

GOLDSTEIN, J. H. (1989), 'Beliefs about Human Aggression', in Groebel and Hinde (1989), 10–19.

GORDON, M. R. (1974), 'Domestic Conflict and the Origins of the First World War: the British and the German Cases', *Journal of Modern History*, 46: 191–226.

GROEBEL, J., and HINDE, R. H. (1989) (eds.), *Aggression and War: their Biological and Social Bases* (Cambridge: Cambridge University Press).

GRUNER, R. (1969), 'Mandelbaum on Historical Narrative: a Discussion', *History and Theory*, 8: 283–7.

GURR, T. R. (1980) (ed.), *Handbook of Political Conflict* (New York: Free Press).

HAAS, M. (1974), *International Conflict* (Indianapolis: Bobbs-Merrill).

HAMMOND, M. (1977), 'Weighting Causes in Historical Explanation', *Theoria: A Swedish Journal of Philosophy*, 43: 103–28.

HANSON, N. R. (1958), *Patterns of Discovery: An Inquiry into the Conceptual Foundations of Science* (Cambridge: Cambridge University Press).

HARRÉ, R. (1964), 'Concepts and Criteria', *Mind*, 73: 353–63.

—— (1972), *The Philosophies of Science: an Introductory Survey* (London: Oxford University Press).

—— and E. H. MADDEN (1975), *Causal Powers: A Theory of Natural Necessity* (Oxford: Basil Blackwell).

HART, H. L. A. (1961), *The Concept of Law* (Oxford: Clarendon Press).

—— and HONORÉ, T. (1985), *Causation in the Law*, 2nd edn. (Oxford: Clarendon Press).

HASTRUP, K. (1992) (ed.), *Other Histories* (London: Routledge).

HAWTHORN, G. (1991), *Plausible Worlds: Possibility and Understanding in History and the Social Sciences* (Cambridge: Cambridge University Press).

HAZLEWOOD, L. (1975), 'Diversion Mechanisms and Encapsulation Processes: The Domestic Conflict–Foreign Conflict Hypotheses Reconsidered', in McGowan (1975), 213–44.

HEISENBERG, W. (1971), *Physics and Beyond: Encounters and Conversations*, trans. A. J. Pomerans (London: Allen & Unwin).

HELLER, A. (1982), *A Theory of History* (London: Routledge & Kegan Paul).

HEMPEL, C. G. (1965a), *Aspects of Scientific Explanation and Other Essays in the Philosophy of Science* (New York: Free Press).

—— (1965b), 'The Function of General Laws in History', in Hempel (1965a), 231–43.

—— (1965c), 'Aspects of Scientific Explanation', in Hempel (1965a), 331–496.

HERBERT, J. (1989), 'The Physiology of Aggression', in Groebel and Hinde (1989), 58–71.

HESSE, M. (1980a), *Revolutions and Reconstructions in the Philosophy of Science* (Brighton: Harvester Press).

—— (1980b), 'The Explanatory Function of Metaphor', in Hesse (1980a), 111–24.

HEXTER, J. H. (1967), 'The Rhetoric of History', *History and Theory*, 6: 3–13.

HINSLEY, F. H. (1977) (ed.), *British Foreign Policy under Sir Edward Grey* (Cambridge: Cambridge University Press).

HOBBES, T. (1651), *Leviathan*, ed. and abridged with introd. by J. Plamenatz (London: Collins, 1962).

—— (1655), *Elements of Philosophy*, ed. Sir William Molesworth (London: John Bohn, 1839).

HOFFMANN, S., KEOHANE, R. O., and MEARSHEIMER, J. J. (1990), 'Correspondence—Back to the Future, Part II: International Relations Theory and Post-Cold War Europe', *International Security*, 15: 191–9.

HOLLIS, M. (1994), *The Philosophy of Social Science* (Cambridge: Cambridge University Press).

—— and SMITH, S. (1990), *Explaining and Understanding International Relations* (Oxford: Clarendon Press).

HOLSTI, K. J. (1989), 'Ecological and Clausewitzian Approaches to the Study of War: Assessing the Possibilities', paper presented at the Annual Meetings of the International Studies Association/British International Studies Association, London, 28 Mar.–2 Apr.

—— (1991), *Peace and War: Armed Conflicts and International Order 1648–1989* (Cambridge: Cambridge University Press).

HOLSTI, O. R. (1990), 'Crisis Management', in Glad (1990), 116–42.

HOWARD, M. (1983*a*), *The Causes of Wars and Other Essays* (London: Temple Smith).

—— (1983*b*), 'The Causes of Wars', in Howard (1983*a*), 7–22.

HUGHES, J. L. (1989), 'The Origins of World War II in Europe: British Deterrence Failure and German Expansionism', in Rotberg and Rabb (1989), 281–321.

HUIZINGA, J. (1955), *The Waning of the Middle Ages: A Study of the Forms of Life, Thought, and Art in France and the Netherlands in the Fourteenth and Fifteen Centuries*, trans, F. Hopman (Harmondsworth: Penguin Books).

—— (1973), 'The Idea of History', in Stern (1973), 289–303.

HUME, D. (1777), *Enquiries Concerning the Human Understanding and Concerning the Principles of Morals by David Hume*, 2nd edn., repr. from the posthumous edn. of 1777 and ed. with introd., comparative tables of contents, and analytical index by L. A. Selby-Bigge (Oxford: Clarendon Press, 1962).

HUNTINGFORD, F. A. (1989), 'Animals Fight, but Do Not Make War', in Groebel and Hinde (1989), 25–34.

IRIYE, A. (1987), *The Origins of the Second World War in Asia and the Pacific* (London: Longman).

JAMES, A. M. (1964), 'Power Politics', *Political Studies*, 12: 307–26.

—— (1986), 'The Emerging Global Society', a review of *The Expansion of International Society*, ed. Hedley Bull and Adam Watson, *Third World Affairs* (1986), 465–8.

—— (1992), 'The Equality of States: Contemporary Manifestations of an Ancient Doctrine', *Review of International Studies*, 18: 377–91.

—— (1993*a*), 'Diplomacy', *Review of International Studies*, 19: 91–100.

—— (1993*b*), 'System or Society?', *Review of International Studies*, 19/3: 269–88.

JANIS, I. L. (1982), *Groupthink: Psychological Studies of Policy Decisions and Fiascoes*, 2nd edn. (Boston: Houghton Mifflin).

JARAUSCH, K. (1969), 'The Illusion of Limited War: Chancellor Bethmann Hollweg's Calculated Risk, July 1914', *Central European History*, 2: 48–76.

JERVIS, R. (1978), 'Cooperation under the Security Dilemma', *World Politics*, 30: 167–214.

—— (1989), 'War and Misperception', in Rotberg and Rabb (1989), 101–26.

—— (1990), 'The Political Effects of Nuclear Weapons: A Comment', in Lynn-Jones, Miller, and Van Evera (1990), 28–38.

JOLL, J. (1972), '1914: The Unspoken Assumptions', in Koch (1972), 307–28.

—— (1979), 'Politicians and the Freedom to Choose: The Case of July 1914', in Ryan (1979), 99–114.

—— (1984), *The Origins of the First World War* (London: Longman).

KAISER, D. E. (1983), 'Germany and the Origins of the First World War', *Journal of Modern History*, 55: 442–74.

KEAT, R., and URRY, J. (1975), *Social Theory as Science* (London: Routledge).

KELSEN, H. (1961), *General Theory of Law and State*, trans. A. Wedberg (New York: Russell & Russell).

—— (1967), *Pure Theory of Law*, trans. from the 2nd (rev. and enlarged) German edn. by Max Knight (Berkeley and Los Angeles: University of California Press).

KENNEDY, P. M. (1979) (ed.), *The War Plans of the Great Powers 1880–1914* (London: Unwin Hyman).

KENNEDY, R. F. (1969), *Thirteen Days: A Memoir of the Cuban Missile Crisis*, with introd. by Robert S. McNamara and Harold Macmillan (New York: Signet).

KEOHANE, R. O. (1986) (ed.), *Neorealism and its Critics* (New York: Columbia University Press).

—— (1989), *International Institutions and State Power: Essays in International Relations Theory* (Boulder, Colo.: Westview Press).

—— and NYE, Jr., J. S. (1987), 'Power and Interdependence Revisited', *International Organization*, 41: 725–53.

KHONG, Y. F. (1984*a*), 'War and International Theory: A Commentary on the State of the Art', *Review of International Studies*, 10: 41–63.

—— (1984*b*), 'A Rejoinder', *Review of International Studies*, 10: 77–8.

KIM, J. (1993), 'Explanatory Realism, Causal Realism, and Explanatory Exclusion', in Ruben (1993), 228–45.

KINGLAKE, A. W. (1877), *The Invasion of the Crimea: Its Origin, and an Account of its Progress Down to the Death of Lord Raglan*, 6th edn. (Edinburgh: Blackwood).

KNEALE, W. (1949), *Probability and Induction* (Oxford: Clarendon Press).

KOCH, H. W. (1971), 'Hitler and the Origins of the Second World War: Second Thoughts on the Status of Some of the Documents', in Robertson (1971), 158–88.

—— (1972) (ed.), *The Origins of the First World War: Great Power Rivalry and German War Aims* (London: Macmillan).

KRIEGER, L., and STERN, F. (1967) (eds.), *The Responsibility of Power: Historical Essays in Honor of Hajo Holborn* (New York: Doubleday).

KUPCHAN, C. A., and KUPCHAN, C. A. (1991), 'Concerts, Collective Security, and the Future of Europe', *International Security*, 16: 114–61.

LAKATOS, I. (1970), 'Falsification and the Methodology of Scientific Research Programmes', in Lakatos and Musgrave (1970), 91–195.

—— and MUSGRAVE, A. (1970), *Criticism and the Growth of Knowledge: Proceedings of the International Colloquium in the Philosophy of Science, London, 1965*, iv (Cambridge: Cambridge University Press).

LAYNE, C. (1994), 'Kant or Cant: The Myth of the Democratic Peace', *International Security*, 19/2: 5–49.

LEICESTER, H. M. (1956), *The Historical Background of Chemistry* (New York: Dover).

LESSNOFF, M. (1974), *The Structure of Social Science: A Philosophical Introduction* (London: Allen & Unwin).

LEVY, J. S. (1986), 'Organizational Routines and the Causes of War', *International Studies Quarterly*, 30: 193–222.

—— (1987), 'Declining Power and the Preventive Motivation for War', *World Politics*, 49: 82–107.

—— (1989*a*), 'The Causes of War: a Review of Theories and Evidence', in Tetlock *et al.* (1989), 209–333.

—— (1989*b*), 'The Diversionary Theory of War: A Critique', in Midlarsky (1989), 259–88.

—— (1989*c*), 'Domestic Politics and War', in Rotberg and Rabb (1989), 79–99.

—— (1991), 'Preferences, Constraints, and Choices in July 1914', in Miller, Lynn-Jones, and Van Evera (1991), 226–61.

—— (1992), 'Prospect Theory and International Relations: Theoretical

Applications and Analytical Problems', *Political Psychology*, 13: 283–310.

—— CHRISTENSEN, T. J., and TRACHTENBERG, M. (1991), 'Correspondence: Mobilization and Inadvertence in the July Crisis', *International Security*, 16: 189–203.

—— and VAKILI, L. (1992), 'External Scapegoating by Authoritarian Regimes: Argentina in the Falklands/Malvinas Case', in Midlarsky (1992), 118–46.

LEWIS, D. (1975), 'Causation', in Sosa (1975), 180–91.

—— (1993), 'Causal Explanation', in Ruben (1993), 182–206.

LINKLATER, A. (1982), *Men and Citizens in the Theory of International Relations* (London: Macmillan/The London School of Economics and Political Science).

—— (1995), 'Neo-Realism in Theory and Practice', in Booth and Smith (1995), 241–61.

LORENZ, K. (1961), *King Solomon's Ring: New Light on Animal Ways*, trans. M. K. Watson (London: Methuen).

LOWE, P. (1986), *The Origins of the Korean War* (London: Longman).

LUARD, E. (1986), *War in International Society* (London: Tauris).

LYNN-JONES, S. M. (1991), 'Détente and Deterrence: Anglo-German Relations, 1911–1914', in Miller, Lynn-Jones, and Van Evera (1991), 165–94.

—— MILLER, S. E., and VAN EVERA, S. (1990) (eds.), *Nuclear Diplomacy and Crisis Management: An International Security Reader* (Cambridge, Mass.: MIT Press).

MCCARTHY, T. (1984), *The Critical Theory of Jürgen Habermas* (Cambridge: Polity Press).

MCGOWAN, P. J. (1975) (ed.), *Sage International Yearbook of Foreign Policy Studies*, iii. (London: Sage).

MACK, A. (1975), 'Numbers are not Enough: A Critique of Internal/External Conflict Behavior Research', *Comparative Politics*, 7: 597–618.

MACKIE, J. L. (1974), 'Causes and Conditions', in Sosa (1975), 15–38.

—— (1980), *The Cement of the Universe: A Study of Causation* (Oxford: Clarendon Press).

MACMILLAN, J. (forthcoming), *On Liberal Peace* (provisional title) (London: British Academic Press).

MACRAE, A. W. (1988), 'Measurement Scales and Statistics: What can Significance Tests tell us about the World?', *British Journal of Psychology*, 79: 161–71.

MAGEE, B. (1978), *Men of Ideas: Some Creators of Contemporary Philosophy—Dialogues with Fifteen Leading Philosophers* (Oxford: Oxford University Press).

MAJESKI, S. J., and SYLVAN, D. J. (1984), 'Simple Choices and Complex Calculations: A Critique of *The War Trap*', *Journal of Conflict Resolution*, 28: 316–40.

MANN, M. (1993), *The Sources of Social Power*, ii. *The Rise of Class and Nation-States*, 1760–1914 (Cambridge: Cambridge University Press).

MANNING, C. A. W. (1942), 'The "Failure" of the League of Nations', reprinted from *Agenda*, 1: 59–72, in Cosgrove and Twitchett (1970), 105–23.

—— (1975), *The Nature of International Society*, reissue (London: Macmillan/The London School of Economics and Political Science).

MAOZ, Z., and ABDOLALI, N. (1989), 'Regime Types and International Conflict, 1816–1976', *Journal of Conflict Resolution*, 33: 3–35.

MARTEL, G. (1986) (ed.), *The Origins of the Second World War Reconsidered: The A. J. P. Taylor Debate after Twenty-Five Years* (London: Allen & Unwin).

MARTIN, R. (1982), 'Causes, Conditions, and Causal Importance', *History and Theory*, 21: 53–74.

MASON, T. W. (1971), 'Some Origins of the Second World War', in Robertson (1971), 105–36.

MATTHEWS, R. O., RUBINOFF, A. G., and STEIN, J. G. (1984) (eds.), *International Conflict and Conflict Management: Readings in World Politics* (Scarborough, Ontario: Prentice-Hall of Canada).

MAYER, A. J. (1967), 'Domestic Causes of the First World War', in Krieger and Stern (1967), 286–300.

—— (1969), 'Internal Causes and Purposes of War in Europe, 1870–1956: A Research Assignment', *Journal of Modern History*, 41: 291–303.

—— (1977), 'Internal Crisis and War since 1870', in Bertrand (1977), 201–33.

MEARSHEIMER, J. J. (1990), 'Back to the Future: Instability in Europe after the Cold War', *International Security*, 15: 5–56.

MIDDLEBROOK, M. (1989), *The Fight for the 'Malvinas': The Argentine Forces in the Falklands War* (London: Viking).

MIDLARSKY, M. I. (1989) (ed.), *Handbook of War Studies* (Boston: Unwin Hyman).

—— (1992) (ed.), *The Internationalization of Communal Strife* (London: Routledge).

MILLER, S. E., LYNN-JONES, S. M., and VAN EVERA, S. (1991) (eds.), *Military Strategy and the Origins of the First World War*, an International Security Reader, rev. and expanded edn. (Princeton: Princeton University Press).

MILNER, H. (1991), 'The Assumption of Anarchy in International Relations Theory: a Critique', *Review of International Studies*, 17: 67–85.

MINK, L. O. (1964), 'The Autonomy of Historical Understanding', *History and Theory*, 5: 24–47.

—— (1967–8), 'Philosophical Analysis and Historical Understanding', *Review of Metaphysics*, 21: 667–98.

MOMMSEN, W. J. (1973), 'Domestic Factors in German Foreign Policy before 1914', *Central European History*, 6: 3–43.

MOREWOOD, S. (1989), 'Anglo-Italian Rivalry in the Mediterranean and Middle East, 1935–1940', in Boyce and Robertson (1989), 167–98.

MORRISON, D. E., and HENKEL, R. E. (1970) (eds.), *The Significance Test Controversy: A Reader* (London: Butterworths).

MOSES, J. A. (1975), *The Politics of Illusion: The Fischer Controversy in German Historiography* (London: Prior).

MOST, B. A., and STARR, H. (1983), 'Conceptualizing "War"', *Journal of Conflict Resolution*, 27: 137–59.

MUELLER, J. (1990), 'The Essential Irrelevance of Nuclear Weapons', in Lynn-Jones, Miller, and Van Evera (1990), 3–27.

NELSON, K. L., and OLIN, Jr., S. C. (1979), *Why War? Ideology, Theory, and History* (Berkeley and Los Angeles: University of California Press).

NETTLESHIP, M. A., GIVENS, R. D., and NETTLESHIP, A. (1975) (eds.), *War, its Causes and Correlates* (The Hague: Mouton).

NICHOLSON, M. (1987a), 'The Conceptual Bases of *The War Trap*', *Journal of Conflict Resolution*, 31: 346–69.

—— (1987b), 'Comment on Bueno de Mesquita's Reply', *Journal of Conflict Resolution*, 31: 383.

—— (1992), *Rationality and the Analysis of International Conflict* (Cambridge: Cambridge University Press).

NISH, I. (1985), *The Origins of the Russo-Japanese War* (London: Longman).

NORTHEDGE, F. S., and DONELAN, M. D. (1971), *International Disputes: The Political Aspects* (London: Europa Publications for The David Davies Memorial Institute of International Studies).

NUTTING, A. (1967), *No End of a Lesson: The Story of Suez* (London: Constable).

OLAFSON, F. O. (1970), 'Narrative History and the Concept of Action', *History and Theory*, 9: 265–89.

—— (1979), *The Dialectic of Action: A Philosophical Interpretation of History and the Humanities* (Chicago: University of Chicago Press).

OLSON, W. C. (1990) (ed.), *The Theory and Practice of International Relations*, 8th edn. (Englewood Cliffs, NJ: Prentice-Hall).

OVENDALE, R. (1984), *The Origins of the Arab–Israeli Wars* (London: Longman).

OWEN, J. M. (1994), 'How Liberalism Produces Democratic Peace', *International Security*, 19/2: 87–125.

PARKER, R. A. C. (1993), *Chamberlain and Appeasement: British Policy and the Coming of the Second World War* (London: Macmillan).

PASSMORE, J. (1962), 'Explanation in Everyday Life, in Science, and History', *History and Theory*, 2: 105–23.

PAUL, T. V. (1994), *Asymmetric Conflicts: War Initiation by Weaker Powers* (Cambridge: Cambridge University Press).

POPPER, K. R. (1961), *The Poverty of Historicism* (London: Routledge).

—— (1972), *The Logic of Scientific Discovery* (London: Hutchinson).

PORK, A. (1985), 'Assessing Relative Causal Importance in History', *History and Theory*, 24: 62–9.

PROPP, V. (1968), *Morphology of the Folktale*, 2nd edn., trans. Laurence Scott, rev. and ed. with a preface by Louis A. Wagner, new introd. by Alan Dundes (Austin, Tex.: University of Texas Press).

QUESTER, G. H. (1984), 'War and Peace: Necessary and Sufficient Conditions', in Matthews, Rubinoff, and Stein (1984), 44–54.

QUINE, W. V. O. (1961a), *From a Logical Point of View: Logico-Philosophical Essays*, 2nd rev. edn. (New York: Harper & Row).

—— (1961b), 'Two Dogmas of Empiricism', in Quine (1961a), 20–46.

RANKE, L. von (1973), *The Theory and Practice of History*, ed. with introd. by G. G. Iggers and K. von Moltke; new trans. by W. A. Iggers and K. von Moltke (New York: Bobbs-Merrill).

RAPOPORT, A. (1968) (ed.), *Clausewitz on War* (Harmondsworth: Penguin Books).

—— (1974), *Conflict in Man-Made Environment* (Harmondsworth: Penguin Books).

—— (1975), 'Approaches to Peace Research', in Nettleship, Givens, and Nettleship (1975), 43–53.

RAY, J. L. (1993), 'Wars between Democracies: Rare, or Nonexistent?' *International Interactions*, 18: 251–76.

REARDON, B. A. (1985), *Sexism and the War System* (New York: Teachers College Press, Columbia University).

REISCH, G. A. (1991), 'Chaos, History, and Narrative', *History and Theory*, 30: 1–20.

REMAK, J. (1959), *Sarajevo: The Story of a Political Murder* (London: Weidenfeld & Nicolson).

REYNOLDS, C. (1973), *Theory and Explanation in International Politics* (London: Martin Robertson).

REYNOLDS, C. (1981), *Modes of Imperialism*. (Oxford: Martin Robertson).

REYNOLDS, P. A. (1961), 'Hitler's War?', *History*, 46: 212–7.

REYNOLDS, V., FALGER, V. S. E., and VINE, I. (1987) (eds.), *The Sociobiology of Ethnocentrism: Evolutionary Dimensions of Xenophobia, Discrimination, Racism and Nationalism* (London: Croom Helm).

ROBERTSON, E. M. (1971) (ed.), *The Origins of the Second World War: Historical Interpretations* (London: Macmillan, St Martin's Press).

—— (1989), 'German Mobilization Preparations and the Treaties between Germany and the Soviet Union of August and September 1939', in Boyce and Robertson (1989), 330–82.

ROTBERG, R. I., and RABB, T. K. (1989) (eds.), *The Origins and Prevention of Major Wars* (Cambridge: Cambridge University Press).

RUBEN, D.-H. (1993) (ed.), *Explanation* (Oxford: Oxford University Press).

RUMMEL, R. J. (1963), 'Dimensions of Conflict Behavior within and between Nations', *General Systems: Yearbook of the Society for General Systems Research*, 3: 1–50.

—— (1968), 'The Relationship between National Attributes and Foreign Conflict Behavior', in Singer (1968), 187–214.

—— (1972), *The Dimensions of Nations* (London: Sage).

—— (1983), 'Libertarianism and International Violence', *Journal of Conflict Resolution*, 27: 27–71.

—— (1985), 'Libertarian Propositions on Violence within and between Nations', *Journal of Conflict Resolution*, 29: 419–55.

RUSSETT, B. (1990), 'Economic Decline, Electoral Pressure, and the Initiation of Interstate Conflict', in Gochman and Sabrosky (1990), 123–40.

—— (1993), *Grasping the Democratic Peace: Principles for a Post-Cold War World*, with the collaboration of William Antholis, Carol R. Ember, Melvin Ember, and Zeev Maoz (Princeton: Princeton University Press).

—— and ANTHOLIS, W. (1992), 'Do Democracies Fight each other? Evidence from the Peloponnesian War', *Journal of Peace Research*, 29: 415–34.

—— LAYNE, C., SPIRO, D. E., and DOYLE, M. W. (1995), 'Correspondence: The Democratic Peace', *International Security*, 19: 164–84.

—— and RAY, J. L., and COHEN, R. (1995), 'Raymond Cohen on Pacific Unions: A Response and a Reply', *Review of International Studies*, 21/3: 319–25.

—— RISSE-KAPPEN, T., and MEARSHEIMER, J. J. (1990–1), 'Correspondence—Back to the Future, Part III: Realism and the Realities of European Security', *International Security*, 15: 216–22.

RYAN, A. (1970), *The Philosophy of the Social Sciences* (London: Macmillan).

—— (1979), *The Idea of Freedom: Essays in Honour of Isaiah Berlin* (Oxford: Oxford University Press).

SAGAN, S. D. (1989), 'The Origins of the Pacific War', in Rotberg and Rabb (1989), 323–52.

—— (1991), '1914 Revisited: Allies, Offense, and Instability' in Miller, Lynn-Jones and Van Evera (1991), 109–33.

SCHOLES, R. (1974), *Structuralism in Literature: An Introduction* (New Haven, Conn.: Yale University Press).

SCHWELLER, R. L. (1992), 'Domestic Structure and Preventive War: Are Democracies More Pacific?' *World Politics*, 44: 235–69.

Science News (1978), 'Chimp Killings: Is it the "Man" in them?', *Science News*, 113: 276.

SCOLNIK, J. M. (1974), 'An Appraisal of Studies of the Linkages between Domestic and International Conflict', *Comparative Political Studies*, 6: 485–509.

SCRIVEN, M. (1959), 'Truisms as the Grounds for Historical Explanations', in Gardiner (1959), 443–75.

—— (1966), 'Causes, Connections and Conditions in History', in Dray (1966), 238–64.

—— (1971), 'The Logic of Cause', *Theory and Decision*, 2: 49–66.

—— (1975), 'Causation as Explanation', *Noûs*, 9: 3–16.

SEABURY, A., and CODEVILLA, A. (1989), *War: Ends and Means* (New York: Basic Books).

SINGER, J. D. (1968) (ed.), *Quantitative International Politics: Insights and Evidence* (New York: Free Press).

—— (1979a) (ed.), *The Correlates of War*, i. *Research Origins and Rationale* (New York: Free Press).

—— (1979b), 'The Historical Experiment as a Research Strategy in the Study of World Politics', in Singer (1979a), 175–96.

—— (1989), 'System Structure, Decision Processes, and the Incidence of International War', in Midlarsky (1989), 1–21.

—— and SMALL, M. (1968), 'Alliance Aggregation and the Onset of War, 1815–1945', in Singer (1968), 247–86.

—— and SMALL, M. (1972), *The Wages of War* (New York: Wiley).

SIVERSON, R. M., and DIEHL, P. F. (1989), 'Arms Races, the Conflict Spiral, and the Onset of War', in Midlarsky (1989), 195–217.

—— and SULLIVAN, M. P. (1983), 'The Distribution of Power and the Onset of War', *Journal of Conflict Resolution*, 27: 473–94.

SMALL, M., and SINGER, J. D. (1976), 'The War-Proneness of Democratic Regimes, 1816–1965', *Jerusalem Journal of International Relations*, 1: 50–69.

—— —— (1982), *Resort to Arms: International and Civil Wars, 1816–1980* (Beverly Hills, Calif.: Sage).

SMITH, J. C., and HOGAN, B. (1992), *Criminal Law*, 7th edn. (London: Butterworths).

SNYDER, J. (1984), 'Civil–Military Relations and the Cult of the Offensive, 1914 and 1984', *International Security*, 9: 108–46.

—— (1990), 'Averting Anarchy in the New Europe', *International Security*, 14: 5–41.

SONTAG, S. (1983) (ed.), *Barthes: Selected Writings*, ed. and with an introd. by Susan Sontag (Glasgow: Fontana Paperbacks).

SOSA, E. (1975) (ed.), *Causation and Conditionals* (London: Oxford University Press).

SPIRO, D. E. (1994), 'The Insignificance of the Liberal Peace', *International Security*, 19/2: 50–86.

STAMPP, K. M. (1965) (ed.), *The Causes of the Civil War* (Englewood Cliffs, NJ: Prentice-Hall).

STANFORD, M. (1986), *The Nature of Historical Knowledge* (Oxford: Blackwell).

STEIN, J. G. (1992), 'Deterrence and Compellence in the Gulf, 1990–91: A Failed or Impossible Task?' *International Security*, 17: 147–79.

STEINER, Z. S. (1977a), *Britain and the Origins of the First World War* (London: Macmillan).

—— (1977b), 'The Foreign Office under Sir Edward Grey, 1905–1914', in Hinsley (1977), 22–69.

STEPHENS, R. (1971), *Nasser: A Political Biography* (London: Penguin Press).

STERN, F. (1973) (ed.), *The Varieties of History: From Voltaire to the Present* (New York: Vintage Books).

STOESSINGER, J. G. (1985), *Why Nations go to War*, 4th edn. (Houndmills, Basingstoke: Macmillan Education).

STOHL, M. (1980), 'The Nexus of Civil and International Conflict', in Gurr (1980), 297–330.

STRANGE, P. (1983), *It'll Make a Man of You . . . : A Feminist View of the Arms Race* (Nottingham: Mushroom Books).

SUGANAMI, H. (1983), 'The Structure of Institutionalism: An Anatomy of British Mainstream International Relations', *International Relations*, 7: 2363–81.

—— (1989a), *The Domestic Analogy and World Order Proposals* (Cambridge: Cambridge University Press).

—— (1989b), 'The Causes of War: A New Framework of Analysis', paper presented at the ISA/BISA Joint Convention, London, 28 Mar.–1 Apr.

—— (1990a), 'Bringing Order to the Causes of War Debates', *Millennium: Journal of International Studies*, 19: 19–35.

—— (1990b), 'The Causes of War: A New Theoretical Framework', in Olson (1990), 229–34.

SUPPE, F. (1977), *The Structure of Scientific Theories*, 2nd edn, ed. with a critical introd. and an afterword by Frederick Suppe (Urbana, Ill.: University of Illinois Press).

TANTER, R. (1966), 'Dimensions of Conflict Behavior within and between Nations, 1958–60', *Journal of Conflict Resolution*, 10: 41–64.

TAYLOR, A. J. P. (1953), Review of Luigi Albertini, *The Origins of the War of 1914*, ii, in *Manchester Guardian*, 6 Oct.: 4.

—— (1964), *The Origins of the Second World War* (Harmondsworth: Penguin Books).

—— (1969), *War by Time-Table: How the First World War Began* (London: Macdonald).

—— (1971), 'War Origins Again', in Robertson (1971), 136–41.

—— (1977a), 'In Defence of Small Nations', *Listener*, 98/2520 (4 Aug.): 138–40.

—— (1977b), 'How War begins—(4) The First World War', BBC2: 23.15–23.45, 1 Aug. 1977.

—— (1977c), 'Accident Prone, or What happened next', *Journal of Modern History*, 49: 1–18.

TAYLOR, D. M. (1970), *Explanation and Meaning: An Introduction to Philosophy* (Cambridge: Cambridge University Press).

TAYLOR, R. (1975), 'The Metaphysics of Causation', in Sosa (1975), 39–43.

TETLOCK, P. E., HUSBANDS, J. L., JERVIS, R., STERN, P. C., and TILLY, C. (1989) (eds.), *Behavior, Society, and Nuclear War*, i. (New York: Oxford University Press).

THUCYDIDES (1954 edn.), *History of the Peloponnesian War*, trans. R. Warner with an introd. and notes by M. I. Finley (Harmondsworth: Penguin Books).

TRACHTENBERG, M. (1991a), *History and Strategy* (Princeton: Princeton University Press).

—— (1991b), 'The Coming of the First World War: A Reassessment', in Trachtenberg (1991a), 47–99.

—— (1991c), 'The Influence of Nuclear Weapons in the Cuban Missile Crisis', in Trachtenberg (1991a), 235–60.

TREVOR-ROPER, H. R. (1971), 'A. J. P. Taylor, Hitler and the War', in Robertson (1971), 83–99.

TURNER, L. C. F. (1968), 'The Russian Mobilization in 1914', *Journal of Contemporary History*, 3/1: 65–88.

—— (1979), 'The Significance of the Schlieffen Plan', in Kennedy (1979), 171–221.

VAN EVERA, S. (1984), 'The Cult of the Offensive and the Origins of the First World War', *International Security*, 9: 58–107.

VASQUEZ, J. A. (1987), 'The Steps to War: Toward a Scientific Explanation of Correlates of War Findings', *World Politics*, 40: 108–145.

—— (1993), *The War Puzzle* (Cambridge: Cambridge University Press).

—— and HENEHAN, M. T. (1992), *The Scientific Study of Peace and War: A Text Reader* (New York: Lexington Books).

VEYNE, P. (1984), *Writing History: Essay on Epistemology*, trans. Mina Moore-Rinvolucri (Manchester: Manchester University Press).

VIVARELLI, R. (1980), Review of Hugo Butler, *Gaetano Salvemini und die italienische Politik vor dem Ersten Weltkrieg*, in *Journal of Modern History*, 52: 539–42.

VON WRIGHT, G. H. (1971), *Explanation and Understanding* (London: Routledge).

WAGNER, R. H. (1984), 'War and Expected-Utility Theory', *World Politics*, 36: 407–23.

WALLACE, M. D. (1979), 'Arms Races and Escalation: Some New Evidence', *Journal of Conflict Resolution*, 23: 3–16.

—— (1980), 'Some Persisting Findings: A Reply to Professor Weede', *Journal of Conflict Resolution*, 24: 289–92.

—— (1982), 'Armaments and Escalation: Two Competing Hypotheses', *International Studies Quarterly*, 26: 37–56.

—— (1983), 'Arms Races and Escalation—A Reply to Altfeld', *International Studies Quarterly*, 27/2: 233–5.

—— (1990), 'Racing Redux: The Arms Race—Escalation Debate Revisited', in Gochman and Sabrosky (1990), 115–22.

—— (1994), Review of Scott D. Sagan, *The Limits of Safety: Organizations, Accidents, and Nuclear Weapons*, in *Millennium*, 23: 187–9.

WALLIS, D. I. (1962), 'Aggressive Behaviour in the Ant, Formica Fusca', *Animal Behaviour*, 10: 267–74.

WALSH, W. H. (1951), *An Introduction to Philosophy of History* (London: Hutchinson).

—— (1977), 'Truth and Fact in History Reconsidered', *History and Theory*, 16: 53–71.

WALTZ, K. N. (1959), *Man, the State and War: A Theoretical Analysis* (New York: Columbia University Press).

—— (1964), 'The Stability of a Bipolar World', *Daedalus*, 93: 881–909.

—— (1979), *Theory of International Politics* (Reading, Mass.: Addison-Wesley).

—— (1986), 'Reflections on Theory of International Politics: A Response to My Critics', in Keohane (1986), 322–45.

—— (1989), 'The Origins of War in Neorealist Theory', in Rotberg and Rabb (1989), 39–52.

—— (1991), 'America as a Model for the World? A Foreign Policy Perspective', *PS: Political Science & Politics*, Dec.: 667–70.

—— (1993), 'The Emerging Structure of International Politics', *International Security*, 18/2: 44–79.

WANDYCZ, P. S. (1986), 'Poland between East and West', in Martel (1986), 187–209.

WANK, S., MASCHL, H., MAZOHL-WALLNIG, B., and WAGNLEITNER, R. (1988) (eds.), *The Mirror of History: Essays in Honour of Fritz Fellner* (Santa Barbara, Calif.: ABS-Clio).

WATT, D. C. (1989), *How War Came: The Immediate Origins of the Second World War, 1938–1939* (New York: Pantheon Books).

WEEDE, E. (1980), 'Arms Races and Escalation: Some Persisting Doubts

(Response to Wallace's Article, *JCR*, March 1979)', *Journal of Conflict Resolution*, 24: 285–7.

—— (1984), 'Democracy and War Involvement', *Journal of Conflict Resolution*, 28: 648–64.

WELCH, D. A. (1993), *Justice and the Genesis of War* (Cambridge: Cambridge University Press).

WENDT, A. E. (1987), 'The Agent–Structure problem in International Relations Theory', *International Organization*, 41: 335–70.

—— (1992), 'Anarchy is what States Make of it: The Social Construction of Power Politics', *International Organization*, 46: 391–425.

WHITE, H. (1973), *Metahistory: The Historical Imagination in Nineteenth-Century Europe* (Baltimore: Johns Hopkins University Press).

—— (1978), *Tropics of Discourse: Essays in Cultural Criticism* (Baltimore: Johns Hopkins University Press).

—— (1984), 'The Question of Narrative in Contemporary Historical Theory', *History and Theory*, 23: 1–33.

—— (1987), *The Content of the Form: Narrative Discourse and Historical Representation* (Baltimore: Johns Hopkins University Press).

WHITE, M. (1965), *Foundations of Historical Knowledge* (New York: Harper & Row).

WIGHT, M. (1978), *Power Politics*, ed. Hedley Bull and Carsten Holbraad (Leicester: Leicester University Press for the Royal Institute of International Affairs).

WILKENFELD, J. (1973*a*) (ed.), *Conflict Behavior and Linkage Politics* (New York: David McKay).

—— (1973*b*), 'Domestic and Foreign Conflict', in Wilkenfeld (1973*a*), 107–23.

WILLIAMSON, Jr., S. R. (1991), *Austria–Hungary and the Origins of the First World War* (London: Macmillan).

WILSON, P. (1989), 'The English School of International Relations: A Reply to Sheila Grader', *Review of International Studies*, 15: 49–58.

WINCH, P. (1958), *The Idea of a Social Science and its Relation to Philosophy* (London: Routledge).

WITTGENSTEIN, L. (1968), *Philosophical Investigations*, trans. G. E. M. Anscombe (Oxford: Blackwell).

WOLFERS, A. (1962*a*), *Discord and Collaboration: Essays on International Politics* (Baltimore: Johns Hopkins Press).

WOLFERS, A. (1962*b*), 'The Goals of Foreign Policy', in Wolfers (1962*a*), 67–80.

WOOLF, V. (1938), *Three Guineas*, orig. pub. 1938; repr. in Woolf (1992): 151–433.

WOOLF, V. (1992), *A Room of One's Own, Three Guineas*, ed. with introd. by M. Shiach (Oxford: Oxford University Press).

WRIGHT, Q. (1964), *A Study of War*, abridged by L. L. Wright (Chicago: University of Chicago Press).

YUDKIN, M. (1982), 'Reflections on Woolf's Three Guineas', *Women's Studies International Forum*, 5/3–4: 263–9.

ZINNES, D. A. (1976), *Contemporary Research in International Relations: A Perspective and a Critical Appraisal* (New York: Free Press).

INDEX

Printed in the United Kingdom
by Lightning Source UK Ltd.
9402800001B